Global Light Cuisine

Carol Devenot

Blue Sea Publishing
Hawaii and Washington

Global Light Cuisine

Copyright 2008 by Carol Devenot

Cover art and illustrations by Carol Devenot

First Edition, First Printing 2008

All rights reserved. No portion of this book may be repro-
duced in whole or in part in any form or by any means
without prior permission from the author or publisher,
Blue Sea Publishing, Post Office Box 25783, Honolulu, HI
96825-0783 or Post Office Box 2371, Oak Harbor, WA
98277.

Library of Congress Control Number 2008933015
ISBN 978-0-9741741-9-8

Printed in the United States by Morris Publishing
3212 East Highway 30
Kearney, NE 68847
1-800-650-7888

Author of **Island Light Cuisine** (2003)

Dedication

Bob, Mark, and Chibi

Acknowledgements

The most important Acknowledgement of all is to God for all his blessings. Throughout this process I have been guided by His Love and Light. I am grateful for having the privilege of living in one of the most beautiful places on the earth, a place where people where people share a true sense of Aloha.

Without all the love, help, and support this cookbook would not be possible. Like the end of the movie, I would like to list all of the people who contributed to this cookbook. Unfortunately, that would take pages. However, there are some key people who played a significant part in this project. I am grateful to the following people who have been a constant help.

Wanda Adams, Food Editor and Columnist for the *Honolulu Advertiser* newspaper, for getting me started in writing the "Light & Local" column in 2004 and for assisting me with her great editing, important suggestions, and catchy captions. I have learned so much about doing research and developing a writing style through her tips and pointers. I am most grateful for her unlimited patience in helping me with details I could include and things that I might have left out. I am still learning and am very grateful to learn even more.

Dr. Bob Lange, M.D., my boyfriend, who has been my greatest source of love and support. At Kaiser Hospital, he is known by my readers as "The Shadow." He doesn't seem to mind being in the background while I describe stories about him in the *Advertiser*. His reward is a healthy meal, sometimes even with dessert.

Mark Devenot, "My Sonny Boy," from the time he was little, he has been my best cooking fan. When he was six years old, he brought me the best present a child could give his mother. He got up early on Mother's Day and stood on his little stool and prepared scrambled eggs *(a little burnt)*, toast, and juice. He even remembered to put some pretty weeds in a bud vase. He paid me the highest compliment as a mother and a little chef by trying to imitate what I do.

My dear friends, Lynne Lee and Jenny Choy, who have given me much encouragement . . . . and their prized recipes.

Mama Claire for her love and her great sense of style and drama.

Mr. and Mrs. Francis Au, my parents, who gave me much love and a great sense of tradition.

My publisher, Janet Foster, has become more than a publisher. Throughout the years she has been very helpful in keeping me current and motivated. She has been a great support to me in business and in my life.

Marge Schembri, my dear neighbor, who has been so supportive with her watercolor techniques, paints, books, and magazines. So many of her ideas were very helpful in developing the cover. She is a sage and has a beautiful soul.

All my relatives, friends, and acquaintances that I have met throughout the years who have shared their stories and recipes. My warmest Maholo to all of you who made this book possible.

Foreword

I well remember the first time I "met" Carol Devenot. It was on the phone and we were doing a phone interview about her new cookbook, *Island Light Cuisine*. I was sitting in my small condo on my ancient Apple laptop with a headphone on listening to this slightly shy but very *akamai (smart)* local girl tell me how she'd managed to take Hawai`i's favorite foods—all of them loaded with fat, salt and sugar and all served in portions that would daunt a sumo wrestler—and turned them into reasonably healthy dishes.

I was fascinated. I've always said of myself that the reason I came home to Hawai`i from the Mainland after a sojourn as a food writer there was that you couldn't get a good plate lunch there. *(Plate lunch, for the unitiated, is an Island favorite meal, eaten at any time of day or night and consisting always of two scoops white rice, macaroni salad with lots of Best Foods® mayonnaise, and a heavy entrée of some kind—anything from beef stew to Filipino adobo, a pickled pork dish.)*

Lighten a plate lunch? This, I gotta see. So, first we take the rice from white to *hapa (half white/half brown)* and then all the way to brown. Then we maybe dispense with it altogether or try couscous or bulgur or barley. And then we change the salad to a tossed green or perhaps a slaw or something actually involving vegetable as more than garnish. And then we make the entrée with fat- and sodium-reduced ingredients. And then we serve it in portions a dietitian could approve.

Hmmm, not rocket science.

I was delighted, some time later, to actually meet Carol, a petite former life skills teacher in the high school system and to see that she lived/walked her talk *(well, more than walked, she's always going to the gym, it seems)*.

Over the years, she's introduced me and readers of *The Honolulu Advertiser* to tamari and brown rice syrup, whole wheat pastry flour, Boca Burgers® *(sorry, still not a fan; I prefer tofu crumbles made at home)*, alternative grains, a world of Chinese ingredients, every local health food store in Honolulu, and how to sneak vegetables and beans into anything without anyone caring. She's taught me to rethink dishes I once savored and suddenly to find them too heavy, too down-bringing. And every dish of hers I've ever made has been at least well-received, if not raved about.

I love the name of this book because it expresses so much more than recipes: The light is not just "lightening" a recipe, it is the light of good health and the light of eating with a spiritual sense that food is mean to nurture the body which is the repository of the soul. I love that her goal is not just to share cooking ideas, but to create cohesiveness between cultures in a divided world.

As you read this book, and cook from it, do as Carol does: be well, and wish well for others.

Wanda A. Adams
Honolulu Advertiser Food Editor

Contents

Foreword

Introduction

🌿 Appetizers

Asia/Chinese

**Chinese Black Mushroom and
Tofu Lettuce Cups** *(Pub. Oct. 18, 2006)* 5

Asia/Filipino

Lazy Lumpia and Dipping Sauce
(Pub. June 16, 2004) 8

Asia/Thai

Summer Rolls with Dipping Sauce
(Pub. July 25, 2007) 10

Caribbean/Puerto Rican

Empanadillas 12

Europe/Italian

Eggplant Caponata *(Pub. July 11, 2007)* 14

Europe/Mediterranean

Mediterranean Spinach Rice Balls
(Pub. Feb. 8, 2006) 16

Hawaii Local Favorite

Dilly Dip 18

Mexico

Guacamole 19

Salsa 20

Ceviche *(Pub. Nov. 10, 2004)* 21

South Pacific/Hawaiian

Lynne's Tofu Poke *(Pub. May 16, 2007)* 23

🌿 Soups

Asia/Chinese

Jenny's Watercress Soup *(Pub. March 23, 2005)*. 27

viii   Contents

Asia/Chinese (continued)

Mom's Comforting Jook (turkey rice soup)
(Pub. Feb. 7, 2007) 29

Asia/Japanese

Low-carb Saimin *(Pub. Sept. 19, 2007)* 31

Mitsuko's Oden *(Pub. Dec. 26, 2007)* 33

Asia/Korean

Korean Chicken Soup *(Pub. July 13, 2005)* 35

Europe/Italian

**Slimmed-Down Tomato-Butternut
Squash Bisque** *(Pub. Sept. 7, 2005)* 37

Europe/Portuguese

Healthy Portuguese Bean Soup 39

Mainland U.S. Favorite

Hearty Turkey Soup *(Pub. May 3, 2006)* 41

Light and Creamy Broccoli Soup
(Pub. Jan. 11, 2006) 43

No Need Ham Split Pea Soup
(Pub. March 8, 2006) 45

Mainland U.S./American Indian

Southwestern Corn Chowder
(Pub. Nov. 15, 2006) 47

Mexico

Mexicano Sop A Con Rose Avos
(Pub. Nov. 9, 2005) 49

Middle East

Harira (Ramadan soup) *(Pub. Sept. 20, 2006)* 51

Salads and Condiments

Asia/Chinese

Oriental Chicken Salad 55

Asia/Filipino

Green Papaya Salad 56

Asia/Japanese

Namasu 58

Asia/Korean
    Quickie Cucumber Kim Chee............................ 59

Europe/Greek
    Greek Couscous Salad *(Pub. July 12, 2006)*.......... 60
    Greek Salad *(Pub. Nov. 17, 2004)*............................ 62

Europe/Italian
    Herbed White Bean Salad *(Pub. May 2, 2007)* 64
    Woodi's Caprese *(Pub. Jan. 10, 2007)*...................... 65

Hawaii Local Favorite
    Good Kine Potato Salad *(Pub. May 5, 2004)*........ 67
    Tofu Mayo *(Pub. May 19, 2004)*.............................. 69
    Tofu Salad.. 70
    Hold da Mayo Cold Slaw...................................... 71

Mainland U.S. Favorite
    Roasted Beet Salad with Sherry Shallot
        Vinaigrette and Candied Pecans
    (Pub. May 30, 2007).. 72

Middle East
    Curried Couscous Salad *(Pub. Jan. 24, 2007)* 75
    Tzatziki *(Pub. Jan. 26, 2005)*.................................... 78

Middle East/Israeli
    Heal Ti Israeli Salad *(Pub. March 22, 2006)* 80

Side Dishes

Asia/Chinese
    Kalakoa Fried Rice 85

Asia/Filipino
    Sitaw 86

Asia/Japanese
    Sekihan (happy red rice) *(Pub. Dec. 27, 2006)*........ 87
    One Giant Sushi.. 89

Asia/Korean
    Watercress Namul 90
    Chop Chae.. 91

x   Contents

Asia/Thai
Yummy Sticky Rice 93
Europe/French
Ratatouille *(Pub. Aug. 8, 2007)* 94
Europe/Greek
Greek Seasoned Roasted Vegetables
(Pub. Oct. 4, 2006) 96
Europe/Italian
Linguine Al Pesto Alla Moda Ligure Redo
(Pub. Oct. 3, 2007) 98
Hawaii Local Favorite
Ceci's Tasty Sweet Potatoes
(imu-flavored potatoes) 100
Hapa Rice (white and brown rice) 101
Long Rice Chicken 102
Mainland U.S. Favorite
Microwaved Brown Basmati or
Long Grain Brown Rice *(Pub. Sept. 8, 2004)* ... 104
Festive Stuffed Butternut Squash
(Pub. Dec. 28, 2005) 106
South Pacific/Hawaiian
Lomi Lomi Tomato 108
Luau Spinach 109
Baked Sweet Potato 110
Baked Taro 110
South Pacific/Samoan
Lani Ulu (breadfruit) 111
Light Palu Sami *(Pub. June 1, 2005)* 112

Entrees
Africa
Bobotie (curried meatloaf) *(Pub. May 31, 2006)* 117
Asia/Chinese
Lynne's Quick Asian Salmon
(Pub. Aug. 23, 2006) 120

Asia/Chinese (continued)

Grilled Hamachi with Black Bean Sauce
(Pub. Nov. 28, 2007) 122

Spicy Szechuan Eggplant *(Pub. June 29, 2005)*... 124

Broccoli Stir Fry 126

Garden Chow Mein 128

Char Siu Chicken and Char Siu Sauce 130

**Garlic Asparagus and Chicken in
Black Bean Sauce** *(Pub. Aug. 25, 2004)* 132

**Chinese Five Spice Chicken and
Vegetables** *(Pub. Sept. 6, 2006)* 134

Shoyu Chicken 136

Sichuan Ma Po Tofu *(Pub. June 14, 2006)* 138

**Sweet and Sour Tofu and Carol's Sweet
and Sour Sauce** *(Pub. Feb. 22, 2006)* 140

Sesame Soy Chicken and Edamame Stir Fry
(Pub. April 18, 2007) 142

Asia/Filipino

Chicken Adobo *(Pub. April 19, 2006)* 144

Veat, Not Meat Guisantes *(Pub. Aug. 24, 2005)*.. 146

Asia/Indonesian

Indonesian Chicken Satay *(Pub. June 28, 2006)*. 148

Asia/Japanese

Wild Salmon Shiro Misoyaki
(Pub. May 17, 2006) 150

Chicken Katsu *(Pub. April 21, 2004)* 152

Simply Nishime 154

Asia/Korean

Enlightened Ja Jang Myun *(Pub. Oct. 5, 2005)* .. 156

Susan's Grilled Chicken *(Pub. July 26, 2006)* 158

Asia/Thai

Thai Shrimp or Tofu Curry *(Pub. Aug. 11, 2004)*. 160

Pad Thai *(Pub. Dec. 15, 2004)* 162

Caribbean/Cuban

Cuban Stuffed Zucchini *(Pub. March 21, 2007)*.... 164

xii   Contents

Caribbean/Puerto Rican

Arroz con Gandules (pigeon peas with rice)
(Pub. June 2, 2004) 166

Europe/French

Spinach and Ricotta Crepes
(Pub. March 7, 2007) 168

Europe/German

Sauerbraten in a Crock-Pot *(Pub. June 13, 2007)*   171

Europe/Greek

Meatless Moussaka *(Pub. Nov. 3, 2004)* 173

Europe/Irish

Savvy (Savoy) Stuffed Cabbage
(Pub. March 9, 2005) 176

Europe/Italian

Chicken Florentine a la Devenot
(Pub. May 2, 2007) 178

Mama Claire's Spaghetti Sauce
(Pub. June 30, 2004) 180

Rav-e-oli *(Pub. July 4, 2004)* 182

Cherry Tomatoes and Penne Pasta
(Pub. Oct. 20, 2004) 184

Zucchini—Swiss Chard Frittata
(Pub. April 5, 2006) 186

Angela's Quickie Veggie Lasagna
(Pub. Feb. 21, 2007) 188

Hawaii Local Favorite

Tuna Tofu Patties *(Pub. Feb. 23, 2005)* 190

Lara's Mahimahi with Mango-Papaya Salsa
(Pub. Aug. 22, 2007) 192

Plate Lunch Curry Stew 194

`Ono Keia Hawaiian Stew *(Pub. April 7, 2004)* ... 196

What the Hekka? 198

Coffee Burger with Wasabi Mayo
(Pub. Sept. 6, 2006) 201

Terry Burger with Teriyaki Sauce 203

India/Indian

Ek Handi Ka Murch Aur Masoor (one-pot chicken, red lentils, and green beans) *(Pub. April 20, 2005)* ... 205

Tandori Chicken *(Pub. July 27, 2005)* ... 208

Mainland U.S. Favorite

Flame-broiled Fish Taco *(Pub. Nov. 1, 2006)* ... 210

Barbecue Roasted Salmon *(Pub. Sept. 5, 2007)* ... 212

Quinoa Spinach Casserole *(Pub. Sept. 21, 2005)* ... 214

Mexico

Chicken Fajitas ... 217

Turkey Chiles Rellenos Casserole *(Pub. Nov. 29, 2006)* ... 219

Carol's Chili ... 222

Woo's Southwest Orzo *(Pub. Sept. 22, 2004)* ... 223

Bostadas ... 225

Middle East

Flab You Less Falafel *(Pub. Jan. 12, 2005)* ... 226

Desserts

Australia/New Zealand

Palagyi's Pavlova *(Pub. June 27, 2007)* ... 231

Asia/Chinese

Mango Pudding *(Pub. July 28, 2004)* ... 234

Warm, Tropical Mango-Lychee Dessert *(Pub. May 18, 2005)* ... 236

Almond Float ... 238

Asia/Filipino

New Kine Banana Lumpia ... 239

Asia/Japanese

Smart Manju ... 241

Okinawan Sweet Potato Poi Mochi *(Pub. Dec. 29, 2004)* ... 242

xiv   Contents

Asia/Thai

Thai Tapioca Pudding *(Pub. April 6, 2005)* 244

**Sweet Brown Sticky Rice with
Mango-Lychee** *(Pub. Aug. 9, 2006)* 246

Europe/French

Chocolate Mousse Pie *(Pub. May 2, 2007)* 248

Hawaii Local Favorite

Okinawan Sweet Potato Pie
(Pub. Aug. 10, 2005) 249

Fo' Real Bread Pudding *(Pub. Dec. 14, 2005)* 252

Mainland U.S. Favorite

Date with a Nut Bread *(Pub. Oct. 6, 2004)* 254

Banana Muffins for Mom *(Pub. May 4, 2005)* 256

Yummy Rummy Oatcakes *(Pub. Dec. 1, 2004)* 258

Easy as 1-2-3 Pumpkin Bars *(Pub. Oct. 19, 2005)*. 260

Raspberry and Chocolate Bars
(Pub. Oct. 17, 2007) 262

Little-Bit-Butter Oatmeal Cookies
(Pub. Jan. 25, 2006) 264

Soy Chocolate Fantasy *(Pub. April 4, 2007)* 266

I Love You Berry, Berry, Berry Much Crisp
(Pub. Feb. 9, 2005) 268

Crispy Apricot Turnovers *(Pub. June 15, 2005)* 270

Mainland U.S. Favorite

Chocolate Swirled Cheesecake
(Pub. Dec. 12, 2007) 272

Banana Almond Cream 275

South Pacific/Hawaiian

Jan's Haupia (coconut pudding) 276

🌿 Snacks and Beverages

Asia/Chinese

My Favorite Fruit Mui *(Pub. Dec. 13, 2006)* 279

Asia/Japanese

"Make Her" Musubi 281

Global Light Cuisine ∞ Carol Devenot   xv

Hawaii Local Favorite
    Banana Wrap... 283
Mainland U.S. Favorite
    Loco `Ono Energy Bars *(Pub. Nov. 23, 2005)* 284
    Banana Smoothie.. 287
    Tri-Berrie Smoothie *(Pub. Dec. 13, 2006)*................ 287
Glossary 289
Index 299

xvi   Contents

Introduction

Note on Cover Art:

I picture our world enlightened with a lei of healthy cuisine and a world that embraces our similarities and differences in our choices of food.

Growing up in Hawai`i, I would always hear familiar phrases like, "Lucky you live Hawai`i" and *"Hawai`i no ka oi"* (*Hawai`i is the best*). When I wrote my first cookbook *Island Light Cuisine (2003)*, I took local recipes and lightened them up. Like Hawai`i itself, my recipes were multicultural, including Chinese, Filipino, Southeast Asian, Hawaiian, Samoan, Japanese, Korean, Mexican, Portuguese, and Puerto Rican. Creating this book made me appreciate another familiar term that "Hawai'i is the melting pot" of the world.

In the spring of 2004 I was asked by Wanda Adams, Food Editor, to write a column in the *Honolulu Advertiser*. I decided to give the "Light & Local" column even more of an international flavor, and I had several sources to draw on. Dining at the many ethnic restaurants in Hawaii has given me an opportunity to taste varied blends of spices that each group has to offer. Many of my relatives, friends, and acquaintances have shared family recipes from around the world. All of these experiences along with a constant focus on food have helped me evolve from a local to a global perspective—hence, the title *Global Light Cuisine*.

This book contains recipes from my "Light & Local" columns from Spring 2004 through 2007, plus favorite recipes from *Island Light Cuisine*.

Learning about the traditions and cultures of the world's cuisine has given me a broader perspective of food and people. Using the same basic foods, each culture has added their own unique seasonings. For example, we have our *chow fun*, and Thailand has their *pad Thai*. Tahiti has their *poisson cru*, and Mexico has their *ceviche*. Perhaps by seeing how related we are through foods we can develop a better understanding of people and their culture throughout the world.

Carol Devenot

Appetizers

Asia/Chinese

Posted on: Wednesday, October 18, 2006

Shiitake give pupu character
Chinese Black Mushroom and Tofu Lettuce Cups

Chinese black mushrooms are sometimes called shiitake or forest mushrooms. They used to be imported from Japan and Korea, but they are now being cultivated in the United States as well. California, Pennsylvania, Vermont, Washington, Virginia, and other states grow shiitake they call "golden oak." Fresh shiitake are the most plentiful in the spring and autumn.

The caps of the mushroom are dark brown, sometimes marked with tan striations. Cap sizes range from 3 to 6 inches in diameter. You can find shiitake fresh in the produce section and dried in the Asian section of the supermarket.

Chinese Black Mushroom and Tofu Lettuce Cups

Serves 6

6 Chinese black mushrooms, dried
Canola oil cooking spray
1 (16-ounce) block lowest fat, firm tofu, cut into 1/2-inch cubes
3 cloves garlic, minced
1 tablespoon fresh ginger root, shaved
1 tablespoon *mirin* (rice wine)
1 teaspoon sesame oil
Black pepper, fresh ground and to taste
1 (6-inch) carrot, peeled and grated with largest holes on grater

1/2 cup fresh or canned water chestnuts, diced
1 (large) head butter or red lettuce, washed and
    drained on paper towels

Garnish:

Sesame seeds, toasted *(optional)*
3 green onions, cut into 1/4-inch slices
Hoisin sauce
Red chili sauce

Boil 2 cups of water and pour over the mushrooms in a heat-proof bowl; set aside for at least 10 minutes. Drain and reserve 1/4 cup of the liquid. Dice mushrooms and set aside.

Heat a wok and spray the surface with canola oil. Fry cubed tofu until lightly browned for approximately 5 minutes.

Add mushrooms, garlic, ginger and *mirin,* and stir-fry for about 30 seconds. Add sesame oil and black pepper and continue to stir-fry for 2 minutes. Add the mushroom liquid and grated carrots and stir-fry for 2 minutes. Add water chestnuts and mix thoroughly. Turn down heat, but keep warm.

Arrange the lettuce leaves on a large platter, and fill each leaf with 2 to 3 tablespoons of filling. Sprinkle with sesame seeds and green onions. Serve with hoisin and red chili sauces to drizzle over.

Global Light Cuisine ∞ Carol Devenot

Per serving (with lettuce and green onions, without sesame seeds and hoisin and red chili sauces): 220 calories, 12 g fat, 1 g saturated fat, 70 mg cholesterol, 280 mg sodium, 16 g carbohydrate, 1 g dietary fiber, 2 g sugar, 12 g protein.

Variations: You can add ground turkey or Boca® Burgers. This filling would also be great for wraps or sprinkled on top of fresh mixed greens as a salad or over brown rice for a filling dinner.

8 Appetizers

Asia/Filipino

Posted on: Wednesday, June 16, 2004

Lumpia need not be fried

Lazy Lumpia

Don't let phyllo intimidate you. All you need to do is keep it from drying out while you work with it. The rolled sheets can be found in the freezer case; allow them to defrost overnight in the refrigerator. Open the package, pull out as many sheets as you'll need and wrap the remainder tightly. Refrigerate or freeze for later use. Lay phyllo out on plastic wrap and cover loosely with more wrap, then with a damp towel while you work.

Lazy Lumpia

Serves 8

- 4 (2.5-ounce) Boca® Burgers, defrosted and chopped up like ground beef
- 4 cloves garlic, minced
- 1 (small) onion, minced
- 1 (12-ounce) package chop suey mix *(carrots, red cabbage, mung bean sprouts, etc.)*
- 2 tablespoons *patis (fish sauce)*
- 4 (14- by 18-inch) sheets lowest fat phyllo dough, defrosted
- Butter-flavored cooking spray

Dipping Sauce:

- 3 cloves garlic, minced
- 1/4 cup cider vinegar
- 1 teaspoon soy sauce
- Black pepper to taste

To prepare the filling, sauté the garlic and onion in a large frying pan or wok in just enough water to keep them from sticking. Add chopped Boca® meatless burgers, vegetables, and *patis*. Cook for 2 minutes. Drain and cool.

Combine the dipping sauce ingredients in a bowl and set aside.

Preheat oven to 400 degrees. Lightly spray a cookie sheet.

To assemble the *lumpia*, cut the phyllo sheets in half along the long side, then place in plastic and under damp towel as described above. Place one cut sheet of phyllo dough with the long side facing you. Spray the entire surface with the butter-flavored cooking spray. Then place 4 tablespoons of the mixture about 2 inches from the bottom edge of the phyllo sheet. Fold in burrito fashion, spraying all surfaces again as you fold and roll. Repeat the procedure with the second half of the phyllo dough sheet. Spray all surfaces evenly.

Place *lumpias* on the cookie sheet and bake for 25 to 30 minutes or until golden brown. Cool slightly and serve warm with the dipping sauce or prepared sweet and sour sauce.

Per serving: *87 calories, 1 g fat, 814 mg sodium, 12 g carbohydrates, 3 g dietary fiber, 8 g protein.*

Asia/Thai

Posted on: Wednesday, July 25, 2007

Press, fold and roll this cool meal

Summer Rolls with Dipping Sauce

These Vietnamese "burritos" are a cool and easy main dish that requires virtually no cooking, and your family can even assemble their own. They are basically a wrap which contains mixed vegetables and bits of pork, shrimp, vermicelli, or other desired ingredients. When you get the wrapping down, you end up with a delicious surprise. Because, unlike spring rolls, they are not deep fried, they are lower in fat and calories but long on taste.

Summer Rolls
Serves 20

- 1 (12-ounce) package Vietnamese rice paper wrappers *(banh trang)*
- 1 (8-ounce) package rice sticks *(vermicelli)*
- 1 (small) bunch basil
- 1 (small) bunch mint
- 1 (small) bunch fresh Chinese parsley *(cilantro)*
- 1 (12-ounce) package chop suey mix *(carrots, red cabbage, mung bean sprouts, etc.)*
- 1 (20-ounce) block firm tofu, cut into 1/2-inch strips

Soften rice paper wrappers in warm water and place between paper towels. Following the directions on the package, cook the rice sticks; drain and plunge into cold water to stop the cooking. Set aside. Wash the basil, mint, and parsley. Strip the leaves from the stems. Lay out rice paper wrappers and fill with rice sticks, basil leaves, mint, parsley, chop suey mix, and tofu. Fold and roll as a burrito, tucking in the ends. Place rolls, seam side down, on a serving tray. Serve with a dipping sauce.

Per serving: 150 calories, 2.5 g fat, 0 g saturated fat, 0 mg cholesterol, 100 mg sodium, 26 g carbohydrate, 2 g dietary fiber, 0 g sugar, 7 g protein.

Dipping Sauce:

- 1/2 cup reduced-fat peanut butter
- 4 teaspoons fresh ginger root, grated
- 8 cloves garlic, minced
- 8 stalks green onions, cut into 1/4-inch pieces
- 2 tablespoons vegetable broth
- 3/4 cup soy sauce or hoisin sauce
- 1/2 cup rice wine vinegar
- 1/2 cup brown rice syrup or other desired natural sweetener
- 3/4 cup fresh Chinese parsley *(cilantro)*, chopped
- Hot sauce to taste

Combine above ingredients and mix until smooth. Adjust seasoning to taste. Makes about 3 cups of sauce.

Per serving (with soy sauce): 35 calories, 1 g fat, 0 g saturated fat, 0 mg cholesterol, 275 mg sodium, 5 g carbohydrate, 0 g dietary fiber, 2 g sugar, 1 g protein.

Per serving (with hoisin): 40 calories, 1 g fat, 0 g saturated fat, 0 mg cholesterol, 90 mg sodium, 7 g carbohydrate, 0 g dietary fiber, 3 g sugar, 1 g protein.

Caribbean/ Puerto Rican

Empanadillas
(pork pastry appetizers or entrée)
Makes 20 and Serves 10

Achiote Oil:

2 ounces annatto seeds or 1 1/2 to 2 tablespoons of *goya* powder or chili powder
1 cup canola oil

Empanadillas:

1/2 pound lean pork, finely diced
1 tablespoon *achiote* oil
1/2 onion, finely chopped
2 (large) cloves garlic, minced
1/2 green pepper, finely chopped
1/2 cup fresh Chinese parsley *(cilantro)*, chopped
1 (7-ounce) jar pimentos, chopped
1 teaspoon dried oregano
1 (8-ounce) can tomato sauce
1 teaspoon salt
1/4 teaspoon red pepper, crushed
2 cans (15-ounce) home-style biscuits
Garlic-flavored oil cooking spray

To prepare the *achiote* oil, put annatto seeds and oil in a small saucepan. Simmer for approximately 5 minutes over low heat or until oil turns a dark red color. Strain immediately into a glass jar and let cool. Makes 1 cup. Cover and store the unused *achiote* oil in the refrigerator.

Preheat oven to 375 degrees.

To prepare the *empanadillas*, brown the pork in *achiote* oil in a large saucepan. Stir in onion, garlic, green pepper, parsley, pimientos, and oregano. Simmer covered for 10 minutes. Add tomato sauce, salt, and red pepper. Simmer over low heat for 1 hour. Stir occasionally. Cool.

Take one biscuit and flatten. Fill with 1 heaping teaspoon of filling. Fold the biscuit in a half-moon and pinch the edges together. Place on a lightly greased cookie sheet. Continue until all 20 biscuits are filled. Bake for 10 to 13 minutes or until golden brown. Serve warm or cold.

Per serving: *89 calories, 4 g fat, 6 g carbohydrates, 1 g dietary fiber, 8 g protein.*

Europe/Italian

Posted on: Wednesday, July 11, 2007

Caponata a delightful appetizer
Eggplant Caponata

Eggplant *caponata* is an eggplant relish that originated in Sicily. It is served as an appetizer at room temperature. Traditionally, it is made from chopped, fried eggplants and peppers and seasoned with green or black olives, capers, and celery. During the 1700s, it was considered a main course. Today it is served as a side dish or appetizer. Restaurants in Sicily add lobster, shrimp, fish, and baby octopus to the sauce.

Eggplant Caponata
Serves 10

1 (large) eggplant, cut into 3/4-inch squares
Extra virgin olive oil spray
1/2 cup red onion, chopped finely
5 cloves garlic, minced
1/4 cup green olives with pimento, chopped
3 tablespoons capers
1/2 teaspoon cocoa powder
3 tablespoons balsamic vinegar
1 tablespoon turbinado sugar
    or sugar substitute
1/4 cup red wine
1 cup Italian tomato sauce with basil
Ground pepper to taste

Lay the eggplant squares in a colander and sprinkle evenly with salt. Put the colander in the sink and place a plate on top of the eggplant. Put a heavy weight on the plate to press on the eggplant for half an hour. This process releases the bitter juices of the eggplant.

Heat the oven to 375 degrees. Wipe off excess salt and juices from the eggplant. Spray olive oil on a baking sheet and spread the eggplant on the surface. Bake for 35 minutes or until golden brown and softened.

Spray olive oil in a frying pan and sauté onions until translucent, about 4 minutes. Add the garlic, green olives, and capers. Cook for 2 to 3 minutes and set aside. Add the roasted eggplant and cocoa powder and cook for 2 minutes.

In a small saucepan, combine the balsamic vinegar and the sugar and heat over medium heat until the sugar dissolves. To this mixture add the red wine, then combine with the eggplant mixture, and reduce the liquid by half. Add the tomato sauce and pepper and simmer for 10 minutes or until it reaches a thick-dip consistency. You can serve it right away, but it is best refrigerated overnight and brought back to room temperature the day you serve it. Serve with *crostini*, garlic toast, or pita bread.

Makes 2 cups *(approximately 2 or 3 tablespoons per serving)*.

Per serving *(without crostini, garlic toast, or pita bread)*: *70 calories, 2.5 g fat, 0 g saturated fat, 0 mg cholesterol, 200 mg sodium, 12 g carbohydrate, 3 g dietary fiber, 7 g sugar, 1 g protein.*

Europe/Mediterranean

Posted on: Wednesday, February 8, 2006

Taste the exotic side of spinach

Mediterranean Spinach Rice Balls

Spinach *(Spinacia olerasea)* is a flowering plant belonging to the family *Chenopodiaceae*. Originally, spinach was cultivated in southwestern Asia. It may have been the Persians who first began to cultivate it as a vegetable, because the root word for spinach, *esfenaj*, comes from their language. Also, the Chinese once referred to it as "the herb of Persia." Spinach found its way to North Africa, Syria, Arabia, and Spain. In the next century, spinach spread through Europe, largely grown in the gardens of monasteries. The first documented use of spinach in England was in 1551. Last year, in a poll of two thousand people, spinach was Britain's eighth most favored vegetable.

Mediterranean Spinach Rice Balls

Serves approximately 9

- 1 (10-ounce) box frozen chopped spinach, steamed for 2 minutes
- 1 cup red onion, minced
- 3 to 4 cloves garlic, minced
- 2 tablespoons Mediterranean seasoning
  (onion, garlic, oregano, mint)
- 2 cups brown rice, cooked
- 2 tablespoons balsamic vinegar
- 2 tablespoons dill, finely chopped, or 2 teaspoons dried dill

1/2 cup reduced-fat feta cheese *(optional)*
Sea salt and ground black pepper to taste
1 cup multigrain bread crumbs *(made from 2 slices bread plus 2 teaspoons Mediterranean seasoning)*
Extra virgin olive oil spray

Preheat the oven to 350 degrees.

Spray a large Dutch oven generously with olive oil. Sauté garlic and onions until transparent. Add spinach, Mediterranean seasonings, rice, balsamic vinegar, dill, and feta. Season with salt and pepper. Stir well, mashing the rice mixture against the sides of the pot with a large spoon until the mixture starts to hold together.

Spray two baking sheets with olive oil spray. Pack an 1 1/4-inch meatball shaper *(or large melon baller or small ladle)* with the rice mixture to form a sphere. Roll in bread crumb mixture. Place 1 inch apart on baking sheets. Spray the tops of the balls with olive oil spray. Bake for 20 to 25 minutes or until golden brown. Balls should by crispy on the outside and heated through the inside. Makes 30 to 35 balls.

Dipping sauce is optional if you don't mind the extra fat. Mix balsamic vinegar and drops of extra virgin olive oil according to personal taste.

Per serving (4 spinach balls without feta cheese or dipping sauce): 180 calories, 8 g fat, 1 g saturated fat, 0 mg cholesterol, 100 mg sodium, 23 g carbohydrate, 4 g dietary fiber, 3 g sugar, 5 g protein.

Per serving (4 spinach balls with feta cheese, without dipping sauce): 220 calories, 11 g fat, 3.5 g saturated fat, 15 mg cholesterol, 270 mg sodium, 24 g carbohydrate, 4 g dietary fiber, 4 g sugar, 7 g protein.

18 Appetizers

Hawaii Local Favorite

Dilly Dip
Serve 6

2 (12.3-ounce) boxes Mori-Nu Silken Lite Extra Firm Tofu
1/4 cup fresh lemon juice
1 teaspoon salt
1 teaspoon sugar
2 teaspoon dried dill leaves
1/2 teaspoon onion powder
1/2 teaspoon garlic powder
2 teaspoons dried basil
1/2 teaspoon Worcestershire sauce

Place all the ingredients into a blender. Blend until smooth. Remove from blender and place into covered container. Refrigerate until ready to use. Serve with raw vegetables. The flavor of the dip improves with age. It can be made a day before.

Per serving: *52 calories, 1 g fat, 4 g carbohydrates, 0.2 g dietary fiber, 8 g protein.*

Note: Tofu is an Asian product that is coagulated soybean curd. The word tofu is derived from the Chinese word *taofu.* You can buy it in soft, firm, and extra firm varieties that are most likely refrigerated, except for shelf varieties like silken tofu. The amount of fat varies from 1.5 to 4 grams.

Mexico

This is also a great dip for vegetables and low-fat chips.

Guacamole

Serves 4

1 (large) ripe avocado, mashed
2 tablespoons red onion, minced
1 clove garlic, minced
Juice of 1/2 lemon or lime
1 teaspoon Hawaiian salt

Mix the above ingredients together.

Per serving: *85 calories, 7 g fat, 5 g carbohydrates, 3 g dietary fiber, 1 g protein.*

Appetizers

Mexico

Other vegetables such as green onions and peppers *(red, yellow, and green)* can be added to this basic recipe. To give it a more tropical flair, add fresh pineapple or mango. Be creative and come up with your own special flavor by using different types of vinegars such as balsamic or raspberry. Beware of the jalapeño pepper—a little goes a long way!

Salsa
Serves 12

- 3 tomatoes, chopped
- 1/2 red onion, minced
- 1/2 bunch fresh Chinese parsley *(cilantro)*, minced
- 2 cloves garlic, minced
- 1 teaspoon garlic salt
- 1/2 teaspoon cumin
- 1 teaspoon chili powder
- Juice of 1 lemon
- 1/4 jalapeño pepper; minced

Combine above ingredients, cover, and refrigerate for several hours or overnight. Serve with tostadas, fajitas, and other Mexican dishes. Makes 3 cups.

Per serving: 16 calories, 0.2 g fat, 3 g carbohydrates, 1 g dietary fiber, 1 g protein.

Global Light Cuisine ∞ Carol Devenot   21

Mexico

Posted on: Wednesday, November 10, 2004
'Cook' `ahi with lime juice
Ceviche

In Hawai`i, we have our *poke*. In
Latin countries and elsewhere, they
have their *ceviche* *("say-vee-shay")*, or pickled fish.

Instead of cooking the fish by means of heat, it is
"cooked" with lime or lemon juice. The acid from the
juice denatures or changes the shape of the protein. I
remember the first time I taught this science concept to
my students, and they were so amazed that you could
actually "cook" the fish this way. I loved teaching food
science because kids really enjoy learning about what
happens when you combine different ingredients.

Ceviche
Serves 6

2 pounds *tombo `ahi* fillet, cut into
    1-inch chunks
1 teaspoon red pepper flakes
1 green jalapeño pepper, seeded and minced
1 yellow pepper, seeded and chopped
2 tablespoons green onions, sliced into
    1/4-inch pieces
1/2 teaspoon garlic powder
1 teaspoon Hawaiian salt
1 teaspoon sugar
1 cup fresh lime juice *(about 4 to 6 limes)*
2 tablespoons fresh Chinese parsley *(cilantro)*,
    chopped

In a large mixing bowl combine ingredients. Place in a glass or ceramic bowl and refrigerate overnight or until the fish turns white and opaque. Drain off the excess liquid. Serve as an appetizer or as the central element of a vegetable salad.

Per serving: *180 calories, 1.5 g fat, 4 g carbohydrates, less than 1 g dietary fiber, 350 mg sodium, 36 g protein.*

Global Light Cuisine ∞ Carol Devenot

South Pacific/Hawaiian

Posted on: Wednesday, May 16, 2007

A lesson on cholesterol, fats, our diet

Lynne's Tofu Poke

All animal life contains cholesterol, which is important to the function of the cells. Our livers produce all the cholesterol our bodies need, so we should avoid consuming additional cholesterol. Fats and cholesterol move throughout the body in bundles called lipoproteins. The LDLs *(I remember them as "lousy dense lipoproteins")* carry the cholesterol to the organs by way of the arteries. Large amounts of LDL can increase the growth of fatty deposits *(plaque)* on artery walls. This can cause atherosclerosis and other heart problems. The HDLs *(I refer to them as "healthy density lipoproteins")*, move cholesterol back to the liver for excretion through the bile. In general, people who exercise, don't smoke, and watch what they eat have higher HDLs. People who keep their cholesterol level at 150 or lower are less likely to have atherosclerosis.

Lynne's Tofu Poke

Serves 4

1 (20-ounce) block firm tofu
1 red onion, diced
2 stalks green onions, sliced into 1/4-inch slices
1/2 to 1 teaspoon Hawaiian salt
1 teaspoon red pepper flakes, crushed
2 tablespoons soy sauce

1 teaspoon black sesame seeds *(goma)*
1 teaspoon sesame oil
1/2 cup *ogo (Hawaiian seaweed)*, chopped

Drain tofu; express as much liquid as possible. Cut the block of firm tofu into 1/2-inch cubes. Place into a bowl and add remaining ingredients. Toss lightly, cover, and chill in refrigerator for at least 1 hour.

Per serving: *180 calories, 11 g fat, 2 g saturated fat, 0 mg cholesterol, 950 mg sodium, 7 g carbohydrate, 3 g dietary fiber, 2 g sugar, 17 g protein.*

Variations: You may use 1 pound `ahi` in this recipe instead of tofu. You can also put the above ingredients in a hot wok with vegetable spray, and you'll come up with a delicious and nutritious stir fry.

Soups

Global Light Cuisine ∞ Carol Devenot

Asia/Chinese

Posted on: Wednesday, March 23, 2005

The soup that makes you better

Jenny's Watercress Soup

Jenny cooks authentic Chinese style. When I asked her where she got her chicken bones she said at the Kaimuki Times Supermarket. Here is a case for knowing the butcher. How you going know, if you no ask? Don't be afraid to ring that little bell for the meat department. In my experience, they have always been some of the most helpful people in the market. If you don't want to go through the trouble of making the soup from scratch, look for the lowest sodium chicken broth at your local supermarket or organic food stores. *(Swanson's Certified Organic in the cardboard container, if you can find it, actually tastes like chicken and has less than 600 mg of sodium per cup.)*

Jenny's Watercress Soup

Serves 4

1 1/2 pounds fresh chicken bones
1 (2-inch) piece *chung choy* *(salted, preserved turnip)*
4 1/2 cups water
1/2 bunch watercress, washed and drained
1/4 to 1/2 pound fish cake *(Chinese style, not kamaboko)*
1/8 teaspoon sesame oil
1 teaspoon peanut oil
Pinch of white pepper
1 to 2 (small) stalks green onions, finely sliced

Place the chicken bones, *chung choy*, and water in a large pot and bring to boil, then reduce heat to simmer and cook for 1 hour. Skim off foam. Cut off about 3 to 4 inches of the watercress stalks above the roots and add these during the last half hour of cooking. Cut the rest of watercress into 1-inch lengths and set aside. When broth is done, discard the bones, *chung choy*, and watercress stalks. Strain the soup and return liquid to the pot and simmer.

While the broth is simmering, combine the fish cake and oils in a bowl and beat until mixture turns white. Add pepper and onion. Using a wet teaspoon, scoop and drop small mounds of fish cake into soup where it will turn white and rise to the surface. Add the 1-inch pieces of watercress, simmer for about 2 minutes, and serve immediately.

Per serving: *100 calories, 5 g fat, 1 g carbohydrates, 1 g dietary fiber, 305+ mg sodium, 12 g protein.*

Global Light Cuisine ∞ Carol Devenot

Asia/Chinese

Posted on: Wednesday, February 7, 2007

A pot of jook is sure to comfort on chilly day

Mom's Comforting Jook
(Turkey Rice Soup)

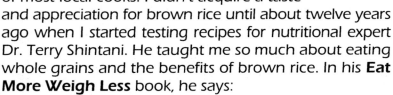

Back then, white rice was the chosen grain of most local cooks. I didn't acquire a taste and appreciation for brown rice until about twelve years ago when I started testing recipes for nutritional expert Dr. Terry Shintani. He taught me so much about eating whole grains and the benefits of brown rice. In his **Eat More Weigh Less** book, he says:

> Any form of brown rice is better than refined white rice. The rice is brown because it is the whole, unprocessed grain, which accounts for its rich, nutty color and chewy texture. That means none of the nutrition has been processed out, and the grain contains its full complement of nutrients, such as vitamin B complex, vitamin E, and fiber.

Mom's Comforting Jook
(turkey rice soup)
Serves 8 to 10

6 to 7 dried Chinese black mushrooms
Leftover turkey or chicken bones
5 quarts water
1 (2-inch) piece *chung choy* (salted, preserved turnip)
1 (1-inch) piece fresh ginger root, peeled and smashed
1 1/2 cups brown rice, washed and drained

2 stalks celery, cut in half
Salt to taste
Soy sauce to taste
Black pepper to taste

Garnish
2 stalks green onions, sliced into 1/4-inch slices
3 to 4 sprigs fresh Chinese parsley *(cilantro)*, chopped
Bamboo shoots, sliced matchstick size

In a small bowl, cover the mushrooms with boiling water to reconstitute.

In a large soup pot, combine the turkey bones, water, *chung choy,* and ginger. Cook over medium heat for 1 hour. Remove the bones, *chung choy,* ginger, and celery from the pot and place in a colander to cool. When cool enough to handle, debone the carcass. Strain the stock and return to the pot. Remove and discard mushroom stems, and slice caps into 1/4-inch slices and add to the stock. Add the rice and deboned turkey meat and cook for 1 1/2 hours. *(I like to do this in a crock pot, but it takes longer.)* To thin out the soup, add chicken broth and cook for another half hour. Serve hot in Chinese soup bowls. Prepare plate of green onions, parsley, and sliced bamboo shoots as garnish.

Per serving:* *200 calories, 3 g fat, 1 g saturated fat, 25 mg cholesterol, 50 mg sodium, 30 g carbohydrate, 2 g dietary fiber, 2 g sugar, 14 g protein.*

* Based on 8 servings, 2 cups of turkey on bones, and without salt and soy sauce to taste.

Asia/Japanese

Posted on: Wednesday, September 19, 2007

Saimin carb count drops, thanks to shirataki

Low-Carb Saimin

Kale's in Hawai'i Kai now carries tofu *shirataki*, a noodle-shaped tofu. It has only 3 grams of carbohydrates, no cholesterol, and 10 percent calcium—plus, it's easy to cook.

Shirataki is made from yam flour *(polysaccharide glucomannan)*. The gelatinous strings made from this product forms the noodle. *Konnyaku* root *(yam flour)* has few calories and is easy to digest. This product can be used in soups, *sukiyaki*, and pasta dishes. *(It tasted so good, I used it in place of spaghetti noodles the next week.)*

Low-Carb Saimin

Serves 4

- 4 cups water
- 2 (8-ounce) packages tofu *shirataki*
- 1 to 2 tablespoons chicken-style vegetarian broth powder
- 1 cup baby bok choy, *choy sum*, or any other greens
- 1 (6-ounce) *char siu* tempura fish cake, julienne style *(optional)*
- 2 green onions, green and white parts, cut into 1/4-inch slices
- 1/2 cup shiitake mushroom, soaked in hot water and sliced

Togarashi or Japanese red pepper flakes
(optional)

In a saucepan, add water and bring to a boil. Sprinkle in the broth and lower the heat. Add the baby bok choy and allow to heat to blanch the greens. In another saucepan, cook the tofu *shirataki* according to the directions on the package.

Divide the tofu *shirataki* in saimin bowls and top with fish cake, shiitake, and green onions. Pour the soup with the vegetables over the garnished noodles. Serve hot. Spice it up with *togarashi*.

Per serving (with fish cake): *400 calories, 16 g fat, 2.5 g saturated fat, 40 mg cholesterol, more than 2000 mg sodium, 29 g carbohydrate, 5 g dietary fiber, 5 g sugar, 39 g protein.*

Asia/Japanese

Posted on: Wednesday, December 26, 2007

An alternative soup for Japanese New Year

Mitsuko's Oden

I have never had this soup before, but after eating it I thought it would be a great soup to serve for Japanese New Year. Traditionally, *ozoni—mochi* soup is served as the first meal of the day, but *oden,* as Mitsuko makes it, might be an easier alternative.

Mitsuko tells me that *oden,* also known as Japanese hot pot, is served year-round in Japan but especially during the winter. They even have *oden* stands *(yatai)*, which resemble our old saimin stands. She says *oden* is not fattening and is easy to digest and children in Japan love it. She remembers that her grandmother always cooked a large pot of *oden, nabe* style *(hot pot style)*, with lots of vegetables. She now is doing just what her grandmother taught her, by serving it to her family, friends, and even fellow employees.

Mitsuko's Oden

Serves 6

- 1/2 daikon radish, peeled and cut into 1 1/2-inch rounds
- 1 block of *konnyaku (yam starch cake)*, cut into 1 1/2-inch pieces
- 1/2 to 1 pound *kibun no kisetsu (oden mix consisting of assorted fish cake)*
- 2 strips *konbu (green Japanese seaweed, a kelp)*

4 hard boiled eggs, peeled
Water
Dashi shoyu (seasoning with dashi, shoyu, and mirin)

Wipe *konbu* with a damp paper towel and cut with scissors into 1 1/2-inch pieces. In a large stock pot, place the daikon, *konnyaku*, *oden* mix, *konbu*, and boiled eggs. Add water to cover. Add *dashi shoyu* to taste and simmer for 40 to 60 minutes. The longer you cook the *oden*, the better the flavor. Taste and add *dashi shoyu* as needed.

Per serving:* *210 calories, 12 g fat, 3 g saturated fat, 185 mg cholesterol, 250 mg sodium, 11 g carbohydrate, 1 g dietary fiber, 1 g sugar, 15 g protein.*

* Without *dashi shoyu* to taste and based on 1 pound *kibun no kisetsu*.

Asia/Korean

Posted on: Wednesday, July 13, 2005

Red pepper, vegetable create healthy Korean chicken soup

Korean Chicken Soup

Kochu karu, Korean hot red pepper powder, is also used in this soup. The Korean variety is one of the hottest, sweetest, and most flavorful powders anywhere. It should be brilliant, flaming red, pungent, and sweet smelling. In some stores you can find three grades of the powder. The fine ground is for cooking and making *kochujang*, coarse ground for making kim chee, and crushed flakes for cooking and garnish. Store in a tightly covered jar or plastic bag in the refrigerator; it stays fresh for several months. Once it loses pungency, discard it.

Korean Chicken Soup

Serves 8 to 10

- 3 chicken breasts, boneless and skinless
- 4 cups water
- 1 (2-inch) piece ginger root, peeled and smashed
- 8 cups low-sodium chicken broth
- 1 to 2 tablespoons *kochujang* (hot red pepper paste)
- 1 to 2 tablespoons *kochu karu* (hot red pepper powder)
- 1 teaspoon sesame oil
- 2 tablespoons low-sodium soy sauce
- 6 to 12 cloves garlic, minced

4 to 5 stalks (large) green onions
1 cup *kosari (packaged fernbracken in water)*
1 (20-ounce) block low-fat tofu, cubed
1/2 pound bean sprouts

In a large Dutch oven, simmer the chicken breasts and ginger with 4 cups of water for about 1 hour. Remove chicken with slotted spoon, cool and shred into large pieces. Remove ginger and add the chicken broth to the same pot; bring back to a simmer. Meanwhile, in a small bowl, mix the *kochujang, kochu karu,* sesame oil, soy sauce, and garlic. Add the pieces of chicken to this mixture and turn to coat. Place the seasoned chicken, green onions, and *kosari (fernbracken)* in the chicken broth. Cook gently for 15 minutes over medium heat. In the last 10 minutes, add the tofu and bean sprouts to the soup. Serve with steamed brown rice.

Per serving for 8: *140 calories, 2.5 g total fat, 0 g saturated fat, 30 mg cholesterol, 800 mg sodium, 10 g carbohydrates, 2 g dietary fiber, 2 g sugar, 21 g protein.*

Per serving for 10: *120 calories, 2 g total fat, 0 g saturated fat, 25 mg cholesterol, 650 mg sodium, 8 g carbohydrates, 2 g dietary fiber, 2 g sugar, 17 g protein.*

Europe/Italian

Posted on: Wednesday, September 7, 2005

Lightening up luscious Tuscan soup
Slimmed-Down Tomato-Butternut Squash Bisque

I was surprised that this soup included butternut squash—a readily available winter squash with a yellowish tan skin and bright orange interior. Roasted, its flavor is sweet and rich, similar to sweet potatoes. Compared to its ridged and bumpy relatives, butternut squash is easy to cut. Butternuts vary from pear-shaped to more cylindrical forms. As for their size, they generally range from 8 to 12 inches and weigh 1 to 4 pounds. This squash is an excellent source of vitamin A, vitamin C and manganese, and contains beta-crytoxanthin, an orange-red carotenoid that may lower your risk of lung cancer.

Slimmed-Down Tomato-Butternut Squash Bisque
Serves 6

- 2 tablespoons butter or extra virgin olive oil
- 1 onion, chopped
- 3 cloves garlic, minced
- 1 (28-ounce) can whole tomatoes, with liquid
- 1/4 to 1/2 cup roasted garlic tomato paste
- 2 cups vegetable or organic chicken stock
- 2 to 2 1/2 cups butternut squash, peeled and diced

Salt and ground pepper to taste
2 tablespoons fresh basil, chopped
1/2 teaspoon dried thyme
1 to 1 1/4 cups nonfat half-and-half
  or nonfat yogurt
Several dashes of Tabasco®
  or other hot pepper sauce

Garnish:

Basil leaves, sliced
Parsley, minced

In a large saucepan, sauté onions and garlic in butter or oil over medium-low heat until soft and golden. Add tomatoes, tomato paste, chicken stock, butternut squash, salt, pepper, basil, and thyme. Bring to a boil, then reduce heat. Partially cover and simmer for about 30 to 35 minutes, or until squash is fork-tender. Purée the soup in a blender, and then pour back into the saucepan. Stir in nonfat half-and-half or yogurt, splash in the hot pepper sauce, and taste for seasoning. Heat the soup just to a boil, then ladle into bowls.

Garnish with sliced basil leaves or minced parsley.

Per serving (without salt): *160 calories, 4.5 g total fat, 2.5 g saturated fat, 10 mg cholesterol, greater than 500 mg sodium, 29 g carbohydrate, 5 g dietary fiber, 12 g sugar, 5 g protein.*

Global Light Cuisine ∞ Carol Devenot

Europe/Portuguese

This becomes a meal in itself when you serve it with rice. For the next day you can boil some macaroni and add to the soup for a different type of dish. For a spicier flavor add Tobasco®.

Healthy Portuguese Bean Soup
Serves 10

4 to 6 cloves garlic, minced
4 stalks celery including leaves, chopped
1 red onion, sliced
1 tablespoon dried oregano
1 tablespoon ground cumin
1 tablespoon chili powder
2 (15-ounce) cans kidney beans
1 (28-ounce) can whole tomatoes
1 (8-ounce) can tomato sauce
2 carrots, peeled and cut into 1 1/2-inch pieces
1/2 head cabbage, sliced
4 red potatoes, peeled and cut into 1 1/2-inch pieces
1 (11.2-ounce) package Smart Links® Italian Vegetarian Sausage
4 cups chicken-style vegetarian broth
Pinch of sea salt

In a large stockpot, water-sauté garlic and onion in 1 cup of broth. Add oregano, cumin, and chili powder. Add the celery, tomatoes, tomato sauce, vegetarian sausage, remaining broth, and salt and pepper and cook on low heat for 1 1/2 hours. In the last half hour, add carrots and potatoes and cook until fork tender

Per serving: 275 calories, 7 g fat, 42 g carbohydrate, 13 g dietary fiber, 16 g protein.

Global Light Cuisine ∞ Carol Devenot

Mainland U.S. Favorite

Posted on: Wednesday, May 3, 2006

Pearl barley fortifies this turkey soup

Hearty Turkey Soup

Pearl barley's puffy grain and thickening quality makes it favorable for soups, stews and side dishes. In the market, you will find two types: hulled and pearl barley. Hulled barley is considered the more nutritious because only the outer hulls are polished off. Pearl barley is polished until the outer bran layer is removed, which makes it less chewy and quicker to cook while still nutritious.

Hearty Turkey Soup

Serves 6 to 8

- 7 (1 1/2 inches in diameter) dried shiitake mushrooms
- Extra virgin olive oil spray
- 3 leeks *(including the green part)*, coarsely chopped
- 3 to 4 cloves garlic, minced
- 1/2 pound button mushrooms
- 2 carrots, peeled and chopped
- 2 celery stalks, peeled and cut into half-moons
- 1/2 cup pearl barley
- 2 turkey breasts or thighs
    (about 1 1/2 pounds, skinless)
- 8 cups organic chicken broth
- 3 tablespoons fresh Chinese parsley *(cilantro)*, chopped
- Sea salt to taste
- Ground pepper to taste

Soak the shiitake mushrooms in boiling water for 30 minutes. Drain the mushrooms and save the liquid. Cut off the stems and chop the mushrooms into 1/2-inch pieces.

Spray a large pot with olive oil and sauté the leeks until soft. Add the garlic, button mushrooms, carrots, celery, and barley and sauté for 1 minute. Remove the mixture from the heat to a small bowl. Spray a little more olive oil in the pot and brown the turkey breasts. Add the sauté mixture and the chicken and mushroom broths. Reduce the heat to low, cover, and cook until the barley is tender, about 1 1/2 hours.

Remove the turkey breasts from the pot and shred the meat into 1-inch chunks; return to the pot. Stir in chopped parsley and simmer for 5 minutes. Season with sea salt and fresh ground pepper. Serve hot with crusty bread.

Per serving (8 servings, without salt): *200 calories, 2.5 g fat, 0 g saturated fat, 60 mg cholesterol, 1000+ mg sodium, 22 g carbohydrate, 4 g dietary fiber, 5 g sugar, 25 g protein.*

Mainland U.S. Favorite

Posted on: Wednesday, January 11, 2006

Broccoli not a yuck veggie at all

Light and Creamy Broccoli Soup

Broccoli comes from the cabbage or *brassicaceae* family, classified as the *Italica Cultivar* group of the species *Brassica oleracea*. Members of this group include cabbage, cauliflower, kale, collard greens, kohlrabi, and Brussels sprouts. It is usually boiled, steamed, or eaten raw. High in vitamin C and fiber, the vegetable also contains an anti-carcinogenic compound, *glucoraphanin*.

Usually grown in cooler climates, broccoli was cultivated in Italy long before it was eaten in other parts of Europe. Thomas Jefferson, an experimental gardener, planted broccoli along with other vegetables in Monticello in 1767. However, broccoli remained an exotic in American gardens for a long time. It wasn't until 1922 that the timing was right. That year, Stephano and Andrea D'Arrigo, immigrants from Messina, Italy, made tentative plantings in San Jose, California, and shipped a few crates to the Boston's North End, the city's Italian community. More than 80 years later, broccoli is now a staple nationwide. Here's one more healthy way to prepare it—perfect for our recent chilly nights.

Light and Creamy Broccoli Soup

Serves 4 to 6

2 tablespoons butter
1 1/2 cups onion, chopped

3 to 4 cloves garlic, minced
2 bay leaves
1 (medium) bell pepper
4 cups broccoli, chopped
2 1/2 cups organic chicken broth
1/4 teaspoon allspice
Dash of dried thyme
1/2 teaspoon dried basil
1 to 2 cups nonfat milk
1/2 cup nonfat sour cream
Salt to taste
Black pepper to taste
White pepper to taste
1 cup broccoli florets, thinly sliced, lightly steamed

In a Dutch oven, melt butter and add the onion, garlic, and bay leaves. Cook until translucent. Add the green pepper, chopped broccoli, chicken broth, allspice, thyme, and basil. Cover and cook over medium heat for 10 minutes or until broccoli is tender.

Remove the bay leaf and purée the soup a cup at a time with the milk in a blender or food processor. Whisk in the sour cream. Heat to desired temperature. Garnish with steamed broccoli florets.

Per serving (6 servings, 1 cup nonfat milk, without salt): *120 calories, 4.5 g fat, 2.5 g saturated fat, 10 mg cholesterol, 330 mg sodium, 15 g carbohydrate, 3 g dietary fiber, 8 g sugar, 7 g protein.*

Mainland U.S. Favorite

Posted on: Wednesday, March 8, 2006

A pea soup with no ham hocks
No Need Ham Split Pea Soup

Provence is in southeastern France, next to Italy. The food of this region is influenced by its warm climate, coastal location, and other neighboring countries. Olive oil plays a greater role in this region than butter, and the cuisine relies on fresh vegetables, herbs, and seafood.

Herbes de Provence is a mixture of aromatic plants. These herbs, either fresh or dried, are grown in the region. Typically, the mixture contains chervil, basil, rosemary, tarragon, savory, thyme, and parsley.

No Need Ham Split Pea Soup
Serves 4 to 6

Extra virgin olive oil spray
2 tablespoons garlic, minced
2 cups sweet Maui onions, coarsely chopped
1 1/2 tablespoons *herbes de Provence*
1 teaspoon whole fennel seeds
1 (large) bay leaf
2 (large) carrots, halved lengthwise and sliced
2 (large) celery stalks, sliced
6 to 7 cups water, boiling
1 (16-ounce) package dried green split peas
1/3 cup fresh Italian flat-leaf parsley, minced
Sea salt to taste
White pepper to taste

Spray a large Dutch oven generously with olive oil. Sauté garlic and onions until transparent. Stir in *herbes de Provence*, fennel, and bay leaf. Add carrots, celery, split peas, and boiling water. Bring to boil and simmer covered until split peas are tender *(about 2 1/2 to 3 hours)*. Remove bay leaf and stir well as you add the parsley and salt and pepper to taste.

Per serving (6 servings, without salt): *330 calories, 1.5 g fat, 0 g saturated fat, 0 mg cholesterol, 300 mg sodium, 0 g carbohydrate, 2 g fiber, 6 g sugar, 21 g protein.*

Per serving (4 servings, without salt): *500 calories, 2.5 g fat, 0 g saturated fat, 0 mg cholesterol, 400 mg sodium, 90 g carbohydrate, 3 g fiber, 9 g sugar, 32 g protein.*

Mainland U.S./American Indian

Posted on: Wednesday, November 15, 2006

Corn chowder packs Southwestern punch

Southwestern Corn Chowder

Southwestern food is a mixture of American Indian, Spanish, Mexican, and Anglo traditions. One of the perks for the partners of convention goers was to attend the Santa Fe Cooking School, which offers classes in New Mexico cuisine, Spanish *tapas*, American Indian, and contemporary Southwestern foods.

The chef who demonstrated our meal taught us many things about these ingredients. He said that the chilies in New Mexico have thick skin, so they should be grilled whole to soften them and bring out the flavor, then chopped. He toasted fresh spices and ground them using a coffee grinder set aside for that purpose. I was so inspired; I bought the school's cookbook and came up with my own version.

Southwestern Corn Chowder

Serves 6

- 1 (small) fresh chili such as jalapeño pepper
  (or less, if you're chili sensitive)
- 1/2 red bell pepper
- 1 cup yellow onions, finely chopped
- 3 cloves garlic, minced
- 1/4 teaspoon sea salt
- 2 teaspoons ground cumin, toasted
- 2 cups russet potatoes, diced

3 cups vegetable or organic chicken stock
3 cups fresh corn or frozen corn kernels
Sea salt to taste
Lime wedges
Fresh Chinese parsley *(cilantro)* for garnish

Grill the chili or jalapeño pepper and the red bell pepper until skin is golden brown. Cool, split in half, and remove seeds. Finely chop each, keeping separate, and set aside.

Sauté the onions and garlic in a little water until translucent. Add 1/4 teaspoon salt. In a small bowl, make a paste of the cumin and 1 tablespoon of stock and stir into sauté. Add the fresh chili to the sauté. Add the potatoes and the stock and simmer until the potatoes are fork-tender, about 10 minutes. Then add the roasted bell pepper and corn and simmer until all the vegetables are tender. Measure out approximately 3 cups of soup and purée in a blender or food processor. Return this mixture to the soup. Salt to taste and serve with lime wedges to squeeze into the soup. Garnish with parsley.

Per serving: *130 calories, 1.5 g fat, 0 g saturated fat, 0 mg cholesterol, 125 mg sodium, 29 g carbohydrate, 4 g dietary fiber, 5 g sugar, 4 g protein.*

Mexico

Posted on: Wednesday, November 9, 2005
Avocado as garnish for soup
Mexicano Sop A Con Rose Avos

Avocados are native to Mexico. The ancient Aztecs call them *ahuacat*. Spaniards called avocados *aguacate* or "alligator pears." The British call an avocado a "butter pear," perhaps they used them in place of butter in warm colonial climates. The avocado is a pear-shaped fruit that tastes more like a vegetable. It is one of the few fruits that contain fat. One average size avocado contains some 335 calories. A larger one would be about 370 calories. However, these calories also come with many beneficial nutrients: protein, calcium, magnesium, phosphorus, potassium, iron, some B vitamins, and vitamin E.

Fortunately, the fat in avocado is of the monounsaturated variety. Research has shown that monounsaturated fats help lower LDL *("bad")* cholesterol.

Mexicano Sop a Con Rose Avos
Serves 6

- 1 tablespoon extra virgin olive oil
- 1 (large) red onion, chopped
- 4 cloves garlic, minced
- 2 (large) chicken breasts, boneless and skinless, cut into l-inch cubes
- 1 cup canned plum tomatoes *(Roma)*, drained or 1 (10-ounce) can tomatoes with green chilies *(if you like it spicy)*

1 teaspoon dried ground cumin
1 (1- by 1-inch) piece ginger root, smashed
Salt and pepper to taste
1 (15-ounce) can hominy
4 cups water
1/4 to 1/2 cup fresh Chinese parsley *(cilantro)*,
    chopped to taste

Garnish:

Avocado slices
1/4 cup low-fat cheddar cheese, grated
Fresh Chinese parsley *(cilantro)*,
    chopped to taste

In a large Dutch oven, sauté onions and garlic in the olive oil until translucent. Add chicken breasts and sauté for 10 minutes. Add tomatoes, cumin, ginger, salt, pepper, hominy, water, and a handful of parsley. Bring to a boil and simmer for 1 hour. Remove the ginger. Serve hot with avocado slices, cheese, and parsley as garnish. Serve with warm whole-wheat, low-carb, low-fat tortillas.

Per serving (with low-fat cheddar, without avocado or tortillas):
170 calories, 4 g total fat, 1 g saturated fat, 35 mg cholesterol, 340 mg sodium, 15 g carbohydrate, 2 g dietary fiber, 3 g sugar, 16 g protein.

Middle East

Posted on: Wednesday, September 20, 2006

Fragrant harira soup celebrates Muslim tradition

Harira (Ramadan Soup)

It's also often referred to as Ramadan soup. Ramadan, the Muslim month of fasting, usually falls on the ninth month of the Islamic calendar. This year, Ramadan begins on September 24. Muslims around the world, including about 8 million in North America, will be acknowledging the month with blessings, prayers, charity, and fasting. Adult, healthy Muslims do not eat or drink, including water, during daylight hours.

During Ramadan throughout the Muslim world, most restaurants are closed during the day. Before the sun rises, families eat a small meal or *suhoor*. When the sun goes down, the fast is broken with a meal known as *iftar*.

Many homes throughout the world prepare *harira* soup. This fragrant soup of Berber origin is flavored with coriander and lemon. *Harira* has many variations, from simple vegetarian to elaborate meat varieties.

Harira
(Ramadan soup)
Serves 6

   6 cups boiling water
   1/4 cup dried lentils
   2 tablespoons brown rice, uncooked

3 tablespoons whole-wheat flour in 1/4 cup cold water
1/2 pound chicken breasts, boneless and skinless, cut into 1/2-inch cubes
2 (medium) onions, chopped
3 cloves garlic, crushed
Extra virgin olive oil spray
1 teaspoon butter
2 tablespoons ground coriander
Sea salt to taste
White pepper to taste
1 (15.5-ounce) can garbanzo beans, drained
1/2 cup fresh Italian flat-leaf parsley, chopped
1 (8-ounce) can tomato sauce
Juice of 1 lemon

In a Dutch oven, simmer lentils and rice for 20 minutes in 6 cups of water. Mix the flour and water thoroughly and add to the simmered lentils and rice, stirring frequently.

In a nonstick frying pan, sauté the onions and garlic in olive oil and butter and remove from pan when done. In the same frying pan, brown the chicken. When the chicken is golden brown, add back the onions and spices and enough water to cover. Simmer until the chicken is tender. Add the meat mixture, beans, parsley, and tomato sauce to the lentils and rice. Simmer 15 minutes. Add lemon juice just before serving.

Per serving (without salt): *250 calories, 9 g fat, 2.5 g saturated fat, 25 mg cholesterol, 300 mg sodium, 31 g carbohydrate, 6 g dietary fiber, 6 g sugar, 15 g protein.*

Salads and Condiments

Global Light Cuisine ∞ Carol Devenot 55

Asia/Chinese

Oriental Chicken Salad
Serves 4 to 6

6 ounces chicken breast, cooked and shredded
3 cups romaine lettuce, shredded
1/2 cup green onions, sliced 1/4-inch thick
1/2 Japanese cucumber, sliced 1/4-inch thick
1 bunch fresh Chinese parsley *(cilantro)*, sliced 1 1/2-inch lengths
1/4 cup slivered almonds or soy nuts

Dressing:

1 tablespoon sugar or honey
1/4 cup cider vinegar
1 teaspoon soy sauce
1 teaspoon sesame oil
1 tablespoon sesame seeds
1/4 teaspoon ground black pepper

Combine vinegar, sugar, soy sauce, sesame oil, sesame seeds, and pepper in a small jar. In a large salad bowl, toss romaine lettuce, green onions, cucumber, and parsley. Garnish with chicken breast and slivered almonds or soy nuts. Shake dressing well and sprinkle on the salad.

Per serving: *158 calories, 7 g fat, 9 g carbohydrates, 2 g dietary fiber, 16 g protein.*

Variations: Fresh celery and bell pepper can be added for additional vegetables, vitamins, and fiber. This is a good recipe for any leftover Char Siu Chicken *(page 130)*, khal-bi chicken, or Shoyu Chicken *(page 136)*. Be creative!

Asia/Filipino

This salad with the shrimp is a main dish and is delicious with sticky rice. Shredded carrots and cucumbers can also be used. For an interesting twist, you can use garlic-roasted peanuts available in Chinatown.

Green Papaya Salad

Serves 4

1 (large) green papaya
4 cherry tomatoes
8 (medium) shrimp, shelled and deveined
1 tablespoon sweet Maui onion, minced
1 head of romaine lettuce, thinly shredded
1 tablespoon peanuts, roasted, for garnish

Vinaigrette Dressing:

1/4 cup lime juice
1/4 cup Japanese rice vinegar
3 cloves garlic, minced
1 to 2 teaspoons chili paste
1 teaspoon *patis (fish sauce)*
1/2 teaspoon Hawaiian salt

Chop peanuts to course ground.

Cook the shrimp briefly in salted boiling water until pink. Drain and set aside.

Cut the papaya in half and remove the seeds. Shred papaya with a fork or mandolin.

Wash and cut the tomatoes in half.

Global Light Cuisine ∞ Carol Devenot   57

Place the papaya, tomatoes, onion, and shrimp in a mixing bowl. Combine the ingredients of the vinaigrette and pour over the salad mixture. Stir the mixture carefully.

Place the shredded romaine on a serving platter and arrange the papaya salad over the shredded romaine. Garnish with ground peanuts.

Per serving: *108 calories, 2 g fat, 17 g carbohydrates, 4 g dietary fiber, 6 g protein.*

Asia/Japanese

Namasu
(condiment)
Serves 4

2 Japanese cucumbers
2 (medium) carrots, peeled
4 stalks celery
1/2 turnip, peeled
1 tablespoon salt

Dressing:

1/2 cup Japanese rice vinegar
1/2 cup brown rice syrup or brown sugar
1 teaspoon salt
1 teaspoon fresh ginger root, grated fine

Slice cucumbers diagonally. Cut the carrots, celery, and turnips in half lengthwise. Slice into thin diagonal pieces. Sprinkle all vegetables with salt and allow it to set for 20 minutes. Rinse, drain, and squeeze the vegetables. Combine vinegar; syrup or sugar; salt, and fresh ginger. Pour over the vegetables. Refrigerate for 1 hour.

Per serving: *125 calories, 0.3 g fat, 28 g carbohydrates, 3 g dietary fiber, 2 g protein.*

Variations: *Wakame (a tender, leafy Japanese seaweed), ogo (Hawaiian seaweed), and other seaweed may be used. Also, small amounts of dried shrimp, canned clams, or abalone may be used. Adding the seafood would increase the fat content. Use sparingly.*

Asia/Korean

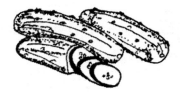

There is an art of making kim chee. It is all in the sauce. This is a quick way to having kim chee that is always fresh and spicy.

Quickie Cucumber Kim Chee
(condiment)
Serves 4

2 (medium) Japanese cucumbers
1/4 to 1/2 cup Huy Fang Faads® Tuang
   or Sriracha Sauce

Wash and slice cucumbers 1/4-inch thick. Mix the sauce with the cucumbers and serve immediately.

Per serving: *23 calories, 0 g fat, 6 g carbohydrates, 2 g dietary fiber, 2 g protein.*

Europe/Greek

Posted on: Wednesday, July 12, 2006

Couscous salad light and fresh
Greek Couscous Salad

Couscous can be made from various grains, though commonly it is a combination of semolina *(durum wheat flour)*, salt, and water. A typical recipe would call for two parts semolina to one part all-purpose flour. Handfuls of semolina are mixed with a little salt water and flour to form a dry, crumbly mixture, which is then passed through a colander to form the characteristic peppercorn-size bits. Finally, a little oil may be added to the rice-shaped "grains." Couscous, a versatile pasta, is usually served with vegetable or meat stews, but also, as here, in a light, fresh salad. You need to cook the couscous first, according to package directions, to soften it up.

Greek Couscous Salad
Serves 6

2 cups couscous, cooked
4 Roma tomatoes, diced
2 cups Japanese or English cucumber, diced
1/2 to 1 cup red onion, minced
1 to 2 cups fresh Italian flat-leaf parsley, chopped
2 cups canned garbanzo beans, drained
Red leaf lettuce *(for presentation)*

Dressing:

- 1 to 2 tablespoons extra virgin olive oil
- 1/2 cup balsamic vinegar
- 2 to 3 cloves garlic, minced
- 1 teaspoon Greek seasoning *(onion, spearmint, oregano, garlic, sea salt)*
- 1 to 3 teaspoons sea salt
- Fresh ground black pepper to taste

In a large mixing bowl, combine couscous, tomatoes, cucumber, red onion, parsley, and garbanzos.

Whisk together olive oil, balsamic vinegar, garlic, Greek seasoning, salt, and pepper. Drizzle over couscous mixture.

Arrange leaf lettuce on plates, top with a serving of salad *(or roll salad in leaf)*. Serve.

Per serving: *400 calories, 7 g fat, 0.5 g saturated fat, 0 mg cholesterol, 850 mg sodium, 72 g carbohydrate, 9 g fiber, 11 g sugar, 14 g protein.*

Europe/Greek

Posted on: Wednesday, November 17, 2004
Use the best olive oil for Greek salad
Greek Salad

I have tried different Greek salads that incorporate green pepper, celery, radishes, broccoli sprouts, watercress, and artichoke hearts. Warm pita bread is a nice accompaniment. If you want to create a dinner salad, add 12 ounces of boneless, skinless rotisserie chicken cut into thin strips or an equal amount of shelled and cooked shrimp. If you are not watching your carbs, you could add a side dish of cooked spinach or whole-wheat pasta.

Good extra virgin olive oil is a must. There is nothing worse than rancid olive oil. In Hawai`i, it helps to store oils in the refrigerator, which cuts down on the oxidation.

This salad goes well with other Greek dishes. It's no wonder Zorba was such a happy fellow!

Greek Salad
Serves 4

3 (medium) ripe tomatoes, cut into wedges
1 (large) English or Japanese cucumber, seeded and cut into 1/2-inch chunks
1 (small) red onion, cut into very thin half-moons
1/8 cup *kalamata* olives, pitted and halved

Global Light Cuisine ∞ Carol Devenot

12 cups salad greens *(arugula, spinach, romaine lettuce, or whatever you like)*, cut into bite-size pieces
1/4 cup feta cheese, crumbled

Lemon Dressing:

1/4 cup fresh lemon juice
1 to 2 teaspoons extra virgin olive oil
1/4 teaspoon salt
1 teaspoon dried oregano or 2 teaspoons fresh oregano leaves, minced
1/8 teaspoon pepper, coarsely ground
2 (small) cloves garlic, smashed

Whisk lemon juice, olive oil, salt, pepper, oregano, and crushed garlic together in a mixing bowl until blended. Set dressing aside.

In a large salad bowl, combine tomatoes, cucumbers, red onion, and olives and toss well. To serve, line a large platter with greens and spoon the tomato mixture over greens. Top with feta cheese and toss salad. Strain dressing into bowl and pour over salad just before serving, or strain dressing into cruet or small pitcher and serve on the side.

Per serving: *140 calories, 7 9 fat, 16.5 g carbohydrates, 5 g dietary fiber, 5.9 g protein.*

Salads and Condiments

Europe/Italian

Posted on: Wednesday, May 2, 2007

Make a meal at home on mom's day

Herbed White Bean Salad

Here's a hearty salad that could serve as a centerpiece for a light lunch or be served alongside chicken as a side dish.

Herbed White Bean Salad
Serves 4 to 6

Extra virgin olive oil spray
1 to 2 tablespoons garlic, minced
1 tablespoon fresh sage leaves, chopped
1 teaspoon fresh thyme leaves, chopped
1 (14.5-ounce) can diced tomatoes with juices
2 (15-ounce) cans white or cannelloni beans, rinsed and drained
4 strips turkey bacon, cooked, drained and sliced into 1-inch pieces
Salt and pepper to taste
3 cups mixed greens

Spray the surface of a large, heavy frying pan with olive oil spray. Sauté the garlic for about 30 seconds. Sprinkle in the sage and thyme. Add the tomatoes, increasing the heat to medium-high for 2 minutes. Add the beans. Simmer this mixture for about 5 minutes. Turn off the heat and add the bacon and season with salt and pepper. On a platter, arrange the mixed greens and spoon the beans over them and serve.

Per serving (4 servings, without salt): *350 calories, 7 g fat, 1.5 g saturated fat, 150 mg cholesterol, 600 mg sodium, 54 g carbohydrate, 11 g dietary fiber, 3 g sugar, 21 g protein.*

Global Light Cuisine ∞ Carol Devenot   65

Europe/Italian

Posted on: Wednesday, January 10, 2007

Mozzarella salad direct from Italy
Woodi's Caprese

In Woodi Carr's recipe, he uses *fleur de sel,* "flower of salt." It is a French salt that can be purchased at gourmet cooking stores, such as Williams-Sonoma or R. Field. Balsamic vinegar gives the salad another dimension. He said you don't have to buy the most expensive brand for this. Woodi starts off with 1 cup of good quality balsamic vinegar around *($10 to $15 a bottle)* and adds 1 tablespoon of brown sugar and begins to slowly cook it down over medium heat so that it begins to reduce but not boil. As this syrup thickens, the flavors become concentrated. Put this reduced balsamic vinegar in a decorative jar, and you will also have created a great gift for that discerning gourmet. You can use this concentrated vinegar in the recipe below, or just use plain balsamic.

Woodi's Caprese
Serves 4 to 6

2 pounds vine-ripened tomatoes, sliced
   1/4-inch thick
1 pound low-fat mozzarella, sliced
   1/4-inch thick
1 pound fresh basil, washed and spun dry
Extra virgin olive oil spray
3 to 4 tablespoons balsamic vinegar

Fleur de sel (French salt) or fine sea salt to taste
Freshly ground pepper

Arrange the tomato, mozzarella, and basil by alternating and overlapping them on a large decorative platter. Spray with olive oil and drizzle with balsamic vinegar. Sprinkle with *fleur de sel* and freshly ground pepper.

Per serving (6 servings): *300 calories, 17 g fat, 10 g saturated fat, 40 mg cholesterol, 425 mg sodium, 17 g carbohydrate, 5 g dietary fiber, 8 g sugar, 23 g protein.*

Hawaii Local Favorite

Posted on: Wednesday, May 5, 2004
Go for the Yukon golds–not russets–for this potato salad

Good Kine Potato Salad

My mom made a great potato salad. It was the best because it was like having egg salad and potatoes mixed together—good old-fashioned home cookin'. For this lighter version, use Yukon Gold potatoes for the taste; they seem to hold their shape better than other types of potatoes. I once made the mistake of using russets and ended up with smashed potato salad.

Good Kine Potato Salad
Serves 4 to 6

- 4 (medium) Yukon Gold potatoes, washed and scrubbed
- 1/2 onion, minced
- 2 stalks celery, peeled and diced
- 1/2 bunch parsley, chopped
- 3/4 pound *kamaboko,* sliced; or imitation crab, flaked; or 1 (6-ounce) can water-packed tuna, drained and flaked
- 2 tablespoons pickle relish, drained
- 1/2 cup reduced-fat mayonnaise dressing or Tofu Mayo *(page 69)*
- Salt and pepper to taste

Fill a large saucepan with cold water. Place the potatoes in the pan and bring to a boil. Turn down the heat and simmer until potatoes are fork-tender. Meanwhile prepare the onion, celery, parsley, and fish cake *(or crab or tuna)*. When potatoes are done, drain and place in a bowl of cold water for about 10 minutes. Peel and dice into 1/2-inch cubes. Place in another large bowl and add onion, celery, fish cake *(or crab or tuna)*, pickle relish, reduced-fat mayonnaise or Tofu Mayo, salt, and pepper. Stir until thoroughly mixed together. Refrigerate until ready to serve.

Per serving: *186 calories, 3 g fat, 26 g carbohydrates, 3 g dietary fiber, 13 g protein.*

Hawaii Local Favorite

Posted on: Wednesday, May 19, 2004

Cut the fat in mayo by making your own
Tofu Mayo

Traditionally, from-scratch mayonnaise is made with egg yolks, dry mustard, salt, pepper, and vinegar or lemon juice. Extra virgin olive oil is beaten in slowly, a half teaspoon at a time. There is no comparison, if made correctly. Next best is your favorite brand.

Tofu Mayo

1 (14-ounce) block firm tofu
2 tablespoons lemon juice
6 tablespoons vinegar, any type
1 teaspoon vegetable oil
1 teaspoon mustard
2 teaspoons Worcestershire sauce
Salt and pepper to taste

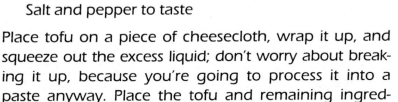

Place tofu on a piece of cheesecloth, wrap it up, and squeeze out the excess liquid; don't worry about breaking it up, because you're going to process it into a paste anyway. Place the tofu and remaining ingredients in a food processor and process until smooth.

Yields 1 1/4 cups.

For the entire 1 1/4 cups (as in a potato salad recipe): 390 calories, 36 g protein, 21 g fat, 18 g carbohydrates, 0 g dietary fiber.

Per 1 tablespoon serving: 19.5 calories, 1.05 g fat, 0.9 g carbohydrate, 0 g dietary fiber, 1.8 g protein.

Hawaii Local Favorite

Tofu salad always is a good potluck recipe because it is so fresh and healthy.

Tofu Salad
Serves 8

- 1 head romaine lettuce, thinly sliced
- 2 tomatoes, diced
- 1 sweet Maui onion, chopped fine
- 1 (20-ounce) block firm tofu, drained and cubed
- 1 (6-ounce) can water-packed tuna or albacore tuna, drained

Dressing:

- 1/4 cup cider vinegar
- 1 tablespoon brown rice syrup or raw sugar
- 1 teaspoon sesame oil
- 1 tablespoon fresh ginger root, grated
- 1 tablespoon garlic, minced
- 2 tablespoons soy sauce

Garnish:

- 4 stalks green onions, sliced 1/4-inch thick
- 2 tablespoons sesame seeds, toasted

Layer lettuce, tomatoes, onion, tofu, and tuna in the order given. Place dressing ingredients in a jar and shake well. Pour the dressing over the salad just before serving. Toss lightly. Garnish with green onions and sesame seeds.

Per Serving: *173 calories, 8 g fat, 11 g carbohydrates, 4 g dietary fiber, 18 g protein.*

Variations: Salmon can be substituted for tuna. Salmon is richer than tuna and much higher in fat. Watercress and sprouts could also be added.

Mainland U.S. Favorite

Hold da Mayo Cold Slaw
Serves 6

2 cups green cabbage, shredded
2 cups red cabbage, shredded
1 cup carrot, grated
1 yellow bell pepper, diced
1/4 cup scallions

Vinaigrette Dressing:

2 tablespoons balsamic vinegar
6 tablespoons red wine vinegar
2 tablespoons Dijon mustard
1 tablespoon tamari
2 teaspoons honey
1/2 teaspoon celery seed
1/4 teaspoon fresh ground pepper

Combine the above vinaigrette ingredients in a small jar and shake. Toss the vegetables in a large bowl. Pour the vinaigrette over the vegetables, toss, and refrigerate at least 1 hour before serving.

Per serving: *52 calories, 0.3 g fat, 11 g carbohydrates, 3 g dietary fiber, 2 g protein.*

Mainland U.S. Favorite

Posted on: Wednesday, May 30, 2007

Vinaigrette is treat with beet salad

Roasted Beet Salad with Sherry Shallot Vinaigrette and Candied Pecans

I've often wondered what "nepenthe" meant. I recently read on the menu of the Nepenthe Restaurant in Big Sur, California, that it is Greek for "the one that chases away sorrow." High above the Pacific, bordered by the Santa Lucia Mountains, the restaurant has served poets, artists, travelers, and free spirits for more than 50 years. The view of the ocean framed by redwoods is a feast in itself. The roasted beet salad was so good. I came away with the recipe for the accompanying sherry shallot vinaigrette.

Roasted Beet Salad
Serves 6

1 pound beets (3 to 4 medium), scrubbed
1 bunch arugula or spinach, well washed and spun dry
1 bunch mixed greens, well washed and spun dry
1/3 cup red onions, thinly sliced
Extra virgin olive oil spray

Garnish:

1/4 to 1/2 cup candied pecans
  (recipe below and optional)

Global Light Cuisine ∞ Carol Devenot   73

1 to 3 ounces Gorgonzola cheese *(optional)*

Heat the oven to 450 degrees. Line a large sheet of aluminum foil with parchment paper. Place the beets in the center of the foil and spray with olive oil spray. Season with salt and pepper. Fold to enclose the beets.

Place on a small baking pan and roast until tender when pierced with a fork, about 1 hour. Remove from oven and cool.

Peel off the skin and cut beets into bite-size wedges. In a large bowl add beets to the arugula, greens, and red onions. Add enough dressing to coat the salad. Garnish with candied pecans and Gorgonzola cheese. *(This will add additional fat and calories.)*

Per serving (without dressing or pecans and cheese garnishes): *50 calories, 1 g fat, 0 g saturated fat, 70 mg sodium, 9 g carbohydrate, 3 g dietary fiber, 6 g sugar, 2 g protein.*

Per serving (2 tablespoon dressing and without pecans and cheese garnishes): *150 calories, 10 g fat, 0.5 g saturated fat, 0 mg cholesterol, 200 mg sodium, 13 g carbohydrate, 3 g dietary fiber, 6 g sugar, 2 g protein.*

Per serving (with 2 tablespoons dressing and 1/4 cup candied pecans, without salt): *360 calories, 31 g fat, 2.5 g saturated fat, 5 mg cholesterol, 200 mg sodium, 20 g carbohydrate, 6 g dietary fiber, 10 g sugar, 5 g protein.*

Sherry Shallot Vinaigrette

1 cup sherry vinegar
1/4 bunch fresh thyme, minced
2 shallots, minced
1 tablespoon Dijon mustard
Sea salt and ground pepper to taste
1/2 cup safflower oil or extra virgin olive oil

Place all ingredients except oil in a bowl and blend with hand blender. Add oil slowly, whisking to emulsify. Makes approximately 1 1/2 cups.

Per 2-tablespoon serving (without salt): *100 calories, 9 g fat, 0.5 g saturated fat, 0 mg cholesterol, 130 mg sodium, 4 g carbohydrate, 0 g dietary fiber, 0 g sugar, 0 g protein.*

Candied Pecans

2 pounds or 1 cup pecan halves
1/2 cup sugar or sugar substitute
1 (large) egg or Egg Beaters®

Heat oven to 375 degrees. Hand whip the egg and sugar together in a large bowl. Gently fold in the pecans. Cover a heavy-duty cookie sheet with foil and put the nuts close together on cookie sheet in single-layer fashion. Bake for exactly 15 minutes in the center rack of the oven. *(Roast 2 pounds in 3 batches.)* Remove from oven, lift foil off cookie sheet into a large bowl, knock nuts off the foil into the bowl, and cool.

Per 1/4 cup serving: *210 calories, 21 g fat, 2 g saturated fat, 5 mg cholesterol, 0 mg sodium, 7 g carbohydrate, 3 g dietary fiber, 4 g sugar, 3 g protein.*

Note: The Candied Pecans recipe will actually coat 2 pounds of pecans, but only one cup is needed for this salad. You have a choice. You can roast all 2 pounds of pecans and store the leftover pecans in glass jars or in the freezer. Or you can put 1 cup of pecans in the egg and sugar mixture knowing you will have to let some of the coating mixture drain off in the bowl before you put the pecans on the cookie sheet. You will also have extra coating left on the cookie sheet after the nuts are roasted.

Middle East

Posted on: Wednesday, January 24, 2007

Dress salad with Naked Cutlets
Curried Couscous Salad

The key ingredient in Quorn™ brand products is mycoprotein. Myco is derived from the Greek word for fungus. The fungus family includes mushrooms, truffles, and morels; this product uses a fungus called *Fusarium venenatum*, a source of protein low in fat and calories.

Find these products in the frozen food section of health food stores. The cutlets and many other Quorn™ offerings are gluten free. However, they contain a small amount of egg white and milk and are not recommended for vegans.

Curried Couscous Salad
Serves 6

The Rub:

2 tablespoons of Ka`iulani Spice Curry Rub
    or
    2 tablespoons mild curry powder
    1 teaspoon Hawaiian salt
    2 tablespoons brown sugar
    1/8 teaspoon red chili pepper flakes

Salad:

Extra virgin olive oil spray
1 (9.7-ounce) package Quorn™ Naked Cutlets
1 lemon
2 to 3 cloves garlic, minced

76 Salads and Condiments

1/2 onion, finely chopped
2 carrots, cut into 1/8-inch-thick rounds
1 cup water
1 cup couscous
1/4 to 1/3 cup cranberries
4 to 6 tablespoons pumpkin seeds
4 to 6 tablespoon sesame seeds
Fresh Chinese parsley *(cilantro)* for garnish

In a small bowl, mix the curry powder, Hawaiian salt, brown sugar, and chili pepper flakes together. Rub 1 tablespoon of this mixture onto the cutlets.

Spray a nonstick frying pan with cooking oil spray and brown the rubbed cutlets on both sides. Remove from the pan. Cut into 1/4-inch diagonal pieces and squeeze the juice of the lemon over the cutlets. Cover and allow the cutlets to cool.

Place the pumpkin seeds and sesame seeds in the same frying pan and toast the seeds until they pop. Be careful not to burn them.

Spray the same frying pan with oil and sauté the garlic, onion, and carrot until the onion is translucent. Add 1/4 cup of water and cover and cook for 3 minutes or until the vegetables are tender.

In a saucepan, bring 1 cup of water to a boil and add the couscous; stir until combined. Remove from heat to prevent burning. Cover and allow the couscous to sit for about 2 minutes or until water has been absorbed. Separate the grains by fluffing them with a fork.

Add the sautéed mixture and heat through. Carefully fold in the cranberries, one third of the pumpkin and sesame seeds, and the rest of the curry rub mixture.

Spoon the entire mix onto a serving platter and place the marinated cutlets on the top. Sprinkle with the remaining pumpkin and sesame seeds. Garnish with parsley.

Per serving: *300 calories, 12 g fat, 2 g saturated fat, 0 mg cholesterol, 500 mg sodium, 40 g carbohydrate, 7 g dietary fiber, 7 g sugar, 13 g protein.*

Salads and Condiments

Middle East

Posted on: Wednesday, January 26, 2005

Tweaked tzatziki still `ana
Tzatziki

Two weeks ago this column served up falafel *(page 226)*, a popular Middle Eastern "fast food" made from ground chickpeas, bulgur wheat, and seasonings. I mentioned that you can eat the falafel accompanied by salsa *(page 20)* or tahini *(sesame butter)* dressing, but it tastes authentic when you serve it with *tzatziki*. This is a creamy yogurt sauce similar to *raita*, an Indian yogurt relish that's often served alongside spicy foods.

Tzatziki (yogurt, cucumber, herbs, and seasonings) rounds out and tames the herbs and spices used in falafel.

Tzatziki
Serves 10

- 1/2 (large) English or Japanese cucumber, peeled
- 3/4 teaspoon kosher salt
- 2 cups low-fat yogurt
- 2 to 3 cloves garlic, minced
- 2 tablespoons dried onion flakes
- 3 tablespoons fresh lemon juice
- 2 tablespoons fresh dill, chopped
- 2 tablespoons fresh mint leaves, chopped
- 1/8 teaspoon ground black pepper

Using the large holes of the grater, grate the cucumber. Place the cucumber in a sieve and toss with 1/4 teaspoon salt. Let stand over a bowl to drain for 30 minutes. Meanwhile, stir in yogurt, garlic, onion flakes, lemon juice, dill, mint, pepper, and the remaining salt. Squeeze the drained cucumber with your hands and discard any juice. Stir into the yogurt mixture. Cover and refrigerate *tzatziki* overnight to blend flavors. Serve with falafel or pita wedges as an appetizer. Yields 2 1/2 cups *(1/4 cup per serving)*.

Per serving: *39 calories, 1 g fat, 5 g carbohydrates, 0 g dietary fiber, 176 mg sodium, 3 g protein.*

Variations: This is a wonderful sauce not just for falafel but to use as a dip, a topping for baked potatoes, or as salad dressing. Instead of chips, buy whole-wheat pita bread at the health food store or at a Greek restaurant. Cut it into wedges and serve with *kalamata* olives and *tzatziki*. Broke the mouth!

Salads and Condiments

Posted on: Wednesday, March 22, 2006

Japanese cukes in an Israeli salad

Middle East/Israeli

Heal Ti Israeli Salad

This salad is served with grilled chicken or fish, falafel in pita bread, or sometimes just with a small wedge of feta cheese. Middle Eastern cucumbers are the favorite choice for this salad. However, the Japanese cucumbers readily available here are an excellent substitute because of their crisp, sweet, and tender skin. This salad also makes use of just a little pickled herring—found in jars in many supermarkets—to add a salty contrast to the sweetness of the fresh vegetables.

Heal Ti Israeli Salad
Serves 4

- 4 Japanese cucumbers, peeled and cut into 1/2-inch cubes
- 1 *(small)* yellow pepper, seeded and finely diced
- 8 plum *(Roma)* tomatoes, finely diced
- 1/2 cup jicama *(Chinese potato)* or celery, sliced
- 2 tablespoons chives or green onions, cut into 1/4-inch slices
- 3 to 4 tablespoons fresh Italian flat-leaf parsley, chopped fine
- 1 to 2 tablespoons balsamic vinegar
- 1 teaspoon extra virgin olive oil
- Sea salt to taste
- Fresh ground pepper
- 2 teaspoons capers, rinsed and drained

Global Light Cuisine ∞ Carol Devenot

   1 (small) piece of pickled herring, cut into
      1/2-inch pieces *(optional)*
   Lettuce leaves

In a mixing bowl, combine cucumbers, peppers, tomatoes, jicama, chives, and parsley. In a small bowl, whisk together the balsamic vinegar, olive oil, salt, and pepper and drizzle over salad. Mix in capers and the cut-up herring. Serve on a bed of leafy green lettuce.

Per serving: *120 calories, 3.5 g fat, 0.5 g saturated fat, 0 mg cholesterol, 150 mg sodium, 20 g carbohydrate, 5 g dietary fiber, 13 g sugar, 5 g protein.*

82 Salads and Condiments

Side Dishes

Asia/Chinese

Kalakoa Fried Rice
Serves 8

Vegetable oil cooking spray
1/4 cup sweet red pepper, diced
1/4 cup celery, diced
2 stalks green onions, sliced 1/4-inch thick
1/2 cup Egg Beaters®, scrambled
3 cups brown rice, cooked
3/4 cup frozen peas and carrots
3 tablespoons Lee Kum Kee® Vegetarian Stir Fry Sauce or Lee Kum Kee® Oyster Sauce

Spray a nonstick wok or frying pan with cooking spray. Scramble in the Egg Beaters® first and set aside. Sauté red pepper, celery, and onion for 2 to 3 minutes over medium-high heat. Stir in rice, peas and carrots, and stir-fry sauce. Add scrambled eggs and stir-fry until heated through. Serve immediately.

Per serving: *105 calories, 1 g fat, 20 g carbohydrates, 2 g dietary fiber, 4 g protein.*

Variations: *Kalakoa* means colorful in Hawaiian slang. You can make this dish more colorful by adding other fresh vegetables such as purple onions, Chinese broccoli, cabbage, or shiitake mushrooms. For additional flavor add *patis* or fish sauce to taste.

Asia/Filipino

Long beans *(called sitaw in Filipino)* may be in your supermarket. If not, Chinatown is a good place to find long beans and any unusual Asian vegetables. Use this recipe as a basis for the many types of beans and greens that you might find in your travels. It's a great way to get vitamins into your diet.

Sitaw
Serves 4

- 1 teaspoon peanut oil
- 3 cloves garlic, minced
- 1 (small) onion, sliced into half-moons
- 12 (medium) shrimp, cooked
- 1 tablespoon *patis (fish sauce)*
- 1 1/2 cups water
- 1 pound long beans, washed and cut into 2-inch lengths
- 1 teaspoon Hawaiian salt

In a nonstick frying pan or wok, sauté garlic and onion in the *patis* and oil. Add water and long beans and stir-fry for 2 to 3 minutes or until tender. Add Hawaiian salt and cooked shrimp. Toss lightly until shrimp is warm.

Per serving: *76 calories, 2 g fat 11 g carbohydrates, 4 g dietary fiber, 6 g protein.*

Asia/Japanese

Posted on: Wednesday, December 27, 2006

Red rice symbolizes happiness
Sekihan (happy red rice)

If you are lucky enough to stumble across a traditional *okazuya,* you may find it shaped as *musubi.* Traditionally, *sekihan* is only made on special occasions, such as New Year's Day, weddings, or birthdays. It is usually made with white *mochi* rice and garnished with dry-roasted sesame seeds and a *shiso* leaf. Lynne made a more healthful version by using unpolished whole-grain *mochi* rice *(with the hull still on).* You can find it in the health food stores.

The adzuki *(also spelled adsuki, azuki, or aduki)* beans that are mixed with the rice produce a reddish color, symbolizing happiness. If you want to be healthy and happy in the upcoming New Year, make *sekihan.*

Sekihan
(happy red rice)
Serves 6

    1/2 cup whole, dried adzuki beans
    1 1/2 cups whole-grain *mochi (sweet)* rice
    1/2 cup brown rice

Garnish:

    1 tablespoon dry roasted sesame seeds
    Shiso leaf or watercress

Soak the two different rices separately in cold water for 15 minutes. Rinse the adzuki beans and place in a saucepan and cover with water. Bring the beans to a rapid boil and lower the heat to medium and cook for 45 minutes, until beans are softened but still whole and not mushy. Drain and reserve the bean cooking liquid, placing the beans in a bowl to cool.

Wash the rice and drain well. Measure liquid from the cooked beans to equal 1 3/4 cups of liquid, adding water if necessary. Mix rice and adzuki beans with liquid and steam in rice cooker or saucepan, as normal. When done, turn off the heat, and let stand for 10 minutes. Garnish with sesame seeds and *shiso* leaf.

Per serving: *290 calories, 2.5 g fat, 0 g saturated fat, 0 mg cholesterol, 5 mg sodium, 62 g carbohydrate, 5 g dietary fiber, 1 g sugar, 9 g protein.*

Global Light Cuisine ∞ Carol Devenot

Asia/Japanese

Pan sushi is like making one giant sushi except without all the rolling and the slicing. Layer with other condiments such as pickled vegetables and *kampyo*. Good for picnics, potlucks, or parties. Serve with pickled ginger.

One Giant Sushi
Serves 9

5 cups Hapa Rice *(page 101)*, cooked
1/2 cup carrots, sliced 1/8- to 1/4-inch thick
1/2 cup Japanese cucumbers, sliced 1/4-inch thick
1 (6-ounce) can water-packed albacore tuna, drained
1 1/2 tablespoons brown sugar or brown rice syrup
1 tablespoon soy sauce or tamari
Salt to taste
1/2 cup seasoned rice vinegar
2 1/4 sheets *nori* seaweed
1/4 cup *furikake*

Cook rice following directions on the package. In a saucepan, cook tuna, brown sugar, and salt. Scoop out the hot rice into a large mixing bowl and fold in the rice vinegar and salt. Line a 9- by 13-inch pan with two sheets of waxed paper. Sprinkle the *furikake* on the bottom of the pan. Spread half of the seasoned rice on the *furikake* and press down. Spread the tuna over the seasoned rice. Alternate the carrots and cucumbers in rows. Layer on the remaining rice. Cover the rice with sheets of *nori*. Press the sushi down with another 9- by 13-inch pan. Cover with waxed paper. Serve from the pan or cut into 2-inch squares.

Per serving: *165 calories, 1 g fat, 32 g carbohydrates, 2 g dietary fiber, 7 g protein.*

Asia/Korean

Watercress Namul
Serves 4

1/2 tablespoons sesame seeds, toasted
1 bunch watercress, washed and cut into
    1 1/2-inch lengths
2 cups water
2 tablespoons soy sauce
1 teaspoon sesame oil
2 tablespoons rice vinegar
1 clove garlic, minced
Red pepper flakes *(optional)*
1/2 teaspoon honey
2 stalks green onions, chopped

Toast the sesame seeds in a frying pan very quickly without burning. In a large pot bring 2 cups of water to boil. Place the watercress in the water and boil for 4 minutes. Drain in a colander and place in a mixing bowl. Combine the soy sauce, sesame oil, vinegar, garlic, red pepper flakes, and honey. Pour over the cooked watercress. Toss in the green onions and chill.

Per serving: *36 calories, 2 g fat, 5 g carbohydrates, 1 g dietary fiber, 1 g protein.*

Variations: Instead of using watercress, you can use spinach, *choy sum,* and bean sprouts. Try different greens for a variety of flavors and great vitamin A and calcium.

Asia/Korean

The shiitake mushrooms give this dish an interesting meat-like texture and taste. You don't even miss the meat. If you really need the extra protein, add either an half pound of chicken breast, shrimp, *aburage* or strips of firm tofu, but remember extra protein adds extra fat.

Chop Chae

Serves 6

- 1 (1.875-ounce) package bean thread *(long rice)*
- 1/2 bunch watercress, cut into 2-inch lengths
- 1 (12-ounce) package chop suey mix *(carrots, red cabbage, mung bean sprouts, etc.)*
- 1 (small) onion, sliced into half-moons
- 3 cloves garlic, minced
- 1 teaspoon fresh ginger root, finely grated
- 1 teaspoon sesame oil
- 1 teaspoon chicken-style vegetarian broth powder
- 6 dried shiitake mushrooms
- 3 tablespoons soy sauce
- 1 tablespoon *ko choo jung* sauce *(hot sauce)*
- 2 teaspoons honey or brown rice syrup
- Salt and pepper to taste

Bring 2 cups of water to a boil in a saucepan. Remove saucepan from burner and place the mushrooms into the water for 20 minutes. Drain, saving the mushroom liquid. Cut off hard stems and slice into 1/4-inch slices.

Add 1 teaspoon of broth powder to the mushroom water to make the broth.

Soak the bean thread, locally known as long rice, in hot tap water for 15 to 20 minutes. Drain and cut into 2-inch lengths. Boil 4 cups of water in a saucepan. Remove from the burner; add the long rice, and allow it to stand for 5 minutes. Drain in colander.

In a wok, sauté onion, garlic, and ginger in sesame oil and 3 tablespoons of broth for 2 to 3 minutes. Add the watercress, chop suey mix, and the remaining broth. Stir-fry until tender but crisp. Mix soy sauce, *ko choo jung* sauce, and honey together. Add to the vegetables. Season with salt and pepper. Stir in mushrooms and long rice. Serve immediately.

Per serving: *76 calories, 1 g fat, 16 g carbohydrates, 2 g dietary fiber, 3 g protein.*

Asia/Thai

Yummy Sticky Rice
Serves 6

2 cups *mochi (sweet)* rice
3 cups water or chicken-style vegetarian broth
1 teaspoon Hawaiian salt

Place the sweet rice in a saucepan. Rinse rice with water and drain thoroughly. Add water or broth and salt. Allow to stand for a half hour. Bring to a boil over high heat for 1 minute. Lower the heat to simmer and cover the saucepan with a tight lid. Cook undisturbed for 20 minutes.

If using a rice cooker, follow the manufacturer's directions.

Per serving: *230 calories, 1 g fat, 49 g carbohydrates, 0.5 g dietary fiber, 6 g protein.*

Variations: Sweet brown rice can be purchased at any large health food store. This rice is delicious just eaten plain. You could add a half cup of adzuki beans to make a Japanese dish called *Sekihan (page 87)*. You could also use this same recipe to make a brown rice *musubi*. Just substitute the water for the broth and eliminate the salt.

Europe/French

Posted on: Wednesday, August 8, 2007
Ratatouille perfect for summer
Ratatouille

Ratatouille *(rat-ah-too-ee)* is a comfort food made in southern France.
It is usually made during the summer, when eggplant, zucchini, onions, peppers, and tomatoes are abundant. Traditionally seasoned with parsley and basil, some recipes call for *herbes de Provence*, mushrooms, black olives, and other flavorings. There are many ways to make this recipe. The method of preparation varies with personal preference. Several chefs have recommended that you cook each ingredient separately and then combine everything. In the following recipe, I have gradually added each ingredient. I have even seen it layered in a casserole. Whatever method you choose, you will end up with a very tasty appetizer, side, or main dish.

Ratatouille
Serves 4 to 6

Extra virgin olive oil spray
5 to 6 cloves garlic, minced
1 (medium) red onion, diced
1 tablespoon tomato paste
3/4 cup organic chicken stock
2 (large) Japanese eggplants, diced
1 (medium) zucchini, diced
1 (medium) bell pepper *(red or green)*, diced
6 shiitake mushrooms, diced

Global Light Cuisine ∞ Carol Devenot

- 1 (14.5-ounce) can diced tomatoes
  or 2 tomatoes, seeded, peeled, and diced
- 2 teaspoons *herbes de Provence*
- Sea salt
- Ground black pepper
- Low-fat Parmesan cheese *(optional)* for garnish

Spray a large Dutch oven with olive oil and sauté the garlic for 1 minute. Add the onion and cook until translucent for about 4 minutes.

Meanwhile, wash remaining vegetables and drain the can of tomatoes.

Add to the Dutch oven 1 tablespoon tomato paste, stirring constantly. Add the chicken stock and stir until the broth begins to simmer. Add the eggplant, zucchini, bell pepper, and mushrooms. Stir frequently for 10 to 12 minutes. Stir in the diced tomatoes and reduce heat to low. Stir in the *herbs de Provence*. Taste and season with salt and pepper. Serve hot or cold on toasted baguettes. Sprinkle with Parmesan cheese if desired for garnish.

Per serving (with salt, cheese, or toasted baguettes): *150 calories, 2 g fat, 0 g saturated fat, 0 mg cholesterol, 400 mg sodium, 32 g carbohydrate, 11 g dietary fiber, 15 g sugar, 6 g protein.*

Europe/Greek

Posted on: Wednesday, October 4, 2006

Toss in some fennel for unique veggie dish
Greek Seasoned Roasted Vegetables

It's the fennel, along with a Greek seasoning blend and garlic, which gives this dish its unique flavor. Most of the fennel being sold in supermarkets is the *finocchio* or Florence variety. This type of fennel has an enlarged pale green bulb at the end of the plant, topped with a delicate spray of leaves, which resembles dill. Because of its pungent licorice flavor, the bulbs are often labeled as "anise." But do not confuse fennel with the true seed spice, which also produces a licorice taste and aroma. Even if you're not particularly fond of licorice, try a little fennel in your next stir-fry or vegetable medley; the flavor is subtle and the crunchy texture adds interest.

The fennel plant is entirely edible and belongs to the *Umbellifereae* family. Its cousins, including dill, parsley, carrots and coriander, share its combination of healthful phytonutrients. In addition to these antioxidants, it is an excellent source of vitamin C and fiber.

Greek Seasoned Roasted Vegetables
Serves 8

1 cup peeled baby carrots
3 teaspoons Greek seasoning*

Global Light Cuisine ∞ Carol Devenot

1 teaspoon Hawaiian salt
1/2 teaspoon ground pepper
2 garlic bulbs, bottoms trimmed, smashed, and peeled
1 (large) sweet Maui onion, cut into wedges
2 red bell peppers, cut into 1-inch triangular shapes
1 green bell pepper, cut into 1-inch triangular shapes
1 yellow squash, halved and cut into half-moons
1 fennel bulb, cut into 1/2-inch triangular shapes
1 (large) zucchini, halved and cut into half-moons
Extra virgin olive oil spray

Adjust one oven rack in the upper third of the oven and the other rack on the lower third of the oven. Preheat the oven to 450 degrees.

Spray a large mixing bowl with cooking spray. Combine the carrots, seasoning, salt, pepper, garlic, onion, peppers, squash, fennel, and zucchini and toss well.

Spray two jelly roll pans with cooking spray. *(A jelly roll pan is a cookie sheet with shallow lip or edge all around it.)* Place evenly divided vegetable mixture in both pans. Bake for 12 minutes; stir the mixture once, then rotate the pans from one shelf to the other. Bake 12 minutes longer or until the vegetables begin to brown. Stir the mixture once again and serve.

Per serving (without salt): *100 calories, 3.5 g fat, 0 g saturated fat, 0 mg cholesterol, 240 mg sodium, 160 g carbohydrate, 4 g dietary fiber, 6 g sugar, 3 g protein.*

* Greek seasoning blends invariably include oregano, salt, pepper, and garlic; often, also, dried parsley, mint, lemon zest, rosemary, and even cinnamon and nutmeg.

Side Dishes

Posted on: Wednesday, October 3, 2007
From ship to shore: an Italian dish

Europe/Italian

Linguine Al Pesto Alla Moda Ligure Redo

While cruising the inland passage of Alaska, my boyfriend and I attended a cooking demonstration aboard the Sapphire Princess. The class was conducted by Master Chef Commendatore Alfred Marzi, who shared *Linguine Al Pesto Alla Moda Ligure*, a dish from his native Italy. His recipes are featured in the Princess Cruises cookbook, **A Culinary Courses Journey** (Princess Cruises, 2006).

Linguine Al Pesto Alla Moda Ligure Redo

Serves 2 to 3

- 1/2 pound red "new" potatoes, scrubbed and cut in halves
- 1/4 pound fresh green beans, washed, trimmed, and cut on diagonal
- 3/4 pound organic whole-grain and flax linguine
- 1 tablespoon extra virgin olive oil

Pesto:

- 2/3 cup vegetable or chicken stock
- 2 to 3 cloves garlic
- 1 cup fresh basil leaves
- 1/3 cup low-fat Parmesan cheese or *Parmigiano-Reggiano* cheese *(which has a higher fat content)*
- 2 tablespoons pine nuts, toasted

Salt and pepper to taste
Fresh basil leaves, shredded, for garnish

Combine the stock and garlic and cook for 5 minutes in a small saucepan. Place in the refrigerator to cool.

Meanwhile, cook the potatoes in simmering water until tender, about 15 minutes. Set aside to cool.

Place the cooled stock with the garlic, basil, cheese, and pine nuts in the bowl of a food processor fitted with a steel blade and process until puréed, pulsing on and off.

Meanwhile, cook the green beans in a quart of briskly boiling water for about 6 minutes, just until bright green and crisp. Drain and plunge into cold water to keep them from overcooking.

Cook the linguine according to package directions. Drain and toss with 1 tablespoon olive oil.

In a large frying pan, combine potatoes, green beans, and pasta and spoon a generous amount of pesto over the mixture to coat it well. *(You may have some pesto left and can use that another day; keep refrigerated up to a week.)*

Heat mixture through and adjust the seasoning, adding salt and pepper as desired. Place in a large warm bowl or platter and garnish with fresh basil.

Per serving (2 servings, without salt): *920 calories, 22 g fat, 3.5 g saturated fat, 10 mg cholesterol, 350 mg sodium, 147 g carbohydrate, 30 g dietary fiber, 6 g sugar, 38 g protein.*

Hawaii Local Favorites

My friend Ceci gave me this as a snack. The only difference in the way she cooked it and mine is that she uses a burned pot to get the same results. I liked the potatoes so much, but I didn't want to sacrifice one of my pots, so this recipe was created. It's a healthy snack that you can take with you and have at those odd hours when you feel like grazing.

Ceci's Tasty Sweet Potatoes
(imu-flavored potatoes)
Serves 6

1 pound Okinawan sweet potatoes
(or any other type of sweet potato)
6 to 8 cups water
1 tablespoon Hawaiian salt
2 tablespoons liquid smoke

Wash and scrub the sweet potatoes with a brush and cut them into halves on the diagonal. Place in a large saucepan and cover with water. Add salt and liquid smoke to the water. Boil uncovered for approximately 40 to 50 minutes on medium-high heat. Serve hot or cold.

Per serving: *79 calories, 0.2 g fat, 18 g carbohydrates, 1 g dietary fiber, 1 g protein.*

Note: The Okinawan sweet potato is a small sweet potato coming from Okinawa, Japan, that has a light beige skin and shaped like a sweet potato. When cooked the skin turns dark brown and the inside is a deep, rich, eggplant purple color.

Hawaii Local Favorite

Hapa Rice
(brown and white rice)
Serves 12

1 cup brown rice
2 cups jasmine rice
4 cups water
Pinch Hawaiian salt

Place both brown and white rice in inner pot of the rice cooker. Rinse with cold water until clear, then drain. Add 4 cups of water and follow manufacturer's directions.

Per serving: *162 calories, 1 g fat, 36 g carbohydrates, 1 g dietary fiber, 3 g protein.*

Hawaii Local Favorite

Long Rice Chicken
Serves 6

2 cups dried shiitake mushrooms
4 cups chicken-style vegetarian broth
2 (medium) chicken breasts, boneless and
    skinless, cut into 1 1/2-inch pieces
1 (1-inch) piece fresh ginger root,
    peeled and crushed
2 to 3 cloves garlic, minced
1 teaspoon peanut oil
2 tablespoons Lee Kum Kee®
    Vegetarian Stir Fry Sauce
1/2 (medium) onion, thinly sliced
2 (1.875-ounce) package bean thread *(long rice)*
2 stalks green onions, sliced into 1-inch pieces
Black pepper, fresh ground to taste
2 (small) bunches baby bok choy, cut into
    1 1/2-inch diagonal slices
Vegetable oil cooking spray

Soak the bean thread, known locally as long rice, in warm water for 10 to 15 minutes. Drain and cut into 3-inch lengths.

Place the mushrooms in a bowl and cover with boiling water. Soak for 15 minutes. Drain and slice the mushrooms 1/4-inch thick, cutting out the hard stem. Save the mushroom water for sautéing.

In a Dutch oven, sauté garlic and onion in peanut oil and set aside. Spray the same pan with cooking spray. Add the mushroom liquid, stir-fry sauce, and chicken.

Cook the chicken, then add back the mushrooms, broth, ginger, long rice, and baby bok choy. Cook the whole mixture with the long rice in it until the long rice is done. Do not overcook the long rice. It should be firm not mushy. Season with pepper and garnish with green onions.

Per serving: *237 calories, 3 g fat, 29 g carbohydrates, 4 g dietary fiber, 25 g protein.*

Side Dishes

Mainland U.S. Favorite

Posted on: Wednesday, September 8, 2004
Microwave brown rice cooks faster
Microwaved Brown Basmati or Long Grain Brown Rice

Every night, my Chinese mom would say, "Go cook rice." I got tired of white rice every night and would have really enjoyed basmati rice, which I now have discovered. It has a popcorn taste, and I usually have it at Indian restaurants.

Its Indian name means "queen of fragrance," and it is known in India as the "king of rice." It is found here more often in its white, polished version rather than the natural, brown rice version, which is the way it grows in the fields.

Microwaved Brown Basmati or Long Grain Brown Rice
Serves 8

- 2 1/2 cups (2 beakers) brown basmati or long-grain brown rice
- 3 cups (4 beakers) water
- 1 1/4 teaspoon salt
- 1 teaspoon extra virgin olive oil
- 1 to 2 inches *konbu (green Japanese seaweed, a kelp)* or *wakame (tender, leafy Japanese seaweed) (optional)*

Global Light Cuisine ∞ Carol Devenot

Immerse the basmati rice in water to soften, 2 to 8 hours. Place the rice, water, salt, olive oil, and *konbu* or *wakame* in the microwave rice cooker. Microwave on high for 22 minutes.

Per serving: *136 calories: 2 g fat, 29 g carbohydrates, 2 g dietary fiber, 90 mg sodium, 3 g protein.*

Side Dishes

Mainland U.S. Favorite

Posted on: Wednesday, December 28, 2005

Wild rice a festive stuffing
Festive Stuffed Butternut Squash

The gorgeous contrast of the orange squash, dark wild rice speckled with cranberries, and slivered almonds is a festive addition to the potluck. Even if you are not vegetarian, you could serve this as a side dish with roast turkey, goose, Cornish game hen, or ham.

Adding a nutty flavor, the wild rice is also very nutritious, high in protein, carbohydrate, and fiber but low in fat *(less than 1 percent)*. The wild rice is high in potassium and phosphorus. It's an excellent source of folate *(folic acid)*, zinc, and the B vitamins *(thiamin, riboflavin, and niacin)*.

Native Americans who lived near the lakes of the upper Midwest and southern Canada gathered the rice by hand from their natural habitats. Today, most wild rice sold on the market is cultivated in paddies. Many crops are grown in Minnesota; it is also cultivated in Northern California, Idaho, and on the East Coast.

Festive Stuffed Butternut Squash
Serves 8

4 butternut squashes *(approximately 1 pound each)*
2 cups water
3/4 cup wild rice, raw and rinsed
Canola oil cooking spay
1 cup sweet Maui onion, chopped
3 cloves garlic, minced

Global Light Cuisine ∞ Carol Devenot

Juice of 1 (medium) orange, fresh squeezed
2 1/2 cups multigrain bread, torn and packed firmly
1 teaspoon poultry seasoning
1/3 cup dried cranberries or currants
   or combination of both
1/4 cup slivered almonds, or pine nuts *(optional)*
Fresh Italian flat-leaf parsley for garnish

Preheat the oven to 375 degrees. Score around the perimeter of the squash using a paring knife. Place the knife in the middle of the long side of the squash and cut the squash in half. Scoop out the seeds and fibers with a grapefruit spoon or any other scraping tool. Cover shallow baking pans with foil and place the squashes cut side up. Cover tightly with more foil. Bake 40 to 50 minutes or until fork tender. Set aside to cool.

In a saucepan, bring water to boil. Add the wild rice, reduce to simmer, and allow to steam for 40 minutes or until all the water is absorbed.

Spray large Dutch oven with cooking spray. Sauté the onion and garlic until the onion is lightly browned. Do not burn. Add the cooked rice, orange juice, bread, cooked wild rice, poultry seasoning, cranberries, and slivered almonds. Scoop out the pulp with a large tablespoon leaving the sides of the squashes about 1/2-inch thick. Gently fold the tablespoons of squash into the rice mixture. Stuff each squash generously with stuffing and place them into foiled-lined pans and cover. Bake for 20 minutes or until well heated through. Garnish with parsley.

Per serving (with almonds): *340 calories, 4.5 g total fat, 0.5 g saturated fat, 0 mg cholesterol, 240 mg sodium, 69 g carbohydrate, 9 g dietary fiber, 12 g sugar, 10 g protein.*

Side Dishes

South Pacific/Hawaiian

Traditionally this dish is served with salmon. The dried shrimp gives it a fish flavor without all the calories. This dish reminds me of my father who used to soak the dried *opai (shrimp)* in the chili pepper water. Another favorite of his was the sweet onions served with Hawaiian salt—so simple, but so ʻ*ono*.

Lomi Lomi Tomato
Serves 6

6 (large) ripe tomatoes, cubed
1 (small) bunch green onions, cut into 1/4-inch slices
1 (medium) sweet Maui onion, chopped
1 to 2 tablespoons cider vinegar
1 teaspoon Hawaiian salt
2 to 6 drops Tabasco®
3 tablespoons dried *opai (shrimp)*

Combine the above ingredients and chill thoroughly.

Per serving: *52 calories, 0.7 g fat, 11 g carbohydrates, 3 g dietary fiber, 3 g protein.*

South Pacific/Hawaiian

Luau Spinach
Serves 3

- 2 bunches fresh spinach
- 1 (small) sweet Maui onion, cut into half-moons
- 3 cloves garlic, minced
- Butter-flavored cooking spray
- 2 tablespoons chicken-style vegetarian broth
- 4 tablespoons light coconut milk
- 1 teaspoon Hawaiian salt to taste

Cut the roots off the spinach near the band that binds the bundle together. Rinse the spinach in a pan of clear water several times to remove any dirt. In a large Dutch oven, sauté the onion and garlic in the cooking spray. Add the spinach leaves and broth. When all the spinach leaves are wilted, add the coconut milk and Hawaiian salt.

Per serving: *55 calories, 1 g fat, 2 g dietary fiber, 4 g protein.*

Note: Look for a light *(or lower fat)* coconut milk for less calories and fat.

Side Dishes

South Pacific/Hawaiian

Baked Sweet Potato
Serves 6

3 pounds sweet potato

Preheat the oven to 350 degrees. Scrub the potatoes thoroughly. Wrap each potato with aluminum foil. Bake for 1 1/2 hours or until fork tender. Serve hot or cold.

Per serving: *234 calories, 0.3 g fat, 55 g carbohydrates, 7 g dietary fiber, 4 g protein.*

South Pacific/Hawaiian

Baked Taro
Serves 6

3 pounds taro root

Preheat the oven to 350 degrees. Scrub the taro root thoroughly. Peel and wrap with aluminum foil. Bake for 1 1/2 hours or until fork tender. Serve hot or cold.

Per serving: *314 calories, 0.6 g fat, 78 g carbohydrates, 12 g dietary fiber, 4 g protein.*

South Pacific/Samoan

Lani Ulu
(breadfruit)
Serves 6

1 (6-inch diameter) breadfruit, ripe
Plastic wrap

Select a ripe, soft breadfruit. Look for a yellow-green color and small sections of the rind flattened and partially brown in color. Scrub the skin of the breadfruit and pierce the outside skin with a fork several times around the diameter of the breadfruit. Remove stem and wrap completely with plastic wrap. Microwave on high for 15 minutes.

Per serving: *66 calories, 0.15 g fat, 17 g carbohydrates, 3 g dietary fiber, 1 g protein.*

Variation: If preferred, spray the breadfruit with butter-flavored cooking spray and then sprinkle it with salt and pepper or brown sugar, or rub on honey before cooking. Breadfruit can be purchased in supermarkets, especially in Chinatown and open markets or farmers' markets at intervals from July to February. You could substitute breadfruit for potatoes in Good Kine Potato Salad *(page 67)*.

Side Dishes

South Pacific/Samoan

Posted on: Wednesday, June 1, 2005

Enjoy taste of palu sami with less fat

Light Palu Sami

The first time I ever had Samoan food was at a friend's house. His neighbors invited us to a *palu sami* and mackerel lunch. They grated coconut with a special grater and then strained the coconut cream through the husk. This freshly grated cream was crushed between a piece of aluminum foil layered with *lu'au* leaves and Hawaiian salt. The bundles were then placed in the oven and baked for an hour. They served this with canned mackerel. Anything canned is referred to as *"pisupo."* One of the first canned foods to arrive in Samoa, the story goes, was pea soup.

You can buy light coconut milk at most supermarkets in the Asian food section. I also use Campbell's Healthy Choice Cream of Mushroom soup to thin down the coconut cream. Add the coconut flavoring to taste, a teaspoon at a time. *Palu sami* is delicious, resembling *laulau* with a coconut twist.

Manuia le aso (have a great day)!

Light Palu Sami

Serves 6

- 3 pounds taro leaves
- 1 sweet Maui onion, thinly sliced
- 1 teaspoon Hawaiian salt
- 1 cup light coconut milk

Global Light Cuisine ∞ Carol Devenot 113

1/2 can (5.5 ounces) light cream of mushroom
    soup
1 teaspoon coconut flavoring
6 (16- x 14-inch) pieces heavy aluminum foil

Wearing gloves, cut the stems off the taro leaves. Fill the sink and soak the taro leaves in cold water, swishing to wash out any dirt. Drain on paper towels.

In a mixing bowl, blend the coconut milk, soup, salt, and coconut flavoring. Lay the six pieces of foil on the counter. Divide up the leaves evenly and layer cleaned taro leaves on each piece of foil. Divide up the onion and lay on top of each pile of leaves. Grab the bottom of the layered leaves pile *(without foil)*, form a cup, and pour approximately 1/3 cup of the coconut mixture into the taro leaves. Fold the leaves over each other to keep the liquid in. Place this bundle in the piece of foil and squeeze the ends tightly to seal and keep in the steam.

Fill a 13- by 9-inch pan with two cups of water. Place a wire rack over the water and place the *palu sami* on the rack and into the oven. Also put a baking bowl filled three-fourths full with water next to the baking pan to ensure moisture during baking.

Set your oven at 325 degrees and bake for 1 1/2 to 2 hours, depending on how soft you like your *lu'au (taro)* leaves. Check the water level in the baking pan and bowl every 30 minutes, and fill with water as needed. When done, remove from the oven, take off the foil, and serve warm.

114 Side Dishes

Per serving: *120 calories, 3 g total fat, 1.5 g saturated fat, 0 mg cholesterol, 400 mg sodium, 18 g carbohydrates, 9 g dietary fiber, 2 g sugar, 12 g protein.*

Note: You can find the prepackage taro leaves in supermarkets. They are sold in 1 pound bundles. Each bag varies as to the number of leaves in each bag. There are approximately 7 to 10 leaves in each bag. Spinach could be substituted for the taro leaves. Serve this with broiled fish and Baked Taro *(page 110)* or *Lani Ulu (page 111)* and you will have a complete Samoan meal.

Entrées

African

Posted on: Wednesday, May 31, 2006
African curried meatloaf makes tasty dinner party entree

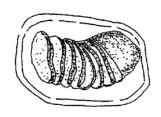

Bobotie (curried meatloaf)

The dish originated in Batavia (now Jakarta) during Indonesia's Dutch colony days. The dish then traveled around the world as the Dutch settled in other countries, notably South Africa, Kenya, Botswana, Zimbabwe, and Zambia. Though now considered an African dish, it is very much a product of the white elite there, not a dish with African roots.

At one time, the dish was made with ground mutton and pork, seasoned with ginger, marjoram, and lemon rind and dried fruit, like a mincemeat and meatloaf hybrid. Today it's made with beef, pork, and lamb. Curry powder is used instead of a homemade spice mixture.

Bobotie
(curried meatloaf)
Serves 9

1 cup coarse crumbs from 2 slices fresh multigrain bread
1 cup skim milk
Butter-flavored spray or extra virgin olive oil spray
1/2 (medium) onion, finely chopped
3 to 4 cloves garlic, minced

118   Entrées

1/2 Granny Smith apple, peeled, cored, and
    finely chopped
1/3 cup raisins or dried currants or cranberries
1/4 cup slivered almonds, blanched
2 tablespoons curry powder
1 teaspoon sugar
3/4 cup Egg Beaters®
1 1/2 to 2 pounds ground turkey
2 tablespoons lemon juice
1/2 teaspoon lemon zest
1 3/4 teaspoon sea salt *(divided use)*
1/4 teaspoon fresh ground pepper
Mango chutney for garnish

In a small mixing bowl, soak the bread crumbs in the skim milk for about 15 minutes, then drain in a sieve over a bowl. Lightly press the bread crumbs to remove the excess milk. Reserve excess milk for the custard topping.

Place an oven rack in the middle of the oven and preheat to 350 degrees. Spray a 9- by 9-inch baking dish with butter-flavored spray and set aside.

In a heavy frying pan, sauté the onion, garlic, and apple with butter-flavored spray until soft, about 12 minutes. Add raisins, almonds, curry powder and sugar, and cook, stirring occasionally, for 1 minute. Remove from heat. In a large bowl, mix together 1/4 cup Egg Beaters®, pressed breadcrumbs, turkey, raisin mixture, lemon juice, lemon zest, 1 1/2 teaspoons salt, and 1/4 teaspoon pepper. Blend until well combined, but do not over mix.

Global Light Cuisine ∞ Carol Devenot

Spread meat mixture evenly in the baking dish and bake for 30 minutes. While the turkey loaf is baking, 1/2 cup Egg Beaters®, reserved milk, and 1/4 teaspoon of salt. Remove the turkey loaf from the oven and pour off excess fat. Using a round chopstick, poke holes in the loaf. Pour the egg mixture over the loaf, return to the oven, and bake for approximately 15 minutes or until set. Serve hot with a dollop of mango chutney.

Per serving (3- by 3-inch): 320 calories, 19 g fat, 5 g saturated fat, 70 mg cholesterol, 650 mg sodium, 17 g carbohydrate, 3 g dietary fiber, 10 g sugar, 22 g protein.

Asia/Chinese

Posted on: Wednesday, August 23, 2006

Salty preserved turnip gives wild salmon Asian flavor

Lynne's Quick Asian Salmon

Lynne is still busy cooking and baking for her family. She is also a Pampered Chef distributor and is sometimes called upon to do healthy food demonstrations for Kapi`olani Medical Center for Women & Children. She shared a salmon recipe she created for her mother-in-law. I tested the recipe the other night and really loved the flavor of the salty *chung choy (preserved turnip)* with the wild salmon. You can find *chung choy* in the Asian section of the supermarket or in Chinatown markets.

Recently, there has been a greater awareness of the benefits of eating wild salmon. It swims free in the waters of the North Pacific, which provide a rich diet of krill and shrimp. This diet is responsible for the natural pink to orange pigment of the salmon. Colorful salmon contains astaxanthin, a strong antioxidant. Salmon is also high in protein and omega-3 fatty acids and relatively low in fat.

Lynne's Quick Asian Salmon

Serves 1

1 (7-ounce) wild salmon fillet
1 tablespoon *chung choy (preserved turnip)*, minced

Global Light Cuisine ∞ Carol Devenot

1 tablespoon green onions, sliced
1 to 2 teaspoons low-sodium soy sauce
   (up to 1 tablespoon if diet allows)
Peanut oil *(place in kitchen spritzer)*
Fresh Chinese parsley *(cilantro)* for garnish

Soak the *chung choy* in cold water for 30 minutes, and squeeze dry. Chop it in 1/4-inch pieces. Place salmon fillet in microwave dish. Spray twice with peanut oil in spritzer. Top with soy sauce, then *chung choy,* and finally with green onions. Cover the dish with microwavable cover, and microwave on high for 1 minute. Remove cover and garnish with parsley. Serve with steamed vegetables, such as choy sum, and brown rice.

Per serving: *300 calories, 14 g fat, 2 g saturated fat, 110 mg cholesterol, 450 mg sodium, 3 g carbohydrate, 0 g dietary fiber, 1 g sugar, 40 g protein.*

Asia/Chinese

Posted on: Wednesday, November 28, 2007

If you score abundance of hamachi, try grilling it

Grilled Hamachi with Black Bean Sauce

The Japanese regard *hamachi* as one of the most desirable fish for *sushi*. It has a rich, smooth, buttery, smoky flavor and is not overly fatty. *Hamachi* is the Japanese name of the yellowtail, a species of amberjack.

This sleek migratory fish is native to the Northwest Pacific. In Japan, *hamachi* are raised in hatcheries and harvested when they weigh between 15 and 20 pounds. Yellowtail caught in Hawaiian waters is usually too lean to be used for sushi. With this prized gift of a fish, I made the following Chinese style with black bean sauce.

Grilled Hamachi with Black Bean Sauce

Serves 4 to 6

5 pounds *hamachi* fillets; cleaned and dressed, with skin on
Teriyaki Sauce *(page 203)* or teriyaki marinade
Cooking spray
Fresh Chinese parsley *(cilantro)* for garnish

Black Bean Sauce:

1 teaspoon peanut oil

3 to 4 tablespoons Teriyaki Sauce *(page 203)*,
   teriyaki marinade, or miso teriyaki sauce
1/2 teaspoon Hawaiian chili pepper, minced
   (optional)
2 tablespoons black beans, rinsed and drained
1/4 cup sherry wine
1 tablespoon Lee Kum Kee® Stir Fry Sauce
3/4 cup vegetarian broth or fish stock
   or chicken broth
2 tablespoon *mochiko* sweet rice flour,
   whisked with 1/4 cup water

In a zippered plastic bag, immerse *hamachi* fillets in teriyaki sauce. Marinate overnight or for at least 30 minutes.

To make the sauce, heat the oil over medium heat in a small saucepan. Add teriyaki sauce, chili pepper, black beans, sherry, stir-fry sauce, and broth. Bring this mixture to a boil and simmer for about 15 minutes. Slowly whisk the *mochiko* slurry into the boiled sauce, stirring until it thickens. Reduce heat to very low; keep warm while you prepare the fish.

Heat barbecue *(briquettes, gas, or wood burning)* to hot. Spray grill with cooking spray. Lay fish—skin side down—on the hot grill; baste during cooking, and watch closely. Remove from heat while midsection is still moist and a little underdone or the thinner ends will be too dry.

Place fish on a serving platter and spoon black bean sauce over the fish. Garnish with parsley.

Per serving (4 servings): *650 calories, 10 g fat, 2 g saturated fat, 200 mg cholesterol, greater than 1,400 mg sodium, 12 g carbohydrate, 1 g dietary fiber, 5 g sugar, 118 g protein.*

124   Entrées

Asia/Chinese

Posted on: Wednesday, June 29, 2005

Szechuan eggplant with less oil

Spicy Szechuan Eggplant

Technically, eggplant is a berry. It comes in a wide range of shapes and sizes, from 2 to 12 inches in length. There are creamy-white, egg-shaped eggplants; thin Japanese eggplants; grape-like small green Thai eggplants; rosy pink and purple-and-white-striped eggplants; and purple eggplant. The most common in the United States is the pear-shaped purple variety.

The Japanese eggplant has a delicate flavor and a thin skin. There is no need to peel the skin because it will soften during the cooking process. Its flesh is smoother and there are fewer seeds than in the common eggplants. You can see why most cooks prefer it.

Wood ear mushrooms, part of the recipe, are also called tree ear and black fungus. They are believed by many to be good for the heart. Wood ears do, indeed, look like ears growing out of trees, hence the name. They are usually sold dried and then reconstituted in warm water. The texture is crunchy and the flavor is mild. They make a nice meat replacement in stir fries and other dishes. You can usually purchase them at large supermarkets and at Asian grocery stores.

Spicy Szechuan Eggplant

Serves 4

1 1/2 pounds Japanese eggplant, peeled and cut into 3-inch strips

1 cup chicken breasts, boneless and skinless, cut into 1 1/2-inch strips
1 cup dried wood ear mushrooms *(or shiitake, straw, or other mushrooms)*, soaked in hot water and sliced into 1 1/2-inch strips
Canola oil cooking spray

Sauce:

1/4 cup lower-sodium soy sauce
1 tablespoon honey
1 tablespoon distilled white vinegar
1 tablespoon cornstarch
2 red chili peppers, minced, or 1/4 teaspoon red chili flakes
2 slices fresh ginger root, peeled
3 cloves garlic, minced

Mix all sauce ingredients and set aside.

Place the sliced eggplant into a microwave-safe bowl and microwave 5 minutes.

Spray a wok or large frying pan with cooking spray and sauté the chicken until golden brown. Set aside.

Spray wok or frying pan with cooking spray again and sauté eggplant over medium heat until golden brown, or desired tenderness is reached. Add the wood ears and chicken, then pour the sauce over everything.

Cook until just heated through. Serve over brown rice.

Per serving: *140 calories, 2 g total fat, 0 g saturated fat, 30 mg cholesterol, 780 mg sodium, 16 g carbohydrates, 8 g dietary fiber, 5 g sugar, 14 g protein.*

Asia/Chinese

Broccoli Stir Fry
Serves 4

1 (1-inch) piece fresh ginger root, crushed
3 cloves garlic, minced
1/2 tablespoon chicken-style vegetarian broth powder plus 2 tablespoons water
Vegetable oil cooking spray
1 teaspoon peanut oil
1 pound chicken breasts, boneless and skinless, cut into 1 1/2-inch pieces
1 tablespoon Lee Kum Kee® Oyster Sauce or Lee Kum Kee® Vegetarian Stir Fry Sauce
1 teaspoon soy sauce
1 (4-ounce) can mushrooms
2 stalks broccoli, sliced diagonally
2 stalks celery, sliced diagonally
1 tablespoon chicken-style vegetarian broth powder plus 1 cup water
1 1/2 tablespoons cornstarch mixed with water

Water-sauté the ginger and garlic with 2 tablespoons reconstituted broth in a frying pan on medium-high heat. Remove from the pan and spray with vegetable oil cooking spray and add the peanut oil. Add the chicken and brown. Add stir-fry and soy sauces. Cook for 2 minutes. Add mushrooms, broccoli, celery, ginger: garlic, and broth. Stir-fry all the ingredients for 10 minutes or until crisp-tender. Add cornstarch mixture to thicken the gravy.

Per serving: *227 calories, 8 g fat, 11 g carbohydrates, 4 g dietary fiber, 28 g protein.*

Variations: This is a good basic stir-fry recipe for any type of vegetable. In place of broccoli, you could use *gai lan (Chinese broccoli)*, Chinese peas, baby bok choy, or *choy sum.* Carrots could be added for color. Green pepper would add a little zest. Rehydrated shiitake mushrooms would be an excellent substitute for the canned mushrooms. Soak the mushrooms in hot water for 20 minutes. Don't throw out the water. It makes a great liquid for sautéing and gravy.

Asia/Chinese

Garden Chow Mein
Serves 12

3 (6-ounce) packages low-fat chow mein noodles
1 teaspoon sesame oil
3/4 to 1 cup Lee Kum Kee® Vegetarian Stir Fry Sauce
8 dried shiitake mushrooms
Vegetable oil cooking spray
4 chicken breasts, marinated in Char Siu Sauce *(page 131)*
4 stalks celery, sliced diagonally
1 (8-ounce) package fresh green beans, sliced diagonally
1/2 cup Chinese pea pods, washed and strings removed
1 (12-ounce) package chop suey mix *(bean sprouts, a little carrot, a little watercress)*
1 to 2 cups vegetable broth
1/2 teaspoon salt
6 stalks green onions, sliced 1/2-inch thick
1 bunch fresh Chinese parsley *(cilantro)* for garnish

Preheat oven to 250 degrees. Place noodles in 13- by 9- by 2-inch baking pan. Sprinkle noodles with sesame oil and 1/4 cup of stir-fry sauce. Heat in oven for 10 minutes.

Reconstitute shiitake mushrooms by placing in a small saucepan with water to cover. Cook on medium heat for 10 minutes and drain, keeping the mushroom water for stir frying. Cut stems from mushrooms; slice caps into 1/4-inch-thick strips.

Spray a wok or frying pan with cooking spray and sauté the chicken breasts until cooked. Remove chicken from the pan and slice into 1/2-inch strips. Set aside. Then stir-fry celery, green beans, Chinese pea pods, and chop suey mix in vegetable and mushroom broths. Season with the remaining stir-fry sauce and salt. Stir in noodles and toss gently. Garnish with chicken, mushrooms, green onions, and parsley sprigs.

Per serving: *205 calories, 5 g fat, 21 g carbohydrates, 2 g dietary fiber, 22 g protein.*

Variations: This is a good recipe for leftover Char Siu Chicken *(page 130).* You can also use *char siu* marinated Boca® Burger. You can add any type of crispy vegetables like jicama and baby corn to the chop suey mix.

Asia/Chinese

Char siu pork is always so tempting to eat because of the beautiful, glazed, reddish-brown color. You can get the flavor without all the fat by substituting chicken breasts. Be careful to check the chicken while roasting because the sugar will cause the chicken to burn. Baste constantly and you'll have a moist and delicious dish.

Char Siu Chicken
Serves 6

2 1/2 pounds chicken breasts, skinless
1 recipe of Char Siu Sauce *(below)*
Vegetable oil cooking spray

Combine all the ingredients for the Char Siu Sauce. Place the chicken and sauce in a zip-type bag and marinate overnight. Heat oven to 400 degrees. Line a baking pan with aluminum foil. Place a wire rack in the foil-lined pan. Spray vegetable oil cooking spray on the wire rack. Lay chicken pieces on top. Place in the oven and roast 15 minutes and baste and roast for another 20 minutes at 375 degrees. Test for doneness by slicing through a piece.

Per serving with sauce: *369 calories, 7 g fat, 14 g carbohydrates, 0 g dietary fiber, 60 g protein.*

Char Siu Sauce

Serves 6

- 1/3 cup sugar
- 1/3 cup soy sauce
- 1/8 to 1/4 teaspoon Chinese five-spice seasoning
- 1 to 2 cloves garlic, minced
- 1 tablespoon fresh ginger root, minced
- 1 tablespoon hoisin sauce
- 1 to 2 teaspoons red food coloring *(optional)*

Combine all the ingredients. Makes enough marinade for 2 1/2 pounds of chicken.

Per serving of sauce: *351 calories, 1 g fat, 81 g carbohydrates, 2 g dietary fiber, 1 g protein.*

Asia/Chinese

Posted on: Wednesday, August 25, 2004
Make black bean sauces healthier
Garlic Asparagus and Chicken in Black Bean Sauce

Perhaps you've wondered if it's possible to recreate the black bean sauce dishes served in Chinese restaurants without all that oil. It can be done. Preparing vegetables in black bean sauce conjures up memories of Mom making bitter melon and black bean sauce. You can try this recipe with bitter melon or any other favorite Asian vegetable, such as baby bok choy or mustard greens. The secret is in the sauce.

Garlic Asparagus and Chicken in Black Bean Sauce
Serves 4

1 tablespoon low-sodium soy sauce
1 tablespoon dry sherry
1/2 teaspoon brown sugar
1/2 pound chicken breasts, skinless
1 pound asparagus, young and tender
1 teaspoon peanut oil
3 cloves garlic, crushed
1 (1 1/2-inch) piece fresh ginger root, crushed
2 tablespoons black beans, cooked and rinsed
3/4 cup chicken broth
1/2 round onion, cut into half-moons

2 tablespoons cornstarch or *mochiko* sweet
   rice flour mixed with 2 tablespoons of water
2 sprigs fresh Chinese parsley *(cilantro)* for garnish

Combine soy sauce, sherry, and sugar in a small bowl and set aside.

Slice the chicken breast in 1 1/2- by 1/4-inch-thick diagonal slices.

Wash asparagus and cut off the tough ends. Slice diagonally every 1 1/2-inch. Parboil tough parts as needed.

Place peanut oil in the wok on high heat, add the chicken, and stir-fry until browned. Set chicken aside. In the same wok, stir-fry the garlic and ginger about 1 minute. Add the rinsed black beans. Add the asparagus and chicken broth and cook for 1 to 2 minutes; do not overcook. Add the onions and soy sauce mixture. Add the chicken. Thicken with the cornstarch mixture. Garnish with parsley and serve immediately.

Per serving: *150 calories, 3 g fat, 20 g carbohydrates, 5 g dietary fiber, 370 mg sodium, 14 g protein.*

Asia/Chinese

Posted on: Wednesday, September 6, 2006

Spices jazz up familiar entrées
Chinese Five Spice Chicken and Vegetables

One of the best open markets on Oahu is held on the grounds of Kapi`olani Community College. Every Saturday morning you can find fresh produce and homemade cooked and baked goods from 7 to 11 a.m. On my first visit, I enjoyed meeting an enthusiastic and creative entrepreneur Ka`iulani Cowell of Ka`iulani Spices.

She blends a total of 21 exotic spices in her 5 different rubs and seasonings using the freshest of ingredients. All her spices are purchased in their natural seed, pod, or stick forms. To maximize their flavors, she has roasted, ground, and mixed them by hand.

Chinese Five Spice Chicken and Vegetables
Serves 6

6 chicken breasts, skinless
Ka`iulani Chinese Five Spice Rub and
    Seasoning *(brown sugar, Hawaiian rock salt, fennel, star anise, cinnamon, and other spices)*
4 Yukon Gold potatoes, peeled and cut in half
    lengthwise
4 (large) carrots, peeled and cut in half lengthwise

Rinse the chicken and pat dry with paper towels. Rub generously with Ka`iulani Chinese Five Spice. Place on roasting pan lined with aluminum foil. Place in the oven and bake at 350 degrees for 20 minutes. Sprinkle the potatoes and carrots with the rub and place them alongside the chicken and bake for 40 to 50 minutes or until chicken is cooked through and vegetables are tender.

Per serving (without rub): *350 calories, 2 g fat, 0.5 g saturated fat, 100 mg cholesterol, 150 mg sodium, 35 g carbohydrate, 2 g dietary fiber, 2 g sugar, 44 g protein.*

Asia/Chinese

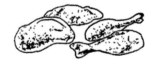

Shoyu Chicken
Serves 6

- 6 chicken thighs, skinless, washed, and dried
- 1 cup soy sauce *(shoyu)* or tamari sauce
- 1 1/2 tablespoons honey
- 1/3 cup brown sugar
- 1 cup chicken broth or chicken-style vegetarian broth
- 2 tablespoons fresh ginger root (1 1/2-inch), minced
- 5 cloves garlic, minced
- 1 star anise or 3 teaspoons anise seed
- 1/4 cup green onions, cut 1/2-inch wide
- 2 tablespoons sherry
- 1/2 to 1 cup shiitake mushrooms, rehydrated in hot water
- 2 tablespoons cornstarch or *mochiko* sweet rice flour
- 4 tablespoons water

Garnish:
- 1/2 cup fresh Chinese parsley *(cilantro)*, chopped
- 1/4 cup green onions, cut into 1/4-inch pieces

In a large pot combine soy sauce, honey, sugar, broth, ginger, garlic, anise, green onions, sherry, and mushrooms. Bring to boil and add chicken. Simmer on medium heat for 40 to 60 minutes. Remove chicken thighs and mushrooms. Combine the cornstarch and water and add to sauce. Bring to boil and simmer for 1 minute on medium heat. Pour over chicken. Garnish with parsley and green onions.

Per serving: *187 calories, 3 g fat, 22 g carbohydrates, 1 g dietary fiber, 18 g protein.*

Asia/Chinese

Posted on: Wednesday, June 14, 2006

Sichuan pepper peps ma po tofu

Sichuan Ma Po Tofu

For the record, Sichuan peppercorns are the fruit of the prickly ash *(Zanthoxylum simulans)*, a member of the citrus family, and have an aromatic, camphor-like flavor and also the ability to cause your lips to go numb or tingle. Ordinary peppercorns *(Piper nigrum)* are an entirely different thing.

Sichuan Ma Po Tofu

Serves 4

2 to 3 tablespoons salted black beans
1 (20-ounce) block of firm tofu
Canola oil cooking spray
1/2 pound ground turkey
1 tablespoon fresh ginger root, grated
4 cloves garlic, minced
1 to 2 tablespoons chili paste *(optional)*
8 stalks green onions, cut in 1/4-inch lengths
1 cup organic chicken stock
2 tablespoons Lee Kum Kee® Vegetarian Stir Fry Sauce or soy sauce
1/2 teaspoon ground Sichuan peppercorns or crushed red pepper
2 teaspoons *mochiko* sweet rice flour or cornstarch, mixed with 2 teaspoons water

Soak the black beans in warm water for 10 minutes. Drain the black beans, place in a bowl, and mash with a fork.

Drain the tofu and place in a pan to catch the water; place a heavy weight on top for 10 minutes.

Spray a large, nonstick frying pan or wok with cooking spray and stir-fry the black beans and ground turkey together for 3 minutes. Add the ginger, garlic, chili paste, and half of the green onions. Stir-fry for 2 minutes and then add the chicken stock and tofu. Simmer for 5 minutes. Add the vegetarian stir-fry sauce and Sichuan peppercorns. Carefully stir the starch mixture into the dish, mixing until the sauce thickens. Sprinkle with reserved green onions and serve over steamed brown rice.

Per serving (without brown rice): 320 calories, 23 g fat, 4 g saturated fat, 40 mg cholesterol, 780 mg sodium, 8 g carbohydrate, 2 g dietary fiber, 1 g sugar, 24 g protein.

Asia/Chinese

Posted on: Wednesday, February 22, 2006
Try tofu with sweet, sour sauce
Sweet and Sour Tofu and Carol's Sweet and Sour Sauce

I think this one is a winner—not too sweet, not too sour, just right. I laugh every time I watch comedian Rap Reiplinger's "Auntie Marialani's Cooking Show." When "testing" the wine, she would say, "Not too sweet, not too rancid, but just right!"

The secret of a sweet-and-sour stir fry is in the sauce. My mom used cider vinegar and dark brown sugar to get the right balance. The ketchup-soy sauce combination I use here gives the sauce richness and color. And I like the sweet rice flour, for a thickener because it has a smoother texture and seems to match, too.

Sweet and Sour Tofu
Serves 4

1 teaspoon peanut oil
1/4 red onion, sliced into half-moons
2 to 3 cloves garlic, minced
1 green pepper, sliced lengthwise
1/2 cup sweet and sour sauce *(recipe follows)*
1 (12.3-ounce) package Mori-Nu Extra Firm Lite Silken Tofu, cut into 1/2-inch cubes
Fresh Chinese parsley *(cilantro)* for garnish

In a wok or large frying pan, fry the peanut oil, red onions, and garlic for 1 minute. Add the green pepper and sauté for about 2 minutes. Pour sweet-and-sour sauce over the mixture. Add the tofu and cook until hot and thickened. Serve immediately.

This is great served over brown or *hapa (brown and white)* rice. Garnish with parsley.

Carol's Sweet and Sour Sauce
Serves 4

- 1/2 cup cider vinegar
- 2 tablespoons soy sauce
- 2 tablespoons cornstarch or *mochiko* sweet rice flour
- 1 cup brown sugar or brown rice syrup
- 6 tablespoons ketchup

Mix the vinegar, soy sauce, and cornstarch or rice flour together. When smooth, add the brown sugar or brown rice syrup and ketchup to the mixture. Cook over medium heat until thick. Bottle, label, and save for any sweet and sour dish. Store in the refrigerator.

Per serving (without rice): 239 calories, 2 g fat, 51 g carbohydrates, 1 g dietary fiber, 676 mg sodium, 7 g protein.

Per serving (sauce only): 185 calories, 0 g fat, 47 g carbohydrates, 0 g dietary fiber, 1 g protein.

Asia/Chinese

Posted on: Wednesday, April 18, 2007
Soy chicken, edamame in stir fry
Sesame Soy Chicken and Edamame Stir Fry

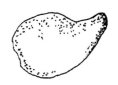

This recipe will be included in the DASH Diet being worked on by Kapi`olani Community College educational specialist Daniel Leung, Alyssa Moreau, and other Kapi`olani Community College culinary school staff.

Daniel Leung explained that DASH, which stands for Dietary Approaches to Stop Hypertension, is designed to help everyone with their eating and exercise habits. He and his staff were given a grant to work with local farmers to develop healthy recipes for the people of Hawai`i. By fall, they'll have a cookbook (*A Dash of Aloha: Healthy Hawaii Cuisine and Life*) and cooking classes to help with weight loss, cholesterol, and blood pressure. The DASH diet is recommended by the American Heart Association.

Sesame Soy Chicken and Edamame Stir-Fry
Serves 3 to 4

1 (8-ounce) package soba noodles
Canola oil cooking spray
A few drops Bragg Liquid Aminos® or low-sodium soy sauce
Few drops sesame oil, toasted
2 cups soy chicken cutlets, sliced into strips

- 1/2 cup red bell pepper, julienned
- 1 tablespoon fresh ginger root, minced
- 1 stalk lemon grass, minced
- 2 cloves garlic, minced
- 1 to 2 tablespoons *mirin*
- 1 tablespoon sesame oil, toasted
- 2 tablespoons Bragg Liquid Aminos® or low-sodium soy sauce
- 1 cup shelled, cooked *edamame (soy beans)*
- 1/2 cup sugar snap peas or snow peas
- 1/4 cup green onions, sliced into 1-inch slices
- 1 tablespoon black sesame seeds, toasted, for garnish

Cook noodles as directed on the package. Rinse and drain well. Toss a few drops of sesame oil and/or Bragg Liquid Aminos® or soy sauce. Set aside.

While noodles are cooking, start the stir fry: Spray a non-stick frying pan with canola spray, stir-fry the soy chicken and red bell pepper a few minutes until cutlets start to brown and bell peppers begin to soften. Add the ginger, lemongrass, and garlic and cook 1 minute. Add the *mirin,* toasted sesame oil, and Bragg Liquid Aminos® and mix well. Then add in *edamame,* snap peas, and green onions. Cook a few minutes or until the snap peas are crisp-tender. Serve over soba noodles garnished with toasted black sesame seeds.

Per serving: *470 calories, 12 g fat, 1 g saturated fat, 0 mg cholesterol, 830 mg sodium, 67 g carbohydrate, 6 g dietary fiber, 6 g sugar, 28 g protein.*

Asia/Filipino

Posted on: Wednesday, April 19, 2006

Bay leaves key to `ono adobo dish

Chicken Adobo

The combination of the cider vinegar, soy sauce, garlic, peppercorns, and bay leaf make this dish distinctive and delicious. Bay leaves make the difference.

There are three major types of bay leaves: Mediterranean, Californian, and Indian. The California type is similar to the Mediterranean leaf but has a stronger flavor. Bay leaves, which come from the laurel family, are one of the most commonly used herbs.

Bay laurels are prized, and this goes back to a story told of the Greek god Apollo. Apollo, the god of prophecy, healing and poetry, was in love with Daphne. Wanting no part of his affections, she turned herself into a bay tree. When he discovered this, he wore a laurel wreath in her memory. He declared the bay leaf sacred, and crowns of these leaves were given to victors in sport and battle. Poets, too, received the honor. And that's why we have poets laureate.

Chicken Adobo

Serves 6

- 3 pounds chicken breasts, boneless and skinless, cut into 2-inch pieces
- 1/2 cup cider vinegar
- 1/4 cup lower-sodium soy sauce or tamari
- 3 to 4 cloves garlic, crushed

1/4 teaspoon peppercorns, crushed
1 or 2 bay leaves
1/2 sweet Maui onion
Sea salt to taste

In a Dutch oven, mix together chicken, vinegar, soy sauce, garlic, peppercorns, bay leaves, onion, and sea salt. Cover and allow to stand for 1 to 3 hours. Bring to boil, then lower the heat and simmer for 30 minutes. Uncover and simmer for 15 additional minutes or until the liquid evaporates and the chicken is golden brown.

Per serving (without salt): 270 calories, 3 g fat, 2 g saturated fat, 130 mg cholesterol, 500 mg sodium, 5 g carbohydrate, 0 g dietary fiber, 2 g sugar, 53 g protein.

Asia/Filipino

Posted on: Wednesday, August 24, 2005
Veat™ beats meat in guisantes
Veat, Not Meat Guisantes

When I was teaching, some of my Filipino students introduced me to *guisantes*—a sort of stew, made with vegetables, tomatoes, and pork. This dish has been one of my favorites because it is so easy to make. But for this column, I didn't want to make an ordinary *guisantes;* I wanted a vegetarian version. So I went to an organic store, Kale's in Hawai`i Kai, and found a new alternative to meat called Veat™ Gourmet Bites. It is made from soy protein and has the flavor and texture you'd expect of meat. It tastes like pork but is cholesterol free and an excellent source of soy protein. It also makes a great sweet-and-sour dish. If you don't care to try Veat™, you can use any meat substitute—or use boneless, skinless chicken breasts.

Veat, Not Meat Guisantes
Serves 4

1 cup Veat™ Gourmet Bites *(soy protein)*, or
   1 cup chicken breasts, boneless and skinless, cooked, and cut into chunks or strips
1 teaspoon extra virgin olive oil
3 to 5 cloves garlic, minced
1 red onion, diced
1 1/2 cups cherry tomatoes
   or 1 (large) tomato, diced
1/8 teaspoon black pepper

Global Light Cuisine ∞ Carol Devenot

- 1/2 cup low-sodium soy sauce
- 2 (medium) red potatoes, diced
- 2 (8-ounce) cans low-sodium tomato sauce
- 1/2 (small) can low-sodium tomato paste
- 1 (6-ounce) package frozen green peas
- 1 green bell pepper, thinly sliced
- 1 red bell pepper, thinly sliced

In a large saucepan, heat olive oil on medium heat and sauté the garlic and onions for 2 minutes. Add the Veat™ or chicken and the tomatoes, black pepper, and soy sauce. Bring to a boil, add potatoes, then lower heat and simmer until potatoes are almost cooked. Add tomato sauce and tomato paste, stirring occasionally. Simmer until potatoes and sauce are cooked. Add green peas and simmer for 5 minutes. Add green and red peppers and simmer for a few minutes. Serve over hot brown rice.

Per serving: *240 calories, 3 g total fat, 0.5 g saturated fat, 25 mg cholesterol, more than 1,400 mg sodium, 36 g carbohydrate, 9 g dietary fiber, 15 g sugar, 20 g protein.*

148   Entrées

Asia/Indonesian

Posted on: Wednesday, June 28, 2006

Satay side dishes from Indonesia still popular centuries later

Indonesian Chicken Satay

Satay *(sate)* is a popular side dish at the Indonesian *rijsttafel*, a Dutch word meaning rice table—a buffet in which rice is the centerpiece accompanied by many other dishes. Comparable to our own large, Asian buffets, as many as 40 to 100 different dishes might be served, including eggs, fish, meat, fruits, vegetables, pickles, and nuts. Traditionally, rice is placed in a soup bowl and side dishes are placed around it. A *sambal*—spicy Indonesian relish or sauce—is served as a seasoning.

Historically, Indonesia has been a center for international trade. For hundreds of years, Chinese, Indian, and African traders bartered for cloves, ginger, mace, nutmeg, and black pepper grown there. Later, European traders came for the same spices and stayed on to colonize the lands. By the 16th century, the Dutch gained control and ruled Indonesia for 320 years. The plantation owners, who enjoyed Indonesian cuisine, introduced it to the Netherlands. Today, this feast is popular both in Indonesia and Holland.

Indonesian Chicken Satay

Serves 4

Dipping Sauce:

3 to 4 tablespoons reduced-fat chunky peanut butter

2 teaspoons fresh ginger root, grated
4 cloves garlic, minced
2 green onions, green part only, finely sliced
2 to 3 tablespoons soy sauce
4 tablespoons rice vinegar
3 to 4 tablespoons brown rice syrup
1 teaspoon hot chili sauce *(optional)*
Fresh Chinese parsley *(cilantro)* for garnish

Satay:

Nonfat vegetable spray
1 (small) onion, finely chopped
1 (l-inch) piece fresh ginger root, peeled and finely chopped
2 to 3 cloves garlic, minced
4 chicken breasts, boneless and skinless, cut into 1 1/2-inch pieces

Combine dipping sauce ingredients, mix, and set aside.

Heat a wok and spray with nonfat vegetable spray. Add the onion, garlic, and ginger and stir-fry for 2 to 3 minutes or until browned. Remove from wok and set aside. Add the chicken pieces to the wok and stir-fry until crisp and golden brown on all sides.

Thread chicken onto bamboo skewers and lay them on a bed of greens; scatter onion, ginger, and garlic over chicken. Pass bowls of dipping sauce garnished with parsley.

Per serving: *430 calories, 15 g fat, 3 g saturated fat, 80 mg cholesterol, 600 mg sodium, 29 g carbohydrate, 2 g dietary fiber, 12 g sugar, 44 g protein.*

Miso flavor dresses up salmon dish

Posted on: Wednesday, May 17, 2006

Asia/Japanese

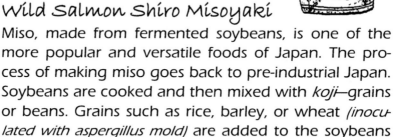

Wild Salmon Shiro Misoyaki

Miso, made from fermented soybeans, is one of the more popular and versatile foods of Japan. The process of making miso goes back to pre-industrial Japan. Soybeans are cooked and then mixed with *koji*—grains or beans. Grains such as rice, barley, or wheat *(inoculated with aspergillus mold)* are added to the soybeans along with salt and water. This mixture is allowed to ferment from one month to three years.

Based on the color and taste, miso can be divided into two groups. *Shiro* or white miso is light in color. *Hatcho* refers to the darker and longer-aged misos. White miso is high in carbohydrates because it has a higher proportion of grains to soybeans than do the darker varieties. Light miso, or sweet miso, is popular in Kyoto and southern Japan.

Wild Salmon Shiro Misoyaki

Serves 4

1 1/2 pounds wild salmon fillets

Marinade:

1 1/2 cups white miso
1 to 3 tablespoons fresh ginger root, peeled and grated
2 to 3 cloves garlic, grated

1/2 cup brown rice syrup
1 cup sake or *mirin* *(sweet rice wine)*
1/2 cup rice vinegar
2 tablespoons tamari or soy sauce

Garnish *(optional):*

Sesame seeds, roasted
2 stalks green onions, chopped in 1/4-inch slices

Combine marinade ingredients in shallow dish.

Slash the surface of the salmon every 1 to 2 inches with a sharp knife. Place the salmon in the marinade and marinate for at least an hour. Broil the salmon, still in the sauce, in the oven for 8 to 10 minutes.

Spoon some of the sauce on the serving plate and lay the broiled salmon on the sauce. Pour additional sauce over the fish. Garnish with roasted sesame seeds and green onions.

Serve immediately with steamed *kabocha* squash and *choy sum* or other steamed greens.

Per serving (with sauce):* *700 calories, 20 g fat, 3 g saturated fat, 100 mg cholesterol, greater than 2,000 mg sodium, 72 g carbohydrate, 6 g dietary fiber, 36 g sugar, 41 g protein.*

* Without garnishes, *kabocha* squash, or *choy sum.*

Entrées

Asia/Japanese

Posted on: Wednesday, April 21, 2004

Leaner chicken katsu hits `ono odometer for taste

Chicken Katsu

I tried to maintain the integrity of the original recipe while reducing the fattening ingredients. Use skinless chicken breasts or lean pork cutlets for this, such as the pork *tonkatsu* cuts you find at many local supermarkets. Garlic or garlic powder enhances the flavors of savory foods. Use egg whites to make the coating stick to the chicken and vegetable spray to keep the chicken from sticking. *Panko* is a very crisp Japanese breading made by a special process and is available in most grocery stores in the Asian section.

Chicken Katsu

Serves 8

4 pounds chicken breasts, skinless, boneless, cut into 8 filets
1 to 2 teaspoons garlic powder
2 egg whites, beaten to soft foam
1/2 cup *panko* flakes
Vegetable oil cooking spray

Katsu Sauce:

1 cup ketchup
6 tablespoons of Worcestershire sauce

Line a 13- by 9-inch pan with aluminum foil and place a wire rack over the foil. Spray the rack with cooking spray. Preheat your oven's broiler.

Place egg whites and *panko* flakes in separate shallow bowls. Sprinkle the chicken with garlic powder, coat both sides in egg white, and then with *panko* flakes. Place chicken on rack and broil 3 to 4 inches from heat source until golden brown on both sides. Serve with *katsu* sauce.

Per serving (without katsu sauce): *296 calories, 9 g carbohydrates, 3 g fat, 0.4 g dietary fiber, 54 g protein.*

Per serving of katsu sauce: *40 calories, 0.5 g fat, 11 g carbohydrates, 0 g dietary fiber. 0.5 g protein.*

Asia/Japanese

A can of *sukiyaki no tomo* should contain sliced bamboo shoots, bean noodle, mushrooms, and water. *Konbu* (green Japanese seaweed, a kelp), *aburage* (deep fried bean curd or tofu slices), and *sukiyaki no tomo* can be found in the Asian section of any local supermarket in Hawaii and the mainland U.S.

Simply Nishime
Serves 4

2 strips *konbu*
6 dried shiitake mushrooms
1 (8.75-ounce) can *sukiyaki no tomo*
3 *aburage*
2 cups Japanese taro *(dasheen)*
1 (large) carrot
1 teaspoon sesame oil
2 1/2 cups vegetable broth
1/2 cup teriyaki marinade or Teriyaki Sauce
   (page 203)

Place *konbu* and mushrooms in a pan and cover with boiling water. Soak for 10 minutes. Save the *konbu* and mushroom water. Tie *konbu* into knots 1-inch apart. Cut between the knots. Slice mushrooms into 1/4-inch strips and set aside.

Scrub the Japanese taro thoroughly, then peel and slice in halves. Peel and cut carrot into 1 1/2-inch pieces. Cut *aburage* into 1-inch pieces.

In a saucepan, sauté taro and carrots in sesame oil. Add vegetable broth and cook covered until taro is fork tender, approximately for 10 minutes. Stir in teriyaki marinade and *konbu* and mushroom water. Toss in the *aburage*. Cook for 2 minutes. Finally, add the shiitake mushrooms, *konbu,* and *sukiyaki no tomo* and cook through for approximately 3 minutes.

Per serving: *266 calories, 9 g fat, 32 g carbohydrates, 5 g dietary fiber, 16 g protein.*

Asia/Korean

Posted on: Wednesday, October 5, 2005

South Korean dish ja jang myun a scene stealer in K dramas
Enlightened Ja Jang Myun

Ja jang myun is actually of Chinese origin but popular all over South Korea. It is said to have originated in the port city of Incheon. Restaurants served it to the Chinese community, but the taste soon caught on and spread to the rest of the country. Every year Incheon celebrates a *ja jang myun*-eating festival.

Today, in urban areas of South Korea, you can make a phone order and your *ja jang myun* will be delivered on the back of a scooter, like pizza in the U.S. This thick noodle dish served with a special, glistening black bean sauce is a favorite of Korean children. The best noodles are handmade, resembling *udon,* and served right after they're boiled.

Enlightened Ja Jang Myun
Serves 4

- 4 quarts water
- 1 tablespoon sea salt
- 1 (18-ounce) package fettuccini-style brown rice pasta
- 1/4 pound very lean ground pork plus 2 (2.5-ounce) Boca® Burgers, chopped
- 1 1/2 to 2 tablespoons garlic, minced
- 1 1/2 to 2 tablespoons fresh ginger root, minced

Global Light Cuisine ∞ Carol Devenot

- 4 tablespoons roasted *ja jang* (black bean paste)
- 2 tablespoon peanut oil
- 2 teaspoons brown sugar or Splenda®
- 2 onions, diced
- 1/4 (small) cabbage, finely chopped
- 2 tablespoons cornstarch
- 2 tablespoons water
- 3/4 cup water or organic chicken or vegetable broth
- 1/4 cucumber, sliced or chopped, for garnish

In a large saucepan, bring 4 quarts of water and 1 tablespoon sea salt to a rapid boil. Add the pasta and cook according to package directions. Drain and set aside.

Meanwhile, stir-fry the ground pork in a nonstick frying pan. Towel off excess oil and add the Boca® Burgers. Add the garlic and ginger and cook for 2 minutes. Mix the *ja jang* sauce with 2 tablespoons of oil to form a glossy, smooth paste. Push the pork mixture to one side in the pan, add the *ja jang* sauce, and mix. Add the sugar, onions, and cabbage and stir-fry, mixing to desired crispiness. Make a smooth paste of cornstarch and water. Add to stir-fry mixture. Add broth, stirring to form a thin gravy. Place pasta in four bowls and pour sauce evenly over noodles. Garnish with cucumber.

Per serving: *730 calories, 15 g total fat, 3 g saturated fat, 140 mg cholesterol, 500 mg sodium, 114 g carbohydrate, 14 g dietary fiber, 12 g sugar, 35 g protein.*

Asia/Korean

Posted on: Wednesday, July 26, 2006

Onolicious chicken breasts

Susan's Grilled Chicken

Actually, the recipe is just a matter of prepping the chicken and marinating it. At Kale's health food store in Hawai`i Kai, I bought free-range chicken because of the deeper chicken flavor and the lack of antibiotics. Even so, I was careful to disinfect my cutting board and hands before moving on to other tasks to avoid cross-contamination.

The rest was simple, because my boyfriend was in charge of the gas grill. He left the lid off the grill. *(Leaving the lid on raises the temperature and causes the chicken to cook too quickly and burn.)* He put the timer on to remind him to turn the chicken every 10 minutes. You can easily forget if you are busy cooking other dishes and entertaining. Nothing is worse than blackened chicken!

Susan's Grilled Chicken

Serves 8

- 4 pounds free-range or organic chicken breasts, boneless and skinless
- 6 tablespoons sake or other white wine
- 5 tablespoons brown sugar or date sugar
- 3 to 6 tablespoons soy sauce or reduced-sodium soy sauce
- 9 tablespoons green onions, chopped
- 6 tablespoons garlic, minced
- 3 to 6 tablespoons sesame seeds, toasted

Global Light Cuisine ∞ Carol Devenot

1 to 3 teaspoons sesame oil
1 tablespoon sea salt
1/4 teaspoon pine nuts *(optional)*
Lettuce leaves, shredded
Nonstick cooking spray

Wash the chicken and pat dry with paper towels. Score the breasts and place them in a bowl. Sprinkle the breasts with the wine and sugar and mix well. In a small mixing bowl, combine the soy sauce with the green onions, garlic, sesame seeds, sesame oil, sea salt, and pine nuts and add to the chicken breasts. Marinate for 1 hour or overnight.

Prepare a bed of medium-hot coals in a charcoal grill. If using a gas grill, heat the unit to medium-hot. Spray the grill rack with nonstick spray. Place the marinated chicken on the grill and cook for about 30 to 45 minutes, turning every 10 minutes. Baste with leftover sauce in the last 10 minutes. Cut into the chicken to check for doneness. The juices from the thickest part of the chicken should run clear. Serve on lettuce leaves.

Per serving: *250 calories, 5 g fat, 1 g saturated fat, 85 mg cholesterol, greater than 1000 mg sodium, 13 g carbohydrate, 1 g dietary fiber, 9 g sugar, 35 g protein.*

160 Entrées

Asia/Thai

Posted on: Wednesday, August 11, 2004

Shrimp, tofu interchangeable in spicy Thai curry dish

Thai Shrimp or Tofu Curry

Here is a curry that can be made with shrimp or tofu *(or both)*, cooked in spicy coconut gravy. I lightened it up by using lower-fat coconut milk. The cherry tomatoes provide a sweet-and-sour flavor. Serve this over brown rice and you have a complete, healthy meal.

Thai Shrimp or Tofu Curry
Serves 4 to 5

1 pound jumbo shrimp or 1 (20-ounce) block firm tofu
10 cherry tomatoes, cut in halves

Sauce:

1 (small) onion, sliced into rounds
3 cloves garlic, minced
1 (13.5-ounce) can light coconut milk
1 tablespoon Thai curry paste *(test for spiciness)*
1 tablespoon fish sauce or 1 tablespoon vegetarian chicken-flavored broth powder
1 teaspoon sugar

Garnish:

Lime juice
Chili peppers, sliced

Global Light Cuisine ∞ Carol Devenot

Jalapeño peppers, sliced
Fresh Chinese parsley *(cilantro)*

Rinse and devein the shrimp. If using tofu, drain and cut into 1-inch cubes. Set aside.

Water-sauté onion and minced garlic until transparent in a wok or frying pan. Add half of the coconut milk and bring to a boil. The curry paste is spicy so add only part of the tablespoon, stir until it blends together, and then test taste. Add the rest if you want spicier curry. Simmer for 10 minutes. Add the fish sauce or broth powder, sugar, and the remaining coconut milk. Simmer for another 5 minutes. Add the shrimp or tofu and the cherry tomatoes and simmer for 5 minutes longer. Do not overcook the shrimp. It should be pink and tender. Serve with lime juice and garnish with sliced chili and jalapeño peppers and parsley.

Per serving (with shrimp): 169 calories, 6 g fat, 8 g carbohydrates, 1 g dietary fiber, 485 mg sodium, 20 g protein.

Per serving (with tofu): 242 calories, 15 g fat, 13 g carbohydrates, 3 g dietary fiber, 365 mg sodium, 20 g protein.

Asia/Thai

Posted on: Wednesday, December 15, 2004

Homemade pad Thai light, `ono
Pad Thai

I found that pad Thai literally means Thai-style fried noodles. Although the name suggests a Thai origin, it really was introduced by a wave of immigrants from southern China to Thailand. The Chinese brought rice noodles and their recipes. The Thais, with their love of hot, sour, sweet and salty flavors, added these to their stir-fried dishes and gave it a fusion name much like Western chefs today.

Pad Thai
Serves 4

Sauce:

1/4 cup fish sauce *(see note below)*
1/2 cup date sugar or unrefined sugar
1 tablespoon garlic chili sauce
1 clove garlic, minced
3 tablespoons fresh Chinese parsley *(cilantro)*, chopped
1 stalk of lemon grass, finely minced, white part only
Juice from 1 lemon or lime

Pad Thai:

1 (7-ounce) package whole-wheat *udon* noodles
1 teaspoon peanut oil

2 chicken breasts, boneless and skinless,
   sliced into strips
1 cup Chinese peas
2 cups chop suey mix
2 egg whites, beaten *(optional)*
20 fresh mint leaves
20 fresh Thai basil leaves
1/4 cup peanuts, chopped *(optional)*

Garnish:
Peanuts, roasted and chopped
Fresh Thai basil leaves

Combine fish sauce, sugar, garlic chili sauce, garlic, parsley, lemon grass, and lemon or lime juice. Set aside.

Cook noodles, following package directions. Drain and set aside.

In a wok, heat the oil and add the chicken. Add the above fish sauce mixture and stir fry for 10 minutes. Combine Chinese peas and chop suey mix, add to stir-fry, and toss. Add the beaten egg whites and noodles. Stir until well combined. Add the mint and basil leaves to the sauce. Garnish with fresh basil leaves and chopped peanuts. Serve immediately on a platter.

Per serving: *419 calories, 8 g fat, 66 g carbohydrates, 9 g dietary fiber, 1627 mg sodium, 28 g protein.*

Note: One tablespoon of fish sauce contains 1,390 milligrams of sodium. Decreasing the amount of fish sauce will decrease the sodium content, but fish sauce contributes a great deal of pad Thai's customary flavor.

Caribbean/Cuban

Posted on: Wednesday, March 21, 2007

Stuffing veggies as Cubans do it

Cuban Stuffed Zucchini

Here's my version of *berenjena*—stuffed eggplant served with Parmesan cheese. *(Yes, Parmesan cheese is Italian, notes Dole, but Cubans like it with this recipe.)*

My boyfriend is not a big eggplant fan, so I used zucchini instead. To cut the fat and calories, I converted the recipe to vegetarian, replacing ground beef and chorizo sausage with Boca® Burger and Soy Rizo. *(You can find Soy Rizo at Kale's Natural Foods in the Hawai`i Kai Shopping Center.)* The original recipe calls for bread stuffing; you can make your own, which would allow you to control the fat and sodium and to increase the fiber content by using whole-grain bread crumbs. However, I took a shortcut with Kraft® Stove Top Stuffing Mix.

Cuban Stuffed Zucchini

Serves 4 to 6

1 package Kraft® Stove Top Stuffing Mix for Pork or 3 cups homemade stuffing
4 (medium) zucchini or eggplant
Extra virgin olive oil spray
1/2 yellow onion, chopped fine
1 bell pepper, finely chopped
8 garlic cloves, mashed and minced

1 pouch of ground Boca® Burger *(meat substitute)*
1/4 pound Soy Rizo *(soy-based chorizo)*
1/2 cup ripe tomatoes, chopped
1 cup tomato sauce
1/2 teaspoon dried oregano
1/4 teaspoon dried cumin
Sea salt to taste
Juice of 1/2 lemon
Low-fat Parmesan cheese *(optional)*

Heat oven to 400 degrees.

Prepare the stuffing according to package directions and reserve.

Cut the zucchini in half lengthwise and scoop out the centers; reserve both the meat and the skins.

Spray a nonstick frying pan with olive oil spray, sauté scooped-out zucchini flesh, onion, and bell pepper until soft. Add the garlic and sauté for 1 minute. Add ground Boca® Burgers and Soy Rizo and cook, stirring occasionally, for 10 minutes. Add tomatoes, tomato sauce, oregano, cumin, salt, and lemon juice. Add the stuffing, stir, and remove from heat. Stuff the zucchini with the mixture. Place the stuffed zucchini in a baking pan and bake for 25 minutes. Sprinkle with Parmesan cheese and bake for 1 more minute.

Per serving: *270 calories, 11 g fat, 1 g saturated fat, 0 mg cholesterol, 900 mg sodium, 35 g carbohydrate, 9 g dietary fiber, 12 g sugar, 15 g protein.*

166   Entrées

Caribbean/Puerto Rico

Posted on: Wednesday, June 2, 2004

A flavorful Puerto Rican favorite, but with way less fat

Arroz con Gandules (pigeon peas with rice)

When it came to *arroz con gandules (ar-ROX con gah-DOO-dez)*, the student cooks would always say, "Gotta have the *achiote*." That's the seed of the annatto tree that reddens oil and lends a musky flavor.

They were right, and what a great use of plant also called "lipstick pod." Pigeon peas *(gandul* or *gandule)* beans are small, tropical, kidney-shaped legumes often used in Puerto Rican cooking. This dish can be a little heavy, with lots of oils and sausage, bacon, fatback or smoked ham, and full-fat broth.

Arroz con Gandules
(pigeon peas with rice)
Serves 8

Achiote Oil:

2 ounces annatto seeds or 1 1/2 to 2 tablespoons
    of goya powder or chili powder
1 cup canola oil

Gandules:

1/2 cup onion, chopped
3 cloves garlic, minced
1 tablespoon *achiote* oil
1/2 cup green pepper, chopped
2 slices turkey bacon, chopped

Global Light Cuisine ∞ Carol Devenot

- 1 (15-ounce) can green pigeon peas *(gandule beans)*, drain and save liquid
- 1 (8-ounce) can tomato sauce
- 3 cups liquid and 3 tablespoons chicken-style vegetarian broth powder
- 1 cup brown rice, uncooked
- 1 cup white rice, uncooked
- 1 bunch fresh Chinese parsley *(cilantro)*, chopped

Put annatto seeds and oil in a small saucepan to make *achiote* oil. Simmer over low heat for approximately 5 minutes or until oil turns a dark red color. Strain immediately into a glass jar and let cool. Makes 1 cup. Cover and store the unused *achiote* oil in the refrigerator.

In a large frying pan, brown onion and garlic in 1 tablespoon of *achiote* oil. Add green peppers and turkey bacon and cook for about 2 minutes. Place pigeon peas' liquid and tomato sauce in a large *(4 cups or more)* measuring cup and add enough water to bring the mixture to 3 cups. Place 2 cups of rice in a rice cooker and stir in the browned onions and garlic, green pepper, turkey bacon, pigeon peas, and liquid mixture. Cover and follow manufacturer's instructions for your rice cooker. It should just turn off when done.

If you don't have a rice cooker, follow above instructions but add enough water to make 4 cups. Place this liquid in a saucepan and bring to a boil, then add remaining ingredients. Return to boil, turn heat down to low, cover and steam until cooked. Serve garnished with parsley.

Per serving: *224 calories, 3 g fat, 43 g carbohydrates, 2 g dietary fiber, 5 g protein.*

Europe/French

Posted on: Wednesday, March 7, 2007

Delicious crepes can be healthy
Spinach and Ricotta Crepes

Crepes *(pronounced "kreps" in France)* are thin pancakes made from a light batter consisting of flour, eggs, milk, and butter. They are not leavened with baking soda or powder. There are two types of crepes: those made with all-purpose flour and a little sweetener and a savory, unsweetened type made with buckwheat flour. Crepes are said to have originated in Brittany in western France. Their popularity has spread throughout the world.

Spinach and Ricotta Crepes
Serves 6

Filling:

1 1/4 pounds fresh spinach or 1 (16-ounce) bag frozen spinach
3/4 cup low-fat ricotta cheese
1/2 block (7 ounces) low-fat tofu
3 tablespoons Parmesan cheese, freshly grated
1 egg or Egg Beaters® equivalent, slightly beaten
1/4 teaspoon nutmeg, freshly ground
Sea salt to taste

Crepes:

1 cup all-purpose flour, not packed down in measuring cup
1/4 teaspoon salt

1 1/2 cups nonfat milk
2 (large) eggs or Egg Beaters® equivalent
Butter-flavored cooking spray

Sauce:

2 tablespoons unsalted butter
1/2 cup all-purpose flour
4 cups nonfat milk
2 to 4 tablespoons dehydrated onions
2 to 4 teaspoons McKay's® Chicken Style
    Instant Broth and Seasoning
Sea salt to taste
White pepper to taste
Parmesan cheese for garnish

To make the filling, steam the spinach in a steamer for about 2 minutes until wilted. Drain well, pressing out excess water. Finely chop the spinach and place in a mixing bowl. Add the ricotta, tofu, Parmesan, egg, nutmeg, and salt. Set aside.

To make the crepes, combine flour and salt in one mixing bowl. Whisk together milk and eggs in another bowl. Add milk mixture to flour mixture and whisk until smooth. Cover the batter and place in the refrigerator for at least 15 minutes.

Heat an 8-inch nonstick frying pan over medium-high heat. Coat pan with cooking spray. Pour 1/4 cup batter into the pan and quickly tilt and turn the pan to cover the entire surface with a thin film of batter. Cook for about 1 minute. Carefully lift the edges of the crepe with a rubber spatula. You can tell if the crepe is ready if it readily comes loose from the pan and is lightly browned. Flip crepe over and cook 30 seconds.

Place crepe on paper towel. Repeat this procedure until all the batter is used.

Heat the oven to 350 degrees.

To make the sauce, melt the butter in a small saucepan over moderate heat. Gradually add the flour, stirring constantly until very smooth. Gradually add the milk and continue stirring constantly until the sauce thickens. Add the onions, chicken broth seasoning, and salt and pepper to taste.

Pour a thin layer of sauce into the bottom of a 12- by 16-inch baking dish. Fill crepes with spinach mixture and roll up. Line crepes up next to each other, seam side down, on top of the sauce in the baking dish. Drizzle remaining sauce over crepes. Bake until the sauce slightly bubbles; about 20 minutes. Pass Parmesan cheese at table.

Per serving: *350 calories, 10 g fat, 5 g saturated fat, 130 mg cholesterol, 775 mg sodium, 43 g carbohydrate, 3 g dietary fiber, 13 g sugar, 22 g protein.*

Europe/German

Posted on: Wednesday, June 13, 2007
Slow-cook sauerbraten for your dad
Sauerbraten in a Crock-Pot

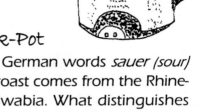

Sauerbraten comes from the German words *sauer (sour)* and *braten (roast meat)*. This roast comes from the Rhineland, Saarland, Silesia, and Swabia. What distinguishes Rhineland's sauerbraten from that of the other regions is the use of raisins and gingerbread, producing a sweet, slightly spicy roast. Traditionally, tougher cuts of meat—even horse meat—were used to make *sauerbraten!*

Sauerbraten in a Crock-Pot
Serves 6 to 8

1 tablespoon pickling spice
2 pounds top round beef steak
2 red onions, chopped
1 cup beef broth
1 cup apple cider vinegar
1/2 (16-ounce) package baby carrots
2 russet potatoes, peeled and cut into fourths
3/4 cup (15 cookies) crushed gingersnaps
2 to 4 tablespoons brown sugar
1/2 cup raisins

Place pickling spice in a small piece of cheesecloth and tie it with string to form a pouch. In a 5-quart slow cooker, place the beef, onions, broth, vinegar, carrots, potatoes, and pickling spices and cook, covered, on low for 8 to 9 hours. At the end of the cooking time, remove the cover and turn up the heat to high and remove the pickling spices.

Add the gingersnaps, brown sugar, and raisins to the mixture. Stir mixture and season by adding more gingersnaps and/or brown sugar. Cover and cook for 30 minutes or until thickened and heated through. Serve with cooked egg noodles or *spatzle (German dumplings)*.

Per serving (6 servings, without noodles): *540 calories, 15 g fat, 5 g saturated fat, 60 mg cholesterol, 350 mg sodium, 63 g carbohydrate, 5 g dietary fiber, 29 g sugar, 39 g protein.*

Europe/Greek

Posted on: Wednesday, November 3, 2004

For this moussaka, go meatless

Meatless Moussaka

Of all Greek dishes, my favorite was moussaka because it was so flavorful and moist. Moussaka *(pronounced moo-sa-ka)* means "casserole" in Greek and is generally made with layered ground  beef or lamb and eggplant, topped with a béchamel *(white)* sauce. But you can make a meatless version using hamburger-style soy products. If you aren't an eggplant fan, you can substitute zucchini. Add sliced, lightly fried potatoes, too, if you are not watching your carbs.

Meatless Moussaka
Serves 8

- 4 pounds round eggplant, peeled and thinly sliced into rounds
- 2 round onions, peeled and thinly sliced
- 4 cloves garlic, minced
- 1 1/2 pounds ground meat alternative like Grilled Boca® Burger, chopped
- 1/2 teaspoon allspice or 1 teaspoon cinnamon *(optional)*
- 1 (large) tomato, skinned and chopped
- 2 to 3 tablespoons tomato paste
- 2 to 3 tablespoons fresh Chinese parsley *(cilantro)*, chopped
- 1/3 to 1 cup dry white wine to taste
- Extra virgin olive oil spray or other nonstick spray

174   Entrées

1 teaspoon Hawaiian or kosher salt

Béchamel Sauce:

4 tablespoons no-trans-fat margarine
4 tablespoons flour
2 cups low-fat milk, hot
Pinch of grated nutmeg
2 egg whites
Salt and pepper to taste
1/3 cup Parmesan cheese, grated *(optional)*

Sprinkle eggplant with salt, place in a colander in the sink, and allow juices to drain for 30 minutes. Pat dry and drain further on paper towels.

Blanch the tomato by plunging into boiling water for 30 seconds, then in cold water for 30 seconds. Skin should pucker easily. Peel away the skin and chop coarsely.

Chop and mince the onions and garlic. Set aside

Preheat oven 375 degrees.

Sauté the onions and garlic until golden yellow in a nonstick frying pan sprayed with olive oil spray. Add the chopped meat alternative and fry until brown. Season with salt and pepper and flavor with allspice or cinnamon. Add the chopped tomato, tomato paste, and parsley. Stir in the wine and cook for about 15 minutes.

If you have a second nonstick frying pan, coat it with the olive oil spray and fry the eggplant pieces until they are browned on both sides. Spray a 9- by 13-inch oblong pan with the nonstick spray and put alternate layers of eggplant and meat alternative mixture starting and ending with a layer of eggplant.

To make the béchamel sauce, place the butter substitute in a saucepan, add flour, and stir over low heat for a few minutes until well blended. Add the hot milk gradually, stirring until it boils and taking care not to allow lumps to form. Season with salt, pepper, a pinch of nutmeg, and the cheese. Simmer until the sauce thickens. Wisk the egg whites directly into the sauce and stir in well. Do not boil the sauce again.

Pour the sauce over the casserole and bake in a preheated oven for 45 minutes. Serve hot! If you eliminate the potatoes, serve with rice pilaf, couscous, brown rice, or other grains. This is best made the day before.

Per serving: *275 calories, 5 g fat, 39 g carbohydrates, 12 g dietary fiber, 808 mg sodium, 24 g protein.*

Europe/Irish

Posted on: Wednesday, March 9, 2005

St. Patrick's Day calls for cabbage

Savvy (Savoy) Stuffed Cabbage

Last year I attended St. Patrick's Day festivities on Merchant Street. A few restaurants were serving corned beef and cabbage. This gave me the idea to come up with a healthier alternative—cabbage stuffed with rice and Boca® Burgers. It's got the green of cabbage but not all the fat and salt of corned beef.

You can find regular cabbage in the supermarket. Select the large heads because the larger leaves make it easier to wrap the filling. But what a nice surprise to find Savoy cabbage next to the regular cabbage heads. Savoy cabbage has ruffled yellow-green leaves that form a less compact head than other types. It contains a significant amount of folate *(folic acid)* and some beta carotene *(five times more than either green and red cabbage)*. It also has a more delicate texture and milder flavor than other cabbages. Great for salads and coleslaw! You can use either type of cabbage for this dish.

Savvy (Savoy) Stuffed Cabbage

Serves 8

8 to 16 (large) cabbage leaves, rinsed
   (number of leaves depends on your love of cabbage)
1 (medium) onion, chopped
1 teaspoon extra virgin olive oil
4 tablespoons date sugar
2 (16-ounce) cans tomato sauce or diced tomatoes

Global Light Cuisine ∞ Carol Devenot

- 4 tablespoons apple cider vinegar
- Salt and pepper to taste
- 1 cup water
- 8 (2.5-ounce) Flamed-grilled Boca® Burgers, thawed and chopped
- 1 cup brown rice, cooked
- 1/4 cup Egg Beaters®
- 1/2 to 1 teaspoon dried basil
- 1 teaspoon Worcestershire sauce
- 4 cloves garlic, minced

Cook the brown rice in a microwave rice cooker or rice maker.

In covered 12-inch frying pan, cook cabbage leaves in 1 inch of boiling water for about 5 minutes. Drain cabbage in colander and set aside. Meanwhile, chop the onions and Boca® Burgers. Measure out the vinegar, olive oil, and date sugar.

Sauté the olive oil and onion for 5 minutes over medium heat in the same frying pan. Add the tomato sauce, date sugar, vinegar, salt and pepper, and water. Simmer.

In a larger bowl, combine chopped Boca® Burgers, cooked rice, Egg Beaters®, basil, Worcestershire, and garlic. In the center of each cabbage leaf, place about 3 to 4 tablespoons of the Boca® mixture.

Fold two sides of leaf toward the center and roll up. Place filled leaves seam sides down in frying pan with sauce. Heat to simmering *(gently bubbling)* over medium heat. Reduce to low; cover, and cook 45 minutes.

Per serving: *200 calories, 4 g fat, 28 g carbohydrates, 5 g dietary fiber, 590 mg sodium, 17 g protein.*

178   Entrées

Europe/Italian

Posted on: Wednesday, May 2, 2007

Make a meal at home on mom's day
Chicken Florentine a la Devenot

Memories of precious moments drift back every Mother's Day. Why not cook something at home for your mother or that special someone on Mother's Day?

Chicken Florentine a la Devenot
Serves 4

4 chicken breasts, boneless and skinless
Sea salt to taste
Black pepper, fresh ground to taste
Whole-wheat pastry flour for dredging
Extra virgin olive oil spray
1 (small) sweet Maui onion
1 tablespoon garlic, chopped
1 1/2 cups dry white wine
1 cup fat-free half-and-half milk
1 tablespoon fresh Italian flat-leaf parsley, chopped
2 (10-ounce) packages frozen cut-leaf spinach, thawed, squeezed
1 tablespoon butter

Season the chicken with salt and pepper. Dredge the chicken in the flour to lightly coat. Spray the olive oil into a large, heavy frying pan over medium heat. Add the chicken and cook until golden brown for about 10 minutes. Remove the chicken from the frying pan, place on a plate, and cover it with aluminum foil to retain the heat.

Global Light Cuisine ∞ Carol Devenot

Spray the olive oil into the same frying pan, and sauté the onion and garlic until translucent. Add the wine and increase the heat to medium-high and bring to a boil to reduce liquid by half. Add the fat-free half-and-half and boil the sauce for three minutes. Sprinkle in the parsley and season with salt and pepper. Add the chicken to the sauce and turn to coat all sides with sauce.

In another large frying pan, spray olive oil and melt butter. Add the spinach, sauté until it is heated and season with salt and pepper to taste. Place the spinach on a platter and cover it with the chicken and sauce. Serve immediately.

Per serving: *400 calories, 7 g fat, 2.5 g saturated fat, 100 mg cholesterol, 300 mg sodium, 21 g carbohydrate, 5 g dietary fiber, 6 g sugar, 47 g protein.*

180   Entrées

Europe/Italian

Posted on: Wednesday, June 30, 2004

Allow seasonings to "marry"

Mama Claire's Spaghetti Sauce

If there was one dish that my mom, Mama Claire, did well, it was spaghetti sauce. She would make tons and then we would have it for the next day. It always tasted better because the seasonings "married." As I grew older, I really appreciated the Tupperware containers filled with this stuff. After a long day teaching, I would just heat and serve over vegetables, pasta, or a potato. Thanks Mama!

Mama Claire's Spaghetti Sauce
Serves 6

1 teaspoon extra virgin olive oil
1 (large) onion, minced
3 cloves garlic, minced
1 green pepper, minced
3 (8-ounce) can tomato sauce
1 (6-ounce) can tomato paste
2 (8-ounce) cans mushrooms with liquid
2 teaspoons dried Italian seasoning
    (oregano, rosemary, and basil)
6 cups spaghetti noodles, cooked,
    or 6 cups spaghetti squash, cooked
Low-fat Parmesan cheese *(optional)*

In a large Dutch oven, sauté the olive oil, garlic, and onion. Add the green pepper, tomato sauce, tomato paste, mushrooms, and herbs. Simmer uncovered on

Global Light Cuisine ∞ Carol Devenot

low heat for 1 1/2 hours or until it reaches a desired consistency. Stir occasionally.

Cook spaghetti noodles according to package instructions. Or cut spaghetti squash lengthwise, remove seeds, poke holes in skin with fork. Bake, cut side down on foil-lined baking pan at 350 degrees for 45 minutes; turn and continue to bake until skin is tender. To microwave squash, place 1/4 cup water in baking dish, place squash skin side down, cover with plastic wrap, and microwave 7 to 10 minutes. Test for doneness by piercing with a toothpick or a fork.

To serve, spoon about a cup of the sauce over the hot noodles or squash and sprinkle low-fat Parmesan cheese.

Per serving (sauce only): 93 calories, 1 g fat, 20 g carbohydrates, 5 g dietary fiber, 206 mg sodium, 4 g protein.

Per serving (with noodles and sauce): 269 calories, 2 g fat, 57 g carbohydrates, 11 g dietary fiber, 210 mg sodium, 12 g protein.

Per serving (with squash and sauce): 137 calories, 2 g fat, 30 g carbohydrates, 7 g dietary fiber, 234 mg sodium, 5 g protein.

Europe/Italian

Posted on: Wednesday, July 4, 2004

Rav-e-oli calls for ready-made wrappers, healthful filling

Rav-e-oli

So what do you do when you have a ton of marinara sauce left over from the spaghetti dinner? You and your family can make ravioli or "rav-e-oli." It's fun to make because it's like wrapping presents.

Inside is a healthy and delicious filling made with spinach, mushrooms, tofu, and seasonings. Instead of making your own pasta, place the filling in the ready-made *mandoo* wrappers. *(Won ton wraps could be used in a pinch—no pun intended.)*

Rav-e-oli

Serves 10

- 1 teaspoon extra virgin olive oil
- 4 cloves garlic, minced
- 1 (medium) onion, minced
- 1 (4-ounce) can of mushrooms, stems and pieces
- 1 (10-ounce) box frozen spinach, chopped
- 1 (12-ounce) block of low-fat firm tofu
- 1 teaspoon dried Italian seasoning *(optional)*
- 50 *mandoo (preferred)* or won ton wrappers

Chop the mushrooms into 1/4-inch pieces and set aside.

Drain and dice the tofu into 1/4-inch cubes and set aside.

Global Light Cuisine ∞ Carol Devenot

In a large frying pan or wok, sauté the garlic and onion in olive oil until transparent. Add mushrooms and spinach and cook on high for approximately 5 minutes. Add tofu and cook for 2 to 3 minutes on medium-low heat. Set aside to cool.

Place 1 tablespoon of filling in the middle of a ready-made *mandoo* or *won ton* wrapper. Moisten the edges, fold the wrapper in half over the filling, and seal the edges, crimping with your fingers.

A faster method, if you have a potsticker press, is to put a wrapper in the press, add the filling, moisten the edges with water, and fold the press to seal the edges.

Cook rav-e-oli in a large pot of boiling water for 3 minutes. Drain and serve with homemade marinara sauce or any choice of jar or canned spaghetti sauce thinned out with a little water. Makes 50 rav-e-oli.

Per serving: *150 calories 1 g fat, 3 g carbohydrates, 2 g dietary fiber, 321 mg sodium, '7 g protein.*

184   Entrées

Europe/Italian

Posted on: Wednesday, October 20, 2004

Waste not: Those cherry tomatoes add zing to penne pasta

Cherry Tomatoes and Penne Pasta

Sometimes I get carried away and buy too many cherry tomatoes in those big cartons at Costco. Here's a great way of using these little morsels. They add a tart and flavorful twist to penne pasta. For those of you counting carbo-hydrates, use whole-wheat pasta or vegetable-based pasta, available at health food stores, low-carb stores, and some larger groceries.

Cherry Tomatoes and Penne Pasta

Serves 6

1 pound whole wheat penne or other pasta
1 tablespoon extra virgin olive oil
3 cloves garlic, thinly sliced
2 cups cherry tomatoes, halved
1 teaspoon dried Italian seasoning or 2 to
      3 teaspoons fresh basil, oregano, and/or
      fresh Italian flat-leaf parsley, chopped
Salt and pepper to taste
1/4 cup black olives, sliced
1/4 cup parsley, chopped
1/4 cup grated fresh Parmesan cheese

Global Light Cuisine ∞ Carol Devenot

Bring a large pot of water to a boil. Cook the penne pasta according the instructions on the package, approximately 10 to 13 minutes. Drain in colander.

In a wok or frying pan, heat the oil over medium heat. Stir-fry the garlic until golden, about 1 minute. Add the cherry tomatoes, Italian seasoning, salt, and pepper. Lower the heat and cook the tomatoes for 3 minutes. Toss in the penne, olives, parsley, and Parmesan cheese. Serve immediately.

Per serving: *321 calories, 4 g fat, 62 g carbohydrates, 7 g dietary fiber, 240 mg sodium, 14 g protein.*

Variation: For a Thai flavor, leave out the Parmesan cheese and use Thai basil and crushed red pepper in place of the Italian seasonings. This dish is so quick and easy, only 25 minutes, and can be either a main dish or filling side dish. Wok On!

186 Entrées

Europe/Italian

Posted on: Wednesday, April 5, 2006

Serve up frittata hot or cooled

Zucchini-Swiss Chard Frittata

Since "real men don't eat quiche," I thought a frittata would be perfect. This is a tasty, healthy recipe and perfect for work at 13,000 feet. A frittata is a baked omelet with a medley of herbs and vegetables. I have also prepared this recipe with broccoli and potatoes. You can substitute any summer squash for the zucchini and spinach for the chard. The red Swiss chard gives a splash of red color. Because it is an Italian dish, I matched it with the Italian seasoning. You could substitute other seasonings, if you prefer. Serve it with whole-wheat French bread, or a multigrain toast. Steve could even serve it with his famous salsa. Leftover frittata can be sliced and served atop a salad, as in the Insalata Contadina at Cafe Sistina in Honolulu, or just munched at room temperature as a snack.

Zucchini-Swiss Chard Frittata

Serves 6

Extra virgin olive oil spray
1 (small) onion, finely chopped
2 to 3 cloves garlic, minced
2 (large) red Swiss chard leaves,
    coarsely chopped
1 (medium) zucchini, coarsely chopped
3 eggs
3/4 cup Egg Beaters®
Sea salt to taste

Ground pepper to taste
1/2 teaspoon dried Italian seasoning
1 cup (3 ounces) grated low-fat Parmesan cheese

Preheat oven to 350 degrees. Spray a nonstick frying pan with olive oil. Sauté the onion, garlic, chard, and zucchini for 5 minutes, stirring occasionally. Remove from heat and allow vegetables to cool for 5 minutes. Beat eggs, then stir in Egg Beaters®, pepper, and Italian seasoning. Stir in the cheese and cooled vegetables. Pour frittata batter into a 9-inch pie pan sprayed with olive oil. Bake for 25 to 30 minutes or until puffed and browned. Serve hot.

Per serving: *160 calories, 9 g fat, 4.5 g saturated fat, 120 mg cholesterol, 430 mg sodium, 5 g carbohydrate, 1 g dietary fiber, 3 g sugar, 15 g protein.*

Europe/Italian

Posted on: Wednesday, February 21, 2007
Ground-meat substitute lightens quick lasagna

Angela's Quickie Veggie Lasagna

Boca® Burgers are veggie burgers made from soy and wheat gluten. You can usually find Boca® products in the freezer section of supermarkets or health food stores. They are a significant source of protein, complex carbohydrates and fiber, and they are easy to prepare. I used to cut the burgers up for my recipes, but now all I have to do is buy the Boca® meatless ground burger.

Angela's Quickie Veggie Lasagna
Serves 6 to 8

- 1 (8-ounce) package whole-wheat lasagna noodles, uncooked
- 3 cups (12 ounces) low-fat mozzarella cheese, grated

Sauce:

- 1 (32-ounce) jar or can spaghetti sauce with mushrooms or 3 1/2 cups homemade sauce
- 1 cup Boca® Meatless Ground Burger
- 8 ounces water

Filling:

- 1 (16-ounce) carton cottage cheese or 1 (20-ounce) block firm tofu, crumbled and drained
- 1/2 cup (2 ounces) Parmesan cheese, grated
- 1 egg, beaten

Global Light Cuisine ∞ Carol Devenot

2 green onions, sliced
1 (10-ounce) box frozen, chopped spinach,
    thawed and squeezed well,
    or 1 (10-ounce) box frozen, chopped broccoli
1/4 teaspoon nutmeg *(optional with spinach)*

Heat oven to 350 degrees.

In a large bowl, combine the spaghetti sauce, Boca® Burgers, and water.

Assemble the filling in a medium-sized mixing bowl.

In a 9- by 13-inch baking pan, layer ingredients in the following sequence: 1 cup *(8 ounces)* sauce, half the noodles, half the filling mixture, 1 1/2 cups *(6 ounces)* grated mozzarella cheese, 1 cup *(8 ounces)* sauce, the other half the noodles, the remaining filing mixture, 1 1/2 cups *(6 ounces)* grated mozzarella cheese *(optional: may omit, after baking, sprinkle with 1/4 cup grated Parmesan cheese instead)*, and finish with 2 cups *(16 ounces)* sauce.

Cover pan tightly with foil to trap moisture so noodles cook in the sauce. Heat in oven for 30 minutes. Let it stand for 10 minutes to set before serving.

Per serving: *520 calories, 17 g fat, 8 g saturated fat, 75 mg cholesterol, greater than 1700 mg sodium, 53 g carbohydrate, 11 g dietary fiber, 12 g sugar, 45 g protein.*

Hawaii Local Favorite

Posted on: Wednesday, February 23, 2005

Quick patty made with tuna, tofu

Tuna Tofu Patties

This recipe brings back memories of making tofu from scratch at Kalaheo High School where I taught food science. For many of the students, who were not used to tofu, this was an excellent dish served with Teriyaki Sauce *(page 203)* and Hapa Rice *(page 101)*.

There are so many brands of tofu on the market. I look for the brands with the lowest fat grams, because the amount of fat grams varies 1.5 to 4 grams. It is important to get all the water out of the tofu when you squeeze it. If you don't get out all the water, the patty will not hold together. For those of you who do not like Egg Beaters®, you can add 2 egg whites instead. In a separate bowl mix the soy sauce, salt, and brown sugar. Minced fresh ginger would be a nice touch. Add it to the tuna-tofu mixture. Fry up a batch tonight, and I am sure that you will please your protein conscious athlete.

Tuna Tofu Patties

Serves 8

1 (20-ounce) block firm tofu, well drained and mashed

1 (6.5-ounce) can tuna, packed in water, or albacore, drained

2 to 3 stalks green onions, sliced into
   1/4-inch pieces
1/4 cup Egg Beaters®
2 tablespoons cornstarch
2 tablespoons soy sauce
2 tablespoons brown sugar
3/4 to 1 teaspoon salt
Garlic-flavored oil cooking spray

Place the tofu in a clean dishtowel or cheesecloth. Bring the sides of the cloth together and squeeze tightly to remove all the water.

Put the tofu in a bowl and add the tuna, green onions, Egg Beaters®, and cornstarch. In a separate, small bowl, mix the soy sauce, salt, and brown sugar together and add to the tuna-tofu mixture. Mix well and shape into 8 patties. Spray the nonstick frying pan with cooking spray and fry the patties on each side for 10 minutes on medium heat until they are golden brown.

Per serving: *153 calories, 6 g fat, 8 g carbohydrates, 2 g dietary fiber, 18 g protein.*

Entrées

Hawaii Local Favorite

Posted on: Wednesday, August 22, 2007

Those lucky dogs enjoy healthy lifestyle, too

Lara's Mahimahi with Mango-Papaya Salsa

If I were a dog, I would love Lara Lasher to come to my house to take care of me. Not only would she feed me delicious snacks, but she can do a mean down dog. Unfortunately *(by dog standards)*, I am just a human in one of Lasher's yoga classes at the Honolulu Club. She is a great teacher and has a calming presence. Lasher has been a yoga instructor for more than six years. Besides teaching yoga at various health centers, she also does pet sitting and dog walking.

When I asked her how she keeps in such good shape, she said it is due to her healthy eating habits and yoga practice. Just as balance is important in yoga, she tries to balance fruits, vegetables, chicken, and fish into her diet.

Lara's Mahimahi with Mango-Papaya Salsa

Serves 4

4 *(6-ounce)* thick *mahimahi* steaks
Garlic powder to taste
Sea salt to taste
Fresh ground pepper to taste

Mango-Papaya Salsa:

2 ripe mangoes, cut into small chunks
2 ripe papayas, cut into small chunks
1 (small) sweet or red onion, chopped
1 hot red pepper, finely minced
   (leave out for a mild salsa)
1 (medium) jalapeño pepper, minced
   (leave out for a mild salsa)
1 yellow pepper, minced
1/4 cup fresh Chinese parsley *(cilantro)*, finely chopped
Juice of 1/2 lime
Sea salt to taste *(optional)*

Mix the ingredients for the salsa and let the flavors blend while you prepare the fish.

Cut a pocket lengthwise in the mahimahi steaks. Generously sprinkle both sides with pepper and garlic powder. Grill 3 to 5 minutes on each side. Stuff with mango-papaya salsa. Place the remainder of the salsa on a serving plate and put the stuffed mahimahi steaks on top of the salsa.

Per serving (without salt): *320 calories, 2 g fat, 0 saturated fat, 125 mg cholesterol, 160 mg sodium, 45 g carbohydrate, 7 g dietary fiber, 30 g sugar, 34 g protein.*

Hawaii Local Favorite

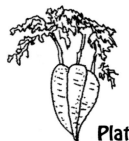

Plate Lunch Curry Stew
Serves 4

2 chicken breasts, boneless and skinless, cut into 1 1/2-inch pieces
2 tablespoons Lee Kum Kee® Vegetarian Stir Fry Sauce
4 red potatoes, scrubbed and cut into 1 1/2-inch chunks
3 (large) carrots, peeled and cut into 1 1/2-inch chunks
4 stalks celery with leaves, cut into 1-inch pieces
4 1/2 cups chicken-style vegetable broth
1 (large) onion, quartered
3 cloves garlic, minced
1 (1-inch) piece fresh ginger root, mashed
1 teaspoon peanut oil
2 to 3 tablespoons curry powder
1 teaspoon brown rice syrup or raw sugar
Salt to taste
2 tablespoons whole-wheat flour dissolved in 2 tablespoons water
Garlic-flavor oil cooking spray

Spray a Dutch oven with cooking spray. Add chicken and stir-fry with vegetarian stir-fry sauce. Remove from pot and set aside.

In the same Dutch oven, sauté onion and garlic in peanut oil and 1/2 cup vegetable broth. Add the chicken, curry powder, carrots, potatoes, celery, broth, ginger, brown rice syrup, and salt. Cook for 20 minutes or until the vegetables are tender. Thicken with whole-wheat flour mixture. Serve with rice or warmed chapatis.

Per serving: *231 calories, 4 g fat. 32 g carbohydrates, 4 g dietary fiber, 19 g protein.*

Variation: To save time you can buy a package of frozen stew vegetables containing potatoes, carrots, onions, and celery. If you use these frozen vegetables, you need to cut down on the amount of onion in the recipe.

Hawaii Local Favorite

Posted on: Wednesday, April 7, 2004
Mother's Hawaiian Stew still `ono without meat, some fat

`Ono Keia Hawaiian Stew

This is a meatless and, therefore, a lower-fat version of my mother's stew made with seitan *(SAY-tan)*, a high-protein food made from boiled or baked wheat gluten, water, and seasonings. It is amazing how much it resembles meat with its chewy texture; find it in health food stores. Or use shiitake mushrooms which can lend a meaty flavor and texture to stew. Our family loved this with rice or poi on a cold and rainy day. It seemed so warm and hearty.

`Ono Keia Hawaiian Stew

Serves 6

- 1 teaspoon extra virgin olive oil
- 3 cloves garlic, crushed
- 1 (1-inch) piece fresh ginger root, crushed
- 1 (medium) onion, sliced
- 5 cups chicken or chicken-style vegetarian broth
- 1 (8-ounce) box seitan *(wheat gluten)* or 1 cup shiitake mushrooms, whole or sliced
- 4 stalks celery with leaves, cut into 1-inch pieces
- 2 (6-ounce) cans tomato paste
- 3 (medium) carrots, peeled and cut in fourths
- 4 red potatoes, peeled and cut in half
- Salt and pepper to taste

2 tablespoons *mochiko* sweet rice flour
2 tablespoons water

Sauté the garlic, ginger, and onions in oil and 3 tablespoons of broth in a heavy-bottomed pot or a large Dutch oven on medium-high heat.

If using seitan, cut into 1-inch pieces and add to the garlic, ginger, and onion mixture.

If using mushrooms, soak them in warm water for 10 to 15 minutes, then drain and add to broth.

Add remaining broth, celery, tomato paste, carrots, and potatoes. Bring stew to a boil, turn heat down to medium, and cook 30 minutes, stirring occasionally, until the vegetables are fork tender. Season to taste with salt and pepper. Combine rice flour and water and stir in to thicken; simmer to combine. If you prefer a thicker stew, add 3 tablespoons rice flour mixed in water.

Per serving: *176 calories, 1 g fat, 33 g carbohydrates, 6 g dietary fiber, 10 g protein.*

Hawaii Local Favorite

The amount of ingredients may seem daunting but it is a meal in itself. You will be able to find the White Wave® Vegetarian Stir Fry Strips in health food stores. They are made from wheat gluten called seitan. It is a low-fat, high-protein alternative to beef and poultry. Its meat-like texture and delicate flavor make it a perfect replacement for beef in your favorite recipes. Another favorite product is Vitamark International's SuperSOY™ Beef Strips made from soy flour and corn. It really tastes like the original local-style *hekka*.

If you choose to use tofu, buy the Mori-Nu Extra Firm Lite Silken Tofu for this recipe because it contains 50 percent less fat and 33 percent fewer calories than regular tofu.

What the Hekka?
Serves 8

1 (8-ounce) box White Wave® Vegetarian Stir Fry Strips *(seitan/wheat gluten),* cut up in 1/4-inch strips or 2 (12.3-ounce) boxes Mori-Nu Extra Firm Lite Silken Tofu

3/4 cup teriyaki marinade or Teriyaki Sauce *(page 203)*

1/4 cup *mirin (cooking wine)*

1 (15-ounce) can bamboo shoots, sliced into half-moons

1 (8-ounce) can water chestnuts, sliced

1 cup dried shiitake mushrooms

Global Light Cuisine ∞ Carol Devenot 199

1 (large) carrot, julienned
1 bunch of watercress, baby bok choy,
    or *choy sum*, sliced into 2-inch lengths
1/2 bunch of green onions, sliced into
    1-inch pieces
1 (medium) yellow onion, sliced into 1/4-inch-
    thick half-moons
1 (1-inch) piece fresh ginger root, peeled
    and grated
3 cloves garlic, minced
1 teaspoon sesame oil
2 (2-ounce) packages bean thread *(long rice)*,
    cooked and cut into 2-inch lengths
3 cups vegetable broth
1 teaspoon white pepper

If using vegetarian stir fry strips, marinate the strips in a bowl for 30 minutes in teriyaki sauce and *mirin.*

If using tofu, cut up the tofu into 1-inch cubes and marinate for 30 minutes in teriyaki sauce and *mirin.* Microwave for 2 minutes.

Open the cans of bamboo shoots and water chestnuts and drain liquids into a small saucepan. Cook mushrooms in these liquids until tender for about 10 minutes. Drain and save liquid for sautéing. Slice mushrooms into 1/4-inch pieces and set aside.

Slice the vegetables and set aside.

Cook the bean threads *(long rice)* in 3 cups of vegetable broth for 10 minutes. Drain the threads and save the broth. Set aside.

Add the mushroom broth to the bean thread broth and set aside.

In a large wok or frying pan, sauté the garlic, onion, and ginger in sesame oil. Add in the remaining ingredients in the following order: carrots, bamboo shoots, shiitake mushrooms, water chestnuts, vegetarian stir fry strips or cooked tofu cubes, marinade, cooked bean threads, watercress, and green onions. As you add each new vegetable, add about 1/4 cup of vegetable broth and stir-fry until the entire mixture is heated through. Season with white pepper and serve immediately. `Ono with rice.

Per serving (with vegetarian strips): *229 calories, 1 g fat, 42 g carbohydrates, 4 g dietary fiber, 12 g protein.*

Per serving (with lite tofu): *215 calories, 1 g fat, 42 g carbohydrates, 4 g dietary fiber, 8 g protein.*

Global Light Cuisine ∞ Carol Devenot

Hawaii Local Favorite

Posted on: Wednesday, September 6, 2006

Spices jazz up familiar entrees

Coffee Burger with Wasabi Mayo

On my first visit to one of the best open markets on O`ahu which is held on the grounds of Kapi`olani Community College, I enjoyed meeting an enthusiastic and creative entrepreneur, Ka`iulani Cowell of Ka`iulani Spices.

We met for lunch over Cambodian food, and I found out that she has been cooking since childhood. Coming from a large family, she had to invent ways to deal with inexpensive ingredients, such as hot dogs, hamburgers, and beans. This early experience developed her passion for food. She attended the Culinary Institute of America in upstate New York. She also has worked in the kitchens of several major hotels.

She blends a total of 21 exotic spices in her five different rubs and seasonings using the freshest ingredients. All her spices are purchased in their natural seed, pod, or stick forms. To maximize their flavors, she has roasted, ground, and mixed them by hand.

Coffee Burger with Wasabi Mayo

Serves 4 to 6

1 pound ground buffalo*, shaped into 3-inch diameter patties or Flame Grilled Boca® Burgers
Extra virgin olive oil spray

- 2 to 3 tablespoons Ka`iulani Hawaiian Coffee Rub & Seasoning *(brown sugar, Hawaiian rock salt, ground Hawaiian coffee, cumin, garlic black pepper and other spices)*
- 4 whole-wheat hamburger buns
- 4 cups romaine lettuce, shredded
- 4 Roma tomatoes, sliced into 1/4-inch slices
- *Wasabi* paste to taste
- 1/2 cup reduced-fat mayonnaise

Mix the *wasabi* paste and low-fat mayo thoroughly and set aside. Sprinkle coffee rub generously over the patties. Grill or fry with olive oil spray. Spread the hamburger buns sparingly with *wasabi* mayo and add the burger of choice. Top with lettuce and tomato.

Per serving (buffalo meat, no rub): *400 calories, 19 g fat, 2.5 g saturated fat, 65 mg cholesterol, 500 mg sodium, 30 g carbohydrate, 5 g dietary fiber, 6 g sugar, 29 g protein.*

* You can find buffalo hamburger at some Star Markets and Safeway stores.

Hawaii Local Favorite

Terry Burger
Serves 4

4 (2.5-ounce) Boca® Burgers
Teriyaki Sauce *(below)*
Vegetable oil cooking spray
1 tomato, sliced into 1/4-inch slices
1/4 sweet Maui onion or red onion, thinly sliced
4 romaine lettuce leaves
4 whole-wheat buns
2 to 4 tablespoons reduced-fat mayonnaise
   or Tofu Mayo *(page 69)*
2 to 4 tablespoons ketchup

Marinate the Boca® Burgers in teriyaki sauce for at least an hour. Spray a nonstick frying pan with cooking spray and fry burgers. Spread mayo on the bun. Place the marinated burger on half of the bun. Top with tomato, onion, lettuce, and ketchup. Cover with the other half of the bun.

Per serving (with Teriyaki Sauce): *323 calories, 9 g fat, 43 g carbohydrates, 6 g dietary fiber, 19 g protein.*

Teriyaki Sauce
Serves 4

1/3 cup soy sauce, tamari, or Bragg® Liquid
   Aminos
2 tablespoons molasses or brown rice syrup
1 tablespoon fresh ginger root, grated
3 to 4 cloves garlic, minced

1 tablespoon *mirin* or sake
2 tablespoons water

In a small saucepan, combine the above ingredients. Bring to a boil and let cool. Use as a sauce or marinade.

Per serving: *49 calories, 0.04 g fat, 10 g carbohydrates, 0 g dietary fiber, 1 gram protein.*

Global Light Cuisine ∞ Carol Devenot

India/Indian

Posted on: Wednesday, April 20, 2005

Fried spices flavor one pot chicken dish

Ek Handi Ka Murch Aur Masoor (one-pot chicken, red lentils, and green beans)

Cooking this dish brought back memories of my Indian friends at the East-West Center in Honolulu. They made incredible curries, chapatis, and chutneys.

I learned a great deal about how to combine the spices from these friends, and I added my own Chinese cooking skills to this dish, using a stir-fry method.

Heating spices is a method used throughout India to bring out the flavors.

In addition to frying the spices, I combined kosher salt, black pepper, and *garam masala* to create a rub for the chicken. *Garam masala* is made up of cardamom seeds, cinnamon, nutmeg, peppercorns, black cumin seeds, and whole cloves. It is much easier to buy it ready-made at the Indian grocer or other store than to put it together yourself.

Ek Handi Ka Murch Aur Masoor
(one-pot chicken, red lentils, and green beans)

Serves 6

- 1 tablespoon extra virgin olive oil
- 3 bay leaves
- 5 whole cloves
- 6 cardamom pods

206   Entrées

1 stick of cinnamon

2 pounds chicken breasts, boneless and skinless

12/3 cups red lentils *(masoor dal)*, washed
   and drained

1/2 teaspoon dried turmeric

5 cups water

2 teaspoons kosher salt

Ground pepper, to taste

11/2 teaspoons *garam masala*

Juice of 1/2 lemon

Nonfat cooking spray

11/2 teaspoons cumin seeds

1 (small) onion, sliced into half-moons

4 cloves garlic, minced

6 ounces fresh green beans, cleaned, destem-
   med, and cut diagonally into pieces

I teaspoon ground coriander

12 cherry tomatoes, cut into halves,
   or 2 (medium) tomatoes cut into wedges

3 dried red hot chilies, diced *(optional)*

Cayenne pepper *(optional)*

In a large Dutch oven, heat 1 tablespoon of olive oil.
When the oil is hot, stir-fry the bay leaves, cloves,
cardamom pods, and cinnamon stick until the bay
leaves darken. Then put the chicken pieces in and
brown on all sides. Meanwhile, measure out the red
lentils, turmeric, and water. After the chicken has
browned, remove meat from the Dutch oven and
reserve. Add the lentils, turmeric, and water. Bring to a
boil, lower the heat to low, and simmer for 10 minutes.

For the rub, mix together the salt, ground pepper,
1/2 teaspoon *garam masala*, and lemon juice and rub

on all sides of the browned chicken. Place the rubbed chicken pieces into the pot with the cooked lentils. Stir and bring to a simmer for 20 minutes, stirring occasionally.

Just before the chicken is done, spray a frying pay with vegetable cooking oil. Stir-fry the cumin seeds for 2 seconds, add the onion and garlic, and fry until browned around the edges. Add the remaining teaspoon of *garam masala*, ground coriander, and tomatoes. Stir-fry for 20 seconds, add the green beans, and stir-fry for another 10 seconds. Place this entire mixture into the Dutch oven with the chicken and lentils. Stir the contents and serve hot.

If you want the dish spicy, add 3 diced dried hot red chilies to the bay leaves, cardamom, and cinnamon stir-fry. And add 1/8 to 1/4 teaspoon of cayenne powder to the cumin seeds, coriander, and *garam masala* mixture. To cool such a dish, some chilled plain yogurt is nice.

Per serving: *387 calories, 5 g fat, 37 g carbohydrates, 10 g dietary fiber, 749 mg sodium, 48 g protein.*

India/Indian

Posted on: Wednesday, July 27, 2005

Tandoori chicken tantalizing

Tandoori chicken

The seasonings make this dish so delectable. You can usually find chili powder and turmeric at the supermarket. I found everything else at the India Market, 2570 South Beretania Street, near University Avenue in Honolulu. *(Asian and some health food stores may carry premixed tandoori seasoning or garam masala.)* Garam masala is an Indian spice mixture that includes cloves, cardamom, cumin, cinnamon, nutmeg, and coriander. The yogurt helps moisturize and tenderize the chicken. No fo'get, put plenty garlic. So *'ono!* If you want more color, as is traditional, add red food coloring to the sauce.

I have read that this elegant dish originated in Punjab State, India. *Tandoori murgh,* as it's called, is one of the most popular dishes there, traditionally cooked in a clay oven called a *tandoor.* Although this authentic *tandoori* flavor is difficult to achieve in conventional ovens, this version still makes a very tasty, moist dish. Microwave basmati rice to go with it and toss in curry powder, dried fruits such as currents or cranberries, and pine nuts. Garnish rice with parsley.

Tandoori Chicken
Serves 6

6 chicken breast halves, boneless and skinless
1 cup plain nonfat yogurt

2 teaspoons extra virgin olive oil
3 tablespoons lime juice
3 tablespoons fresh ginger root, peeled and grated
6 garlic cloves, crushed
1 1/2 to 2 teaspoons chili powder
1/2 to 1 teaspoon turmeric
1 tablespoon *garam masala*
2 sprigs fresh Chinese parsley *(cilantro)*, chopped
1 tablespoon Hawaiian salt

Garnish:

Salad greens
Lime juice
Tomatoes

Rinse and pat dry the chicken breast. Make two slits into each piece. Rub each piece with Hawaiian salt and place in a glass bowl and set aside. Mix together yogurt, olive oil, lime juice, ginger, garlic, chili powder, turmeric, *garam masala* and parsley and beat so ingredients are blended. Pour this mixture over the chicken breast and marinate at least three hours *(overnight is better)*. Heat oven to 425 degrees. Place chicken pieces on a wire rack over a baking pan and bake for 20 to 25 minutes, basting occasionally. Chicken should be cooked through and browned on top. Transfer to serving dish and garnish with salad greens, lime, and tomato. Serve with basmati rice flavored with dried fruits and nuts.

Per serving (without rice): 210 calories, 3.5 g fat, 1 g saturated fat, 85 mg cholesterol, greater than 1200 mg sodium, 6 g carbohydrate, 1 g dietary fiber, 4 g sugar, 36 g protein.

Mainland U.S. Favorite

Posted on: Wednesday, November 1, 2006

Fresh wahoo tacos? Make your own

Flame-broiled Fish Taco

It all started after my spinning class, at the Honolulu Club. Spinning instructor Stephanie Pietsch and I were discussing exercise, diet and health. In the course of the conversation, I was surprised to learn that she also owned and operated Wahoo's Fish Taco. This discussion continued over lunch the following week.

The outlet at Ward and `Auahi streets in Honolulu is one of forty in the U.S., launched in 1988 by three brothers with business sense and a love of the ocean. Their first spot was a small taco restaurant in Costa Mesa, California. One of the brothers asked Stephanie to open up the first Wahoo's in Hawai`i. Having a degree in health and sports medicine from Boston College and a consulting practice, she was well qualified to fill the position.

Flame-broiled Fish Taco
Serves 6

1/2 pound fresh *'ono (wahoo)*, cut into two fillets
Pinch garlic salt and pepper to taste
8 corn tortillas or whole-wheat and spinach tortillas
2 ounces cabbage, shredded
1 ounce cheese *(jack/cheddar mix)* or nonfat or low-fat cheese, shredded

4 ounces Salsa *(page 20 or bottled)*

Garnish:

2 limes, quartered
Fresh Chinese parsley *(cilantro),* chopped *(optional)*

Season the fish with garlic salt and pepper. Prepare a barbecue grill *(wood burning, charcoal, or gas)* and grill fillets over medium heat, a few minutes on each side, until done.

Meanwhile, in a dry frying pan over medium-low heat, heat tortillas, cover, and keep warm.

When fish is done, cut into four equal portions. Fill warm tortillas with cabbage and top with fish, cheese, and salsa. Serve with lime and parsley, if desired.

Per serving: 210 calories, 4.5 g fat, 2 g saturated fat, 35 mg cholesterol, 360 mg sodium, 28 g carbohydrate, 4 g dietary fiber, 3 g sugar, 16 g protein.

Mainland U.S. Favorite

Posted on: Wednesday, September 5, 2007

Easy, tasty salmon dish friend's fave salmon

Barbecue Roasted Salmon

Joe loves to meet with old and new friends to talk story. I am sure the racquetball guys want to know what techniques he used to win the U.S. Open Men's 55 in Memphis last year.

He grew up in Georgia and joined the Army at 18. After serving for 21 years, he is now working for the Feds at Schofield Barracks. He also owns a small car dealership in Hawai`i. Joe has a commitment to contributing to the growth and development of the youth in his community, and to this end he has sponsored youth church groups at events such as bowling. He enjoys working out and cooking healthy food. He shared a favorite recipe with me.

Barbecue Roasted Salmon
Serves 4

1/4 cup pineapple juice
2 tablespoons fresh lemon juice
2 teaspoons lemon zest
4 (6-ounce) wild salmon filets
2 tablespoons brown sugar
4 teaspoons chili powder
3/4 teaspoon ground cumin
1/2 teaspoon sea salt
1/4 teaspoon ground cinnamon

Global Light Cuisine ∞ Carol Devenot

    Extra virgin olive oil spray
    Lemon wedges for garnish

Combine the pineapple juice, lemon juice, lemon zest, and salmon in a zip-closure plastic bag; seal; and marinate in the refrigerator for 1 hour, turning occasionally. Preheat the oven to 400 degrees. Remove fish from the bag and discard marinade. Combine sugar, chili powder, cumin, salt, and cinnamon in a bowl. Rub over the fish and place in a 7- by 11-inch baking dish coated with cooking spray. Bake for 12 minutes or until fish flakes easily with a fork. Serve with lemon wedges.

Per serving: *400 calories, 23 g fat, 4.5 g saturated fat, 100 mg cholesterol, 350 mg sodium, 10 g carbohydrate, 1 g dietary fiber, 7 g sugar, 38 g protein.*

Mainland U.S. Favorite

Posted on: Wednesday, September 21, 2005

Casserole with a difference
Quinoa Spinach Casserole

My daughter-in-law, August, had some cooked quinoa on hand, so we decided to use it in a casserole.

Quinoa *(pronounced key-NO-ah or KEEN-wah)* contains up to 20 percent high-quality protein. This grain is also high in B vitamins, iron, zinc, potassium, calcium, and vitamin E. It is a member of the goosefoot family *(Chenopodiaceae)*, so named because its three-lobed leaf is shaped like a foot of a goose.

Quinoa is believed to have been first cultivated in South America thousands of years ago. U.S. distributors still import the grain from South America. The imported variety is large, about the size of millet, and uniformly buff or cream colored. It has been well processed so that most of the bitter *saponin* coating is removed. *Saponin* acts as a natural pesticide, discouraging predators with its "off putting" flavor. Although quinoa is processed, it still needs to be washed before cooking. To wash the quinoa, place it in a deep bowl and cover with cold water. Gently rub the grains between your palms for about 6 seconds, then drain into a fine mesh strainer. If using the domestic variety, repeat until the water runs clear.

Domestic quinoa is smaller, with a richer, deeper color from off-white to dark tan. This type of quinoa requires extra washing, producing a less dry and fluffy grain.

Quinoa Spinach Casserole

Serves 6

2 cups chicken or vegetable stock

1/4 teaspoon sea salt or 2 teaspoons tamari
(soy sauce)

Freshly ground pepper to taste

Nonfat cooking spray

1 cup imported quinoa or 11/3 cups domestic
quinoa, well washed

1 tablespoon extra virgin olive oil

2 cups sweet Maui onion, minced

6 cloves garlic, minced

1 cup portobello mushroom or shiitake
mushroom, chopped

2 pounds fresh spinach, stemmed and finely
chopped

2 to 4 tablespoons low-sodium soy sauce

4 to 6 teaspoons of Greek seasoning blend
(onion, spearmint, oregano, garlic, sea salt)

Salt to taste

1 cup Egg Beaters®

1 cup nonfat milk

11/2 cups low-fat cheese, grated

1/4 cup sunflower seeds

Paprika

In a 1-quart saucepan, over high heat, combine the stock, salt (or tamari), and pepper. Bring to rapid boil, add the washed quinoa, cover, and lower heat to simmer. Cook for 12 minutes or until all the water has been absorbed. The grain should be translucent with a thin, white curlicue around it. Remove from heat and let it rest 5 minutes, covered. Fluff with a fork.

Preheat the oven to 350 degrees. Spray a 9- by 13-inch baking pan with nonstick spray.

Heat the olive oil in a deep frying pan. Sauté the onion and garlic until soft. Add the mushrooms and cook until soft. Add spinach, soy sauce, and Greek seasoning and cook for 5 minutes more over medium heat, stirring frequently. Place the quinoa in a large bowl and add the cooked vegetables. Taste and add salt, if desired.

Beat together the Egg Beaters® and milk and stir this into the quinoa-spinach mixture along with the grated cheese. Spread this mixture in the sprayed pan and sprinkle with sunflower seeds and paprika. Bake uncovered for 35 to 40 minutes or until heated through and lightly browned on top.

Per serving (without salt): *350 calories, 11 g fat, 2.5 g saturated fat, 10 mg cholesterol, 1200 mg sodium, 44 g carbohydrate, 7 g fiber, 6 g sugar, 22 g protein.*

Mexico

My tortillas of choice are the locally made Sinaloa Hawaii Wraps™ Whole Wheat.

Chicken Fajitas
Serves 4

4 whole-wheat tortillas or chapatis
1/2 red onion, diced
3 cloves garlic, minced
1 red bell pepper, thinly sliced
2 green bell pepper, thinly sliced
3 ounces chicken breast strips, cooked
1 tablespoon chili powder
Juice *(about 2 ounces)* 1 lime
Extra virgin olive oil spray
Hawaiian salt to taste
3 plum tomatoes, diced
1 cup Salsa *(page 20)*
1 cup Guacamole *(page 19) (optional)*

Place the tortillas or chapatis in a toaster oven set at 200 degrees to heat while you prepare the filling.

Spray a medium frying pan with olive oil, add the onion, and stir-fry over medium-low heat until transparent. Add the garlic and peppers and cook for 5 minutes. Add the chicken, chili powder, lime juice, and salt. Lower the heat and simmer 5 minutes.

Remove the tortillas or chapatis from the oven and place under a napkin to keep warm while assembling the fajitas. On each plate, lay the warmed tortilla and place the cooked mixture on one side. Sprinkle each fajita with the fresh tomatoes, salsa, and guacamole *(optional)* over the mixture. Fold like a burrito and bite into this delicious Mexican favorite.

Per serving (without guacamole): *180 calories, 3 g fat, 35 g carbohydrates, 6 g dietary fiber, 12 g protein.*

Per serving (with guacamole): *265 calories, 11 g fat, 40 g carbohydrates, 8 g dietary fiber, 13 g protein.*

Mexico

Posted on: Wednesday, November 29, 2006

Spice up leftover turkey for chiles rellenos casserole

Turkey Chiles Rellenos Casserole

Although they are called peppers, chiles *(chilies, chillies)* are not members of the same family as black pepper. They belong to the genus *Capsicum,* for the Greek word meaning "to bite." The bite or burn you get from some chiles is caused by the alkaloid capsaicin. Even when dried, cooked or frozen, the heat level remains stable. However, not all members of this species are hot and spicy; some are sweet and mild. Peppers grown in New Mexico are rated mild to moderate in heat.

Chiles are known to have been cultivated in Central Mexico as long ago as 7000 BC. In 1493 Christopher Columbus, while searching for the countries that grow black pepper and other spices, found other peppers used by the Native Americans. He called them pimientos *(Spanish for peppers).* The popularity of chiles has been spreading ever since.

Turkey Chiles Rellenos Casserole

Serves 6

Extra virgin olive oil spray
1 cup onion, chopped
3 cloves garlic, minced
1 1/2 teaspoons ground cumin
1 1/2 teaspoons dried oregano

220   Entrées

1/4 teaspoon sea salt

1/4 teaspoon ground pepper

2 cups roast turkey *(white meat)*, shredded into 1 1/2-inch pieces

1 (16-ounce) can fat-free refried beans

2 (4-ounce) cans whole green chiles, sliced into quarters lengthwise or fresh green chilies *(grilled whole and quartered lengthwise)*

1 cup 2% fat Mexican cheese, grated*

1/3 cup whole-wheat flour

1/4 teaspoon sea salt

1 1/3 cup skim milk

1/8 teaspoon Tabasco® or other hot sauce

2 (large) eggs, lightly beaten

2 (large) egg whites lightly beaten

Garnish *(optional)*:

Fresh Chinese parsley *(cilantro)*
Black olives
Cherry tomatoes

Heat the oven to 350 degrees.

Spray a nonstick frying pan with olive oil and sauté the onion and garlic for 2 minutes. Add the cumin, oregano, salt, pepper, turkey, and refried beans. Stir until well combined and remove from heat.

Spray a 9- by 13-inch baking dish with olive oil and place half of the green chilies on the bottom of the dish. Top with 1/2 cup grated cheese. Gently spoon the turkey mixture onto the cheese, and spread evenly. Place the other half of the green chilies over the turkey mixture, and sprinkle with remaining cheese.

Global Light Cuisine ∞ Carol Devenot

Combine flour and salt in small bowl and gradually whisk in milk, hot sauce, eggs, and egg whites. Stir with a wire whisk until well blended. Pour this mixture over the casserole and bake at 350 degrees for 1 hour. Cool casserole briefly before serving. Garnish with sprigs of parsley, sliced black olives, and/or sliced cherry tomatoes. Serve with hot sauce or salsa if desired.

Per serving: *260 calories, 8 g fat, 3 g saturated fat, 100 mg cholesterol, greater than 1000 mg sodium, 27 g carbohydrate, 6 g dietary fiber, 5 g sugar, 21 g protein*

* I found low-fat Mexican cheese at Safeway; you can substitute any reduced-fat cheese.

Mexico

My fondest memory of eating chili was at the lunch wagon parked in front of Bowls, Ala Moana, Honolulu. The surfers always ordered chili and rice after surfing and a shower. The most delicious way to eat chili is over rice.

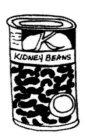

Carol's Chili
Serves 6

- 3 cloves garlic, minced
- 1 (medium) red onion, finely chopped
- 1 (large) celery stalk with leaves, chopped
- 2 tablespoons chicken-style vegetarian broth
- 1 teaspoon extra virgin olive oil
- 1/2 (small) green pepper; diced
- 1/4 teaspoon red chili flakes *(optional)*
- 2 tablespoons chili powder
- 1 teaspoon dried cumin powder
- 2 (2.5-ounce) Boca® Burger patties, chopped
- 2 (15-ounce) cans kidney beans
- 2 (6-ounce) cans tomato sauce
- Salt and pepper to taste

In a large saucepan, sauté the garlic, onion, celery, and chopped up Boca® Burger patties in olive oil and broth. Add green pepper; chili flakes, chili powder; cumin, kidney beans, tomato sauce, and salt and pepper to taste. Simmer for 10 minutes. Serve with brown rice and a tossed green salad.

Per serving: *246 calories, 2 g fat, 42 g carbohydrates, 17 g dietary fiber, 16 g protein.*

Mexico

Posted on: Wednesday, September 22, 2004

Southwest orzo dish excellent
Woo's Southwest Orzo

A few weeks ago, we were invited to a party of Spanish speakers who meet every month to share their language and culture. There were many different Mexican dishes such as *empanadillas* and *quesadillas*, as well as the typical local-style buffet.

After I took my first bite of an orzo dish from the buffet, I wanted to get the recipe. It was delicious. Mike Woo, the creator, was very happy to share this recipe with us. He says he usually cooks this with hamburger meat, red peppers, and mushrooms. To cut the fat, I tried making a vegetarian version with Boca® brand vegetable protein burger, and it worked well. Or you can just leave the meat out.

Woo's Southwest Orzo
Serves 10

1 teaspoon extra virgin olive oil
1 (large) round onion
5 to 6 cloves garlic, minced
1 green or red bell pepper, diced
4 to 5 teaspoons chili powder
2 teaspoons ground cumin
1/2 teaspoon pepper
3 teaspoons Hawaiian salt
2 to 3 fresh tomatoes, diced
1 (8-ounce) can tomato sauce

- 1 (19-ounce) can black beans, drained
- 1 (15.25-ounce) can whole kernel corn, drained
- 4 (2.5-ounce) Boca® Burgers, microwaved and diced *(optional)*
- 1 (16-ounce) package orzo
- 1/4 to 1/2 cup fresh Chinese parsley *(cilantro)*, chopped, for garnish

In a large wok or frying pan, sauté the onion, garlic and bell pepper in olive oil on high heat. Add the seasonings, tomatoes, tomato sauce, black beans, corn, and Boca® Burgers.

In a large pot, bring 4 quarts of water to a rolling boil. Add the orzo and cook for 8 minutes. Drain in a colander. Return pasta to the large pot, pour sauce over orzo and mix, taking care not to mash the pasta. Garnish with parsley. Serve immediately.

Per serving (with Boca® Burgers): *300 calories, 3 g fat, 55 g carbohydrates, 8 g dietary fiber, 390 mg sodium, 16 g protein.*

Mexico

Here's a way of making an open-faced taco without the fat. The plum tomatoes and romaine lettuce give you more nutritive value than the regular tomatoes and iceberg lettuce. There are several different types of low-fat cheeses. There are fat free, 2% milk, and low-fat varieties. I find that the fat-free cheese works best with recipes that have strong flavors.

Bostadas

Serves 4

- 4 whole-wheat tortillas
- 4 (2.5-ounce) Boca® Burger patties, microwaved and chopped
- 1/2 red onion, chopped
- 1/2 cup plum tomatoes, chopped
- 1 cup romaine lettuce, shredded
- 1/2 cup low-fat mozzarella cheese or low-fat soy cheese
- 1 cup taco sauce or Salsa *(page 20)*

Preheat oven at 350 degrees. Place tortillas on a cookie sheet and bake until crisp for about 5 to 7 minutes. Meanwhile chop the remaining ingredients. Spread the chopped Boca® Burger patties on the crisp tortillas. Top with onion, tomatoes, lettuce, cheese, and taco sauce or salsa.

Per serving: 254 calories, 7 g fat, 27 g carbohydrates, 6 g dietary fiber, 21 g protein.

226   Entrées

Middle East

Posted on: Wednesday, January 12, 2005

Low-fat version of falafel a hit

Flab You Less Falafel

Falafel (fah LAH fel) is to the Middle East, and especially Israel, as hamburgers are to the United States—fast food found everywhere. These are little rounded cakes, patties, or croquettes made from ground chickpeas, bulgur *(steamed, dried and crushed whole-wheat kernels)*, herbs, and spices. Each *falafel* stand has its own style and condiments: cucumbers, radishes, peppers, and alfalfa sprouts among them.

Flab You Less Falafel

Serves 6

1/3 cup bulgur wheat

3 cloves garlic, minced

1 (small) red onion, chopped

1 (19-ounce) can garbanzo beans *(chickpeas)*, drained

1 cup whole-wheat bread cubes

2 teaspoons lemon juice

1 teaspoon dried cumin

1/4 teaspoon salt

1/4 teaspoon pepper

1 shake of hot pepper sauce

1/2 cup fresh Chinese parsley *(cilantro)*

6 pita pocket breads

Extra virgin olive oil spray

Garnish:
Tomato, sliced or chopped
Lettuce, shredded
Onion, chopped
Salsa *(page 20)*

Heat oven to 400 degrees. Place bulgur in a mixing bowl and pour 2 cups boiling water over it; let stand for 30 minutes.

In the food processor or blender, purée the chickpeas. Add garlic, onion, lemon juice, cumin, salt, pepper, and hot pepper sauce. Purée for 1 minute. Drain the bulgur wheat, squeezing out excess moisture. Add to the processed mixture along with bread cubes and parsley. Process briefly.

Place *falafel* mixture on a dinner plate and cut up into 12 sections *(like 12 pie slivers)*. Roll one sliver at a time and shape into about 2- by 1/2-inch-thick patties. Flatten the patties with a spatula.

Spray cookie sheet with olive oil. Place the *falafel* patties on the sheet and spray with olive oil. Bake for 20 minutes turning halfway through, spraying the new side up. Then broil for 2 minutes per side or until golden and crispy.

Split a pocket bread in half and pass it over a flame. Fill each half with a *falafel* patty, shredded lettuce, tomato, onion, and salsa. Instead of salsa, you also can use tzatziki *(page 78)*, tahini, or low-fat ranch dressing.

Leftover patties can be refrigerated for up to 2 days. To serve, cover with foil and bake for 10 minutes at 400 degrees.

Per serving: *326 calories, 3 g fat, 66 g carbohydrates, 11 g dietary fiber, 734 mg sodium, 13 g protein.*

Desserts

Australia/New Zealand

Posted on: Wednesday, June 27, 2007

Baked meringue, fruit in pas de deux
Palagyi's Pavlova

This dessert is a baked meringue with a soft marshmallow center and a crispy outer crust. It is so airy, your mouth feels like it is dancing on a cloud. So appropriately named, the dessert was first prepared for the late Russian ballerina Anna Pavlova when she was on tour Down Under. Different sources suggest that this dessert originated in New Zealand, while others claim it was created in Australia.

Palagyi's Pavlova
Serves 8

- 3/4 cup *(about 4 to 5 eggs)* egg whites
- 1 1/2 teaspoon pure vanilla extract
- 2 teaspoons distilled white vinegar
- 1 1/2 tablespoons cornstarch
- 1 cup baker's sugar *(ultrafine sugar)**
- Pinch of salt
- 1 1/2 to 2 cups cup fruit, sliced
- 1 to 2 cups Cool Whip® or canned whipped topping

For best results, separate eggs while they are cold. Cover them with plastic wrap and allow them to sit at room temperature for at least 30 minutes. *(Egg yolks may be reserved for other uses.)* To get the maximum

232   Desserts

volume from egg whites, make sure to start with clean mixing bowls and utensils.

Place oven rack in the center of the oven. Heat the oven to 250 degrees.

Line a large baking sheet with parchment paper. Draw 8 circles on the parchment paper with a light pencil using a 3-inch plate for a template.

Pour the vanilla and vinegar into a small cup. In a small bowl, mix the cornstarch and sugar. In a large bowl, using an electric mixer, whip egg whites and salt. Start the mixing speed at low and then move to medium for approximately 2 to 3 minutes until the egg white bubbles are small. Increase the speed to medium-high and gradually add the sugar-cornstarch mixture 1 tablespoon at a time. After 2 to 3 minutes, pour in the vanilla-vinegar mixture. Increase speed and whip until the mixture forms stiff peaks when the beater is raised *(4 to 5 minutes)*.

Spoon the meringue into 8 round mounds on the parchment paper. Form an indentation in the middle of each mound to hold the filling.

Place the baking sheet in the oven and bake for 50 to 60 minutes. Check on the meringues during the baking process. If they look as though they are getting too dark and cracking, reduce the temperature 25 degrees and turn the baking pans. The meringues should be crispy on the exterior and marshmallow-like on the interior.

When they're done, use a thin, metal spatula to carefully lift them from the baking sheet and place on a wire rack. When completely cooled, spread with a layer of whipped topping and sprinkle the sliced fruit over the top. Add another layer of topping. Serve immediately.

Meringues can be made days in advance; store in a covered container, but they don't hold up well in very hot, humid weather.

Per serving (based on 2 cups each of fruit and whipped topping): 200 calories; 3 g fat; 3 g saturated fat; 0 mg cholesterol, 0 mg sodium, 0 g carbohydrate, 0 g dietary fiber, 0 g sugar, 0 g protein.

* To make your own superfine sugar, place ordinary white sugar in a food processor or blender and process until the sugar granules are reduced to a fine consistency.

Desserts

Asia/Chinese

Posted on: Wednesday, July 28, 2004

Mango memories in pudding
Mango Pudding

Last week, I took two of my friends to lunch at a delightful Chinese restaurant in Chinatown. We ordered an assortment of dishes, family style. Being the *niele* cook that I am, I wanted to try their mango pudding—not a pudding, really, but a gelatin dessert, also known as mango *doufu*.

It brings back memories of growing up in Kaimuki. My dad used to pick ripe mangoes with his homemade hook. He used to put the half-ripe ones in a paper bag to ripen quicker. Later, when I became a food science teacher, I found out this ripening trick is actually based on science. The paper bags tend to keep the gases from the fruit in, but are porous enough to allow oxygen to pass through.

To take it over the top, sprinkle the mango pudding with *li hing* powder, a Chinese seasoning made with prunes, salt, water, sugar, dextrose, preservatives, and food coloring.

Mango Pudding
Serves 8

2 (0.2-ounce) envelopes unflavored gelatin
3/4 cup fructose
1 cup hot water
3 cups fresh or frozen mangoes, thawed
1 cup evaporated fat-free milk

8 ice cubes
1/8 cup fresh mango, hand diced,
    or 32 lychee halves *(16 whole lychees)*

Garnish:

Li hing powder *(optional)*
8 sprigs mint

Cut up fresh mangoes to fill 3 cups, or use 3 cups thawed frozen mangoes, and process them in food processor until smooth. *(You can try keeping it a little chunky and see how you like it.)*

Put the gelatin and fructose in a small bowl, add hot water, and stir until thoroughly dissolved.

In a bowl, mix processed mangoes, evaporated milk, and ice cubes. Pour gelatin mixture into mango mixture and stir until all the ice cubes are melted.

Pour mixture into 8 glass cups and chill for at least 3 hours. Garnish with fresh, hand-diced mangoes or lychee halves, lightly sprinkled *li hing* powder and a sprig of mint.

Per serving: *151 calories, 0.18 g fat, 36 g carbohydrates, 1 g dietary fiber, 4 g protein.*

Variation: To thicken the mixture, use unflavored gelatin or kanten *(seaweed-based, vegan jelling agent)*. Ice cubes hasten the chilling process.

Asia/Chinese

Posted on: Wednesday, May 18, 2005
Mangoes marvelous as dessert
Warm, Tropical Mango-Lychee Dessert

My parents had two large Haden mango trees in the back yard. My dad even designed his own mango hook to pick the fruit. Our relatives used to drive all the way from "the country" *(Pearl City and Waikane)* to pick up their mangoes. In good years, even the neighbors would get their share.

I miss our old neighborhood where we used to climb the mango trees and eat the fruit right off the branches. Any *kine*—green, half ripe, and ripe but NOT overripe.

Warm, Tropical Mango-Lychee Dessert
Serves 8

1 1/2 cups mango juice
16 ounces mangoes, sliced
1 cup lychees, shelled, pitted, and halved
2 teaspoons lemon zest
1/4 cup lemon juice
1 cup whole-wheat pastry flour
1 1/2 teaspoon baking soda
1 1/4 cup Vanilla Rice Dream® or low-fat vanilla soy milk
Nonfat cooking spray

    2 teaspoons *li hing* powder
    Mint for garnish

Preheat the oven to 350 degrees.

Combine the mango juice, mangoes, lychees, lemon zest, and lemon juice. Set aside.

Mix the whole-wheat pastry flour and baking soda in a bowl. Add Vanilla Rice® Dream and stir until just moistened.

Spray a 1-quart, round casserole dish with cooking spray. Spread the batter into the casserole dish. Spoon the juice and fruit mixture over the batter. Place in the oven and bake for 40 to 45 minutes or until golden brown. Remove from the oven and allow to cool just to warm. Sprinkle the *li hing* powder over the surface. It tastes great warm with a nonfat whipped topping. Garnish with a sprig of mint.

Per serving: *150 calories, 1.5 g total fat, 0 g saturated fat, 0 mg cholesterol, 300 mg sodium, 34 g carbohydrates, 2 g dietary fiber, 21 g sugar, 2 g protein.*

Asia/Chinese

You will be able to find the fat free condensed milk at any large supermarket. There are no grams of fat in a 1.4-ounce container. You can use fresh mangoes, papayas, pineapple, and other combinations of fruit in season.

Almond Float
Serves 6

2 (0.2-ounce) envelopes unflavored gelatin
3 2/3 cups water
1/3 cup fat free sweetened condensed milk
2 1/2 teaspoons almond extract
2 (11-ounce) cans Mandarin oranges
1 (20-ounce) can lychees
Mint sprigs for garnish

In a medium saucepan, sprinkle gelatin over water and heat until the solids dissolve. Stir in the condensed milk and almond extract. Mix thoroughly and pour into a glass pan and cover. Refrigerate until firm. Cut into 1-inch pieces and top with Mandarin oranges and lychees. Garnish with a sprig of mint.

Per serving: *220 calories, 0.4 g fat, 51 g carbohydrates, 1 g dietary fiber, 4 g protein.*

Asia/Filipino

New Kine Banana Lumpia resembles the original Filipino *lumpia,* but a lighter and "kinder" version. Make sure to get ripe bananas, but not bruised bananas. Serve with 0 gram fat whipped cream in the aerosol can and you'll have friends begging for more. It is so easy to make, you can show them how to create their very own. Maybe they will create a new recipe. You may need to compare nutritional analyses on the phyllo dough packages to find the lowest fat phyllo dough.

New Kine Banana Lumpia
Serves 5

5 (14- x 18-inch) sheets lowest fat phyllo dough
5 ripe bananas *(not apple bananas if you like a sweeter dessert)*
Butter-flavored cooking spray
2 1/2 tablespoons honey
1 1/4 teaspoons apple pie spice

Allow the frozen phyllo dough to thaw in refrigerator overnight. Allow the unopened package to stand at room temperature for 2 hours. *(You won't use the whole package for this recipe.)* Carefully unroll 5 sheets onto a smooth, dry surface. Cover the sheets completely with plastic wrap, then a damp towel and keep the phyllo sheets covered until needed. Do not leave them uncovered for more than a couple of minutes to avoid drying out.

Preheat the oven 400 degrees. For each lumpia, cut one sheet of phyllo dough in half so you have two 9- by 7-inch pieces. Lay one-half sheet on the work surface with a 7-inch end facing you. Spray this half sheet with cooking spray and put the other half on top of it. Spray the top half sheet also.

Peel the bananas one at a time *(to avoid browning)* and roll each banana in 1/2 tablespoon of honey placed on a plate. Sprinkle each banana with about 1/4 teaspoon of apple pie spice.

Place the honeyed and seasoned banana about 1 1/2-inch from the top 7-inch side of the phyllo sheets and wrap the banana burrito style by folding over the top edge first, then fold in the sides, and roll the banana toward you until the end of the phyllo sheets. Seal the lumpia flap with the cooking spray and lay seam side down on the ungreased cookie sheet. Repeat the process four more times and bake for 15 to 20 minutes or until golden brown. Serve warm.

Per serving (without whipped cream): *215 calories, 1 g fat, 51 g carbohydrates, 3 g dietary fiber, 3 g protein.*

Asia/Japanese

I like to use the whole-wheat phyllo dough found in the freezer section of the health food store.

Smart Manju
Serves 6

3/4 cup *tsubushi-an* (prepared red beans)
6 sheets phyllo dough
Butter-flavored cooking spray

Preheat oven to 400 degrees. Lay one phyllo sheet at a time on the work surface, with narrow ends towards you. Keep remaining sheets covered with damp towel to prevent the phyllo from drying out. Spray with cooking spray. Fold sheet in thirds lengthwise. Spray again. Spoon 2 tablespoons of *tsubushi-an* about 1 1/2-inch from the bottom edge of the sheet. Fold up the 1 1/2-inch flap to cover the filling. Fold the lower left-hand corner of phyllo diagonally to right side of dough, covering the filling. Continue folding in flag style until the end of the sheet. Spray both sides of the *manju* and lay on baking sheet. Repeat with remaining phyllo and *tsubushi-an*. Bake for 15 minutes or until golden brown.

Per serving: 106 calories, 1 g fat, 21 g carbohydrates, 1 g dietary fiber, 3 g protein.

Asia/Japanese

Posted on: Wednesday, December 29, 2004

Homemade mochi delightful
Okinawan Sweet Potato Poi Mochi

Some of my fondest memories of New Year's Day are centered around invitations by my friends to celebrate in the Japanese fashion. I loved joining the family in the kitchen to help roll, shape, and fill the *mochi* cakes. Families used to pound the soaked and steamed sweet rice to make the *mochi* "dough"—a rather tricky and potentially dangerous process involving a huge stone mortar and wood pestle with one person pounding and the other turning the ball of *mochi* and feeling for lumps. The silky smooth dough was then filled with a paste of sweetened red adzuki beans.

Okinawan Sweet Potato Poi Mochi
Serves 8

Filling:

1 cup Okinawan sweet potato, cooked and diced
4 tablespoons fresh *poi*
4 tablespoons water

Mix fresh *poi* and water thoroughly. Add sweet potato. For a smooth filling, place all the ingredients for the filling in a food processor and process until smooth. Set aside.

Mochi:

1 1/2 cups *mochiko* sweet rice flour
1 cup sugar
1 1/2 cups water
1 teaspoon vanilla
1 to 2 cups potato starch or cornstarch
Vegetable oil cooking spray

Combine *mochiko* flour and sugar in a medium bowl. Slowly add water, stirring until smooth. Add vanilla and mix well. Spray a 5-cup microwave tube pan with cooking spray. Pour batter into greased pan. Cover with plastic wrap. Microwave on high for 10 minutes, rotating pan several times during cooking. Don't cook the *mochi* too long or you won't be able to form it into cakes.

Turn out into a plate dusted with potato starch. Cool. Cut into 3-inch rounds and roll flat with a rolling pin dusted with potato starch. Place 3 to 4 tablespoons of filling into the middle of the flattened round. Gather up the sides to the middle of the round and pinch to seal. Smooth out any rough edges. Roll rounds in potato starch.

Per serving: *378 calories, 0.2 g fat, 91 g carbohydrates, 3 g dietary fiber, 3 g protein.*

Asia/Thai

Posted on: Wednesday, April 6, 2005

Thai-style lite tapioca pudding
Thai Tapioca Pudding

This is one of the easiest desserts to make. All you need is a double boiler. If you don't have one, improvise by setting a smaller pot inside a larger one, or nesting a heat-proof bowl inside a pot.

Fill the outer part with water and bring to a simmer. Place the milk in the smaller pot or bowl and heat until scalded. Scalding is different from boiling: you heat the milk over medium-high heat and watch for tiny bubbles that form around the edge of the pan. Then it's ready to use.

In this case, you add the tapioca—a perfect time to start singing Don Ho's famous song. No fo'get to keep one eye on the pot and stir every so often. It only takes 15 minutes to cook.

Thai Tapioca Pudding
Serves 8

2 cups light coconut milk
2 cups light soy milk
1/2 cup tapioca pearls
1/2 cup sugar or 5 tablespoons fructose
1 tablespoon vanilla extract

In the top of a double boiler, combine the coconut and soy milks. On the bottom, add about 1 1/2 cups of water and bring to a rolling boil. Heat the milk until scalded. Add the tapioca and cook, stirring constantly to prevent the pearls from sticking to the bottom of the pan.

Cook this mixture until the tapioca is clear in color *(about 10 minutes)*. Add the sugar or fructose and cook for 5 minutes longer. Cool in the pot by emptying the hot water out of the lower pot and replacing it with cold water. Stir in vanilla. Cool for about 20 minutes. Transfer the pudding to individual-serving glass cups. Serve warm or chilled. Garnish with a sprig of mint or strawberry leaf.

Per serving: *149 calories, 3 g fat, 29 g carbohydrates, 0 g dietary fiber; 60 mg sodium, 2 g protein.*

Variations: To enjoy this with a Thai curry, try adding red or black-eyed beans to the pudding, and you can duplicate what they sell in Chinatown without all the fat and white sugar. It makes a wonderful pudding base for fresh fruits such as papayas, mangoes, and lychees. I served it with canned mandarin oranges for a book signing session. It was a hit.

Asia/Thai

Posted on: Wednesday, August 9, 2006

Making most out of mango
Sweet Brown Sticky Rice with Mango-Lychee

Sweet brown rice is one of the glutinous rices of Thailand. It is grown and cultivated on the high northern plains of the country. Often referred to as sticky rice, it is the staple of northern and northeastern Thailand. Unlike the white rice grown in the central lowlands, glutinous brown rice requires less water for cooking.

Sticky rice is chewier in consistency and sweeter than regular rice. The sticky quality comes from two different substances in the rice kernels: *amylase* and *amylopectin*. A larger amount of *amylopectin* is responsible for the stickiness.

Sweet Brown Sticky Rice with Mango-Lychee

Serves 3

- 1 cup sweet brown rice, rinsed and immersed in water to cover overnight
- 2 cups water
- 3 ripe mangoes, chilled, peeled, and sliced into crescent shapes
- 12 lychees, fresh or canned, drained
- 2 to 3 tablespoons fat-free sweetened condensed milk
- 1/2 teaspoon coconut extract

Garnish:

1 to 3 teaspoons sesame seeds, toasted *(optional)*
3 sprigs of mint

Cook the rice in a rice cooker following the manufacturer's directions or bring water and rice, uncovered, to a boil. Turn heat down to low, cover, and steam until tender. After the rice has been cooked, fill a dry measuring cup with one cup of hot rice and press to form a cup-shaped ball. Place the slices of mango and lychee on top of the rice. Mix the condensed milk with the coconut extract and pour over the fruit. Sprinkle each serving with toasted sesame seeds and a sprig of mint. Serve warm.

Per serving: *470 calories, 5 g fat, 1.5 g saturated fat, 5 mg cholesterol, 35 mg sodium, 105 g carbohydrate, 7 g dietary fiber, 47 g sugar, 8 g protein.*

Europe/French

Posted on: Wednesday, May 2, 2007
Make a meal at home on mom's day
Chocolate Mousse Pie

For the chocolate mousse pie below, I use Madhavi Organic Agave Nectar *(found at the health food store)* or you can use organic honey.

Chocolate Mousse Pie
Serves 8

- 2 (12-3-ounce) boxes Mori-Nu Silken Lite Extra Firm Tofu
- 3/4 cup honey or honey replacer
- 3 teaspoons of vanilla or amaretto extract
- 1/2 cup cocoa powder
- 1 (9-inch) graham cracker pie crust
- 1 to 2 cups Cool Whip® Free *(the nonfat kind)*
- Strawberries or raspberries *(optional)*

Place tofu in a food processor and blend until smooth. Add the honey and blend again. Add the cocoa powder and extract, and blend again. Pour into graham cracker crust, cover, and refrigerate. Top it off with Cool Whip® Free and strawberries or raspberries.

Per serving: *350 calories, 11 g fat, 2.5 g saturated fat, 0 mg cholesterol, 220 mg sodium, 57 g carbohydrate, 2 g dietary fiber, 41 g sugar, 9 g protein.*

Global Light Cuisine ∞ Carol Devenot

Hawaii Local Favorite

Posted on: Wednesday, August 10, 2005

Okinawan sweet potato pie goes lite

Okinawan Sweet Potato Pie

This pie is fairly simple to make. You can start the sweet potatoes steaming and make the crust while they cook. Make sure you completely cool the crust before adding the filling, otherwise you will have a soggy layer.

For the final presentation, you could sprinkle a few slivered almonds on the top and add a sprig of mint and a purple orchid. It looks so beautiful and tastes so ʻono. People will be asking you to bake one for them. I have already received several orders.

Okinawan Sweet Potato Pie
Serves 8

Crust:

1 cup grape nuts® cereal *(wheat and barley nuggets)*
2 tablespoons Splenda® or other sweetener
1/8 teaspoon almond extract
3 tablespoons Egg Beaters®
Nonfat cooking spray

Filling:

1 tablespoon Smart Beat® *(low-fat margarine)*
1/2 cup Splenda®
1/2 cup Egg Beaters®

1/2 cup nonfat evaporated milk
2 cups Okinawan sweet potato, peeled,
    cooked, and mashed
1 teaspoon vanilla extract
1/2 teaspoon salt
1/2 teaspoon cinnamon

Haupia:

1 cup Splenda®
6 tablespoon cornstarch
2 cups 1% milk
4 teaspoons coconut extract

Preheat oven to 350 degrees. Combine cereal, sweetener, and almond extract in a small bowl and mix well. Stir in the Egg Beaters®. Coat a 9-inch pie pan with non-stick cooking spray and use the back of the spoon to press the crust mixture across the bottom and sides of the pan to form an even crust. Bake at 350 degrees for 12 to 14 minutes or until the edges are lightly browned. Set aside to cool.

In a bowl, beat the margarine and Splenda® until lightened and smooth-textured. Add Egg Beaters® and nonfat evaporated milk and mix. Add mashed sweet potato, vanilla, salt, and cinnamon and mix well. Pour into baked crust and bake fo r 40 minutes. Cool completely before adding the *haupia* topping.

To make *haupia* topping, in a medium mixing bowl, thoroughly mix the Splenda®, cornstarch, milk, and coconut extract. Place in a medium saucepan and stir constantly until the mixture thickens. Pour this mixture over the sweet potato filling and chill long enough to cool the *haupia*.

Per serving: *230 calories, 4 g fat, 1 g saturated fat, 5 mg cholesterol, 260 mg sodium, 39 g carbohydrates, 3 g dietary fiber, 12 g sugar, 8 g protein.*

Note: The Okinawan sweet potato is a small sweet potato originally from Okinawa, Japan, that has a light beige skin and shaped like a sweet potato. When cooked the skin turns dark brown and the inside is a deep, rich, eggplant purple color.

Desserts

Hawaii Local Favorite

Posted on: Wednesday, December 14, 2005
Haven't tried breadfruit yet? Maybe it's time you did
Fo' Real Bread Pudding

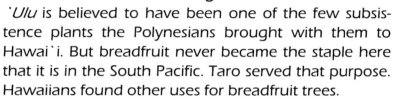

'*Ulu* is believed to have been one of the few subsistence plants the Polynesians brought with them to Hawai`i. But breadfruit never became the staple here that it is in the South Pacific. Taro served that purpose. Hawaiians found other uses for breadfruit trees.

A member of the fig family, breadfruit *(Artocarpis altilis)* is believed to have originated on Java. From there, voyagers took it to Malaysia, then on to the Marquesas, from where it spread to the rest of Polynesia. '*Ulu's* "super food" reputation spread throughout the British colonies by the 18th century,

Here's an interesting side note: In 1787 Captain William Bligh and his Bounty set sail to Tahiti and gathered more than a thousand breadfruit starter plants to bring back to the West Indies. These plants required more than their fair share of the water, and Bligh reduced the ration for his crew. His men set Bligh, a few loyalists, and the breadfruit plants adrift in a small boat, but Bligh and his men survived, and the rest is history.

Fo' Real Bread Pudding
Serves 8

1 (large) ripe breadfruit *(to yield 4 cups of fleshy fruit)*
1 cup ripe apple bananas, mashed
1/4 cup walnuts, chopped

1/2 cup dates, chopped
1 tablespoon baking soda
2 to 3 teaspoons apple pie spice
1 teaspoon sea salt
Nonstick cooking spray

Preheat the oven to 350 degrees. Cut the breadfruit open lengthwise and cut out the seeds and sponge-like flesh. Spoon the ripe flesh away from the skin, place in a bowl and mash with a potato masher. Blend in the remaining ingredients. Pour into an 8-inch square baking pan sprayed with nonstick cooking spray. Bake for about 40 minutes or until the top is brown.

Serve warm with light vanilla yogurt.

Per serving (without yogurt): *190 calories, 3.5 g total fat, 0 g saturated fat, 0 mg cholesterol, 760 mg sodium, 43 g carbohydrate, 7 g dietary fiber, 15 g sugar, 2 g protein.*

254   Desserts

Mainland U.S. Favorite

Posted on: Wednesday, October 6, 2004

Dates, brown sugar, applesauce sweeten nut bread

Date with a Nut Bread

I tried the following date nut bread recipe the other day. I have to admit I would have loved more nuts, but this is nutty enough if you are on a low-fat diet.

Nuts are nutritious but loaded with calories, so a few take you a long way. The dates, applesauce, and brown sugar give the bread natural sweetness and moisture. Canola oil helps with the tenderness. Instead of whole eggs, use egg whites; the combination of baking soda and beaten whites causes the bread to rise. Using whole-wheat pastry flour also lightens the bread.

Date with a Nut Bread

Serves 12

1/2 cup walnuts, chopped
1 cup dates, chopped
1 1/2 teaspoons baking soda
1/2 teaspoon salt
3 tablespoons canola oil
1 cup applesauce
3 egg whites, beaten
1 teaspoon vanilla
3/4 cup brown sugar or honey
1 1/2 cups whole-wheat pastry flour

In a medium-size mixing bowl, combine walnuts, dates, baking soda, salt, oil, and applesauce. Allow mixture to stand for 20 minutes. Preheat the oven to 350 degrees. Grease a 9- by 5-inch loaf pan or spray with nonstick oil spray. Beat together eggs, vanilla, sugar, and flour. Add date mixture, mixing until just blended. Bake for 1 hour. Test for doneness by plunging a toothpick or bamboo skewer into the center of the loaf. The bread is done if the tester emerges clean, with no batter clinging to it.

Per serving: *220 calories, 7 g fat, 38 g carbohydrates, 3 g dietary fiber, 270 mg sodium, 5 g protein.*

Mainland U.S. Favorite

Posted on: Wednesday, May 4, 2005

Making muffins for Mom

Banana Muffins for Mom

One of the most precious memories I have is of the Mother's Day when my 6-year-old son surprised me with breakfast in bed. I woke up to the most beautiful breakfast a mother could dream of. On his modest, little tray were some scrambled eggs, burnt toast with butter and jelly, instant coffee, and orange juice. He couldn't find any flowers in the yard, so he picked some weeds and wildflowers and put them in a little bud vase. I am still touched by this memory, though he's grown up now.

Why not create this same magic and make Mom breakfast, but instead of burnt toast try my Banana Muffins for Mom?

Banana Muffins for Mom

Serves 10 to 12

- 3/4 cup whole-wheat flour or whole-wheat pastry flour
- 1/2 cup all-purpose flour
- 2 teaspoons non-aluminum baking powder
- 1/8 teaspoon salt
- 1 1/4 teaspoon pumpkin pie spice
- 1/2 cup date sugar
- 1/4 cup Smart Balance™ margarine
- 2 egg whites, beaten
- 1/2 cup low-fat soy milk
- Grated rind of 1 (medium) orange

1 ripe banana
1/4 cup rolled oats *(regular oats)*
1/4 cup walnuts, chopped
Nonfat cooking spray

Preheat the oven to 400 degrees. Spray the muffin pans with nonfat cooking spray.

In a mixing bowl, sift together whole-wheat and all-purpose flours, baking powder, salt and spice. Stir in the sugar. Microwave the margarine in a mixing bowl for a few seconds. Cool margarine slightly and then beat in egg whites, soy milk, and grated orange rind.

Carefully fold in the dry ingredients. Mash the banana with a fork and add to the mixture. Be careful not to overmix. Spoon the batter into the muffin tins and fill each to about three-fourths to the top.

Combine the rolled oats and walnuts. Sprinkle a little of the mixture over each muffin and bake for 20 minutes or until the muffins are golden.

Check for doneness by inserting a toothpick through the center of a muffin. If the toothpick comes out clean, transfer muffins to a wire rack. Serve warm or cold.

Per serving: 127 calories, 5 g fat, 20 g carbohydrates, 1.5 g dietary fiber, 107 mg sodium, 3 g protein.

Mainland U.S. Favorite

Posted on: Wednesday, December 1, 2004

Oatcakes offer a healthy yet festive baked holiday treat

Yummy Rummy Oatcakes

After going through a few batches of dog biscuits and hockey pucks, I finally came up with an oatcake recipe that is just what I am looking for—not too large, not too gummy, crispy on the outside, moist and dense on the inside.

Yummy Rummy Oatcakes
Serves 12

1/2 cup cranberries, soaked in rum
1/2 cup raisins, soaked in rum
1/3 cup rum
2 1/2 cups whole-wheat pastry flour
2 cups rolled oats *(regular oatmeal)*
1 cup date sugar
1 teaspoon salt
1 tablespoon baking powder
1/2 teaspoon non-aluminum baking soda
1 tablespoon of apple pie seasoning
8 tablespoons of Smart Balance™ Light, very cold
1 cup orange juice
1 teaspoon real vanilla
1/2 cup walnuts, coarsely chopped
1/4 cup flax seed, ground
2 egg whites, stiffly beaten

4 tablespoons soy milk for topping
2 tablespoons date sugar for topping

Place the cranberries and raisins in a bowl and cover with the rum. Line a cookie sheet with parchment paper. Heat the oven to 425 degrees.

In a food processor, mix flour, rolled oats *(regular oatmeal)*, date sugar, salt, baking powder, baking soda, and apple pie seasoning. Cut in the Smart Balance™ to make a mealy mixture. Place orange juice and vanilla in a bowl, stir, and add this to the flour mixture. Add the soaked cranberries and raisins, walnuts, and flax seed. Fold in the stiffly beaten egg whites.

Turn out onto a lightly floured board and knead for a few minutes. Roll out or pat to a thickness of 1/2-inch. Use a 2 3/4-inch diameter biscuit cutter and cut into 12 rounds. Place on lined cookie sheet, brush with 3 to 4 tablespoons soy milk; and sprinkle with 1 to 2 tablespoons of date sugar. Bake 18 to 20 minutes, until browned.

Per serving: *289 calories, 6 g fat, 52 g carbohydrates, 6 g dietary fiber, 247 mg sodium, 8 g protein.*

Variations: For that Christmas magic, plump the cranberries and raisins soaked briefly in just enough rum to cover. Add more apple pie spice if you like. Walnuts and flax seed add crunch. To release the healthful flax seed oils, grind up the seeds using a mortar and pestle. Give these away for presents at Christmastime, and your family and friends will definitely have a *Mele Kalikimaka!*

260   Desserts

Mainland U.S. Favorite

Posted on: Wednesday, October 19, 2005

Pumpkin bars with fat carved out

Easy As 1-2-3 Pumpkin Bars

Every Halloween, I look forward to seeing the Great Pumpkin in our neighbor's front yard. The sight reminds me of the pumpkin bars I make this time of year, and the anticipation of the upcoming holidays.

I can already smell the spices: cinnamon, ginger, nutmeg, and allspice. I used unbleached flour for this recipe because I thought it would be less heavy than whole wheat. Unbleached flour is a slightly off-white color and has not been put through a chemical whitening process. Otherwise, there's little difference in bleached and unbleached flour, nutritionally or in how it's used.

Easy as 1-2-3 Pumpkin Bars

Serves 24

Baker's Joy® nonstick spray
41/2 cups unbleached flour
2 tablespoons baking soda
1 teaspoon salt
11/2 tablespoons pumpkin pie spice
1 (30-ounce) can pumpkin *(about 31/4 cups)*
2/3 cup dates, chopped
1/4 cup pecans or walnuts, chopped
21/2 cups fructose
1 tablespoon vanilla
5 teaspoons egg replacer*, or 6 egg whites,
    or 3/4 cup Egg Beaters®
5 tablespoons water

Global Light Cuisine ∞ Carol Devenot

Preheat the oven to 350 degrees. Spray the 13- by 9-inch pan with Baker's Joy® *(nonstick spray that contains flour)*. Place the flour, baking soda, salt, and pumpkin pie spice in a large mixing bowl and set aside.

Combine the pumpkin, dates, walnuts, fructose, and vanilla in another bowl. In a small bowl, whisk together egg replacer, egg whites, or Egg Beaters® and water until foamy. Fold the egg foam into the pumpkin mixture, then add the flour mixture. Spread in prepared pan.

Bake for 35 minutes or until toothpick comes out clean. Allow to cool slightly, then cut into bars. This recipe is best when served warm. You can add whipped topping or drizzle with some apricot or peach fruit spread. Makes 24 bars.

Per serving: *220 calories, 1.5 g total fat, 0 g saturated fat, 0 g cholesterol, 480 mg sodium, 50 g carbohydrate, less than 1 g dietary fiber, 25 g sugar, 3 g protein.*

* See Glossary for Egg Replacer information.

262   Desserts

Mainland U.S. Favorite

Posted on: Wednesday, October 17, 2007

Enjoy recipe for sweet bonding time with child

Raspberry and Chocolate Bars

A few weeks ago, we celebrated Aloha Festivals, and now we are getting ready for Halloween. It seems life is accelerating so rapidly. After we put the costumes away, it will be time for Thanksgiving and Christmas. For many of us, the holidays have a special place in our memories. I can still recall how much fun my mother and I would have when we baked for the holidays. My mother's butter cake, date bars, and fruit-cake were da best! Recently, I read an article in the newspaper about children not having enough "down time." They're involved in sports, music lessons, and other activities after school. Then they have to wade through tons of homework. There is barely time for families to do things together.

Raspberry and Chocolate Bars

Serves 16

Nonstick cooking spray
1/2 cup unbleached all-purpose flour
1/2 cup whole-wheat flour
1 cup quick cooking oats
1/2 teaspoon baking soda
1/2 teaspoon salt
1/3 cup turbinado sugar
6 tablespoons butter or Smart Balance™

1/2 cup chocolate chips or 1/4 to 1/3 cup dark chocolate chunks

5 to 10 ounces *(half to full jar)* raspberry all fruit preserves

Heat oven to 375 degrees. Spray an 8-inch square baking pan with nonstick cooking spray.

In a small mixing bowl, whisk together flours, oats, baking soda, and salt; set aside. In a medium bowl, combine sugar and butter and beat with an electric mixer at medium speed. Gradually add the flour mixture to the butter mixture and blend well. Remove 3/4 cup dough to a small bowl and stir in chocolate chips or chunks. Set aside.

Press the remaining dough into the sprayed baking pan and spread the all fruit preserves evenly over the surface. Crumble the chocolate chip mixture over the fruit. Bake at 375 degrees for 30 minutes or until golden brown. Cool bars completely on a wire rack. Makes 16 bars.

Per serving: *160 calories, 7 g fat, 4 g saturated fat, 10 mg cholesterol, 175 mg sodium, 22 g carbohydrate, 2 g dietary fiber, 12 g sugar, 2 g protein.*

Desserts

Mainland U.S. Favorite

Posted on: Wednesday, January 25, 2006

Buttery oatmeal cookies to feel good about

Little-Bit-Butter Oatmeal Cookies

Rapadura is made from organically grown sugar cane in South America. Harvesting is by hand without burning the dry leaves first. *Rapadura* is unrefined; the sugar cane is squeezed, dried and ground, which retains its natural vitamins and minerals. It is high in magnesium, calcium, iron, silicon, and manganese and a perfect sweetener for baking. Substitute one cup of *rapadura* for one cup of white sugar. Store in a moisture-free environment and it will keep indefinitely.

Little-Bit-Butter Oatmeal Cookies

Makes 20 Cookies

3/4 cup unbleached flour
1/4 cup whole-wheat flour
1/2 teaspoon baking soda
2 teaspoons apple pie spice
1/8 teaspoon cloves
1/2 teaspoon grated whole nutmeg
2/3 cup rolled oats *(regular oats)*
3/4 cup dried cranberries
2/3 cup brown sugar or *rapadura*, packed
5 tablespoons butter, softened
1 teaspoon pure vanilla extract
6 tablespoons egg whites

Global Light Cuisine ∞ Carol Devenot

1/4 cup walnuts, chopped *(optional)*
Parchment paper or nonfat cooking spray

Heat the oven to 350 degrees. In a large bowl, mix the flours with baking soda, apple pie spice, cloves, nutmeg, rolled oats, and cranberries. In a second bowl, using a mixer at medium speed, beat together the sugar, butter, and vanilla until light and fluffy.

Add the egg whites and beat well. Stir in the mixed dry ingredients. Drop by a level tablespoon each, 3 inches apart, onto the parchment-papered or coated baking sheet. Press a walnut pieces on the top of each cookie.

Bake for 12 minutes or until crisp. Remove from baking sheet and cool on wire racks.

Per cookie (without nuts): *100 calories, 4.5 g fat, 2 g saturated fat, 10 mg cholesterol, 70 mg sodium, 17 g carbohydrate, 2 g dietary fiber, 10 g sugar, 2 g protein.*

Per cookie (with nuts): *110 calories, 3.5 g fat, 2 g saturated fat, 10 mg cholesterol, 70 mg sodium, 17 g carbohydrate, 2 g dietary fiber, 10 g sugar, 2 g protein.*

Mainland U.S. Favorite

Posted on: Wednesday, April 4, 2007

Something sweet for Easter that's heart healthy

Soy Chocolate Fantasy

Fortunately, a month ago I attended Kapi`olani Community College cooking classes where vegetarian chef Alyssa Moreau taught me how to make Soy Chocolate Fantasy.

I attended two Moreau classes—*Eating Heart Healthy* and *The Joy of Soy*. The class packet included the latest information on controlling cholesterol, healthy oils, *acai* and pomegranate juices, coconut milk, and genetically modified foods.

Moreau is now a personal chef who cooks for four or five families who have health concerns. Each week, she goes to their homes to cook several different dishes. Moreau is now a personal chef who cooks for four or five families who have health concerns. Each week, she goes to their homes to cook several different dishes. Her rules of thumb for any recipe are that it should be nutritious and tasty and would she eat it.

Soy Chocolate Fantasy
Serves 2 to 4

1 (12.3-ounce) box Mori-Nu Silken Tofu
   (firm or extra firm)
2 tablespoons reduced-fat peanut butter
1/4 cup honey
1 teaspoon vanilla

1 (5-inch) frozen banana, peeled and cut
   into chunks
1/4 cup chocolate chips
2 tablespoons almonds, sliced and toasted

Blend the tofu, peanut butter, honey, and vanilla until smooth. Fold in the banana and chocolate chips and top with sliced almonds. Cover and refrigerate for one hour.

Serve as is, with oatmeal cookies, or double the recipe and place the chocolate fantasy in a graham cracker crust.

Per serving (4 servings): *300 calories, 12 g fat, 3.5 g saturated fat, 0 mg cholesterol, 100 mg sodium, 40 g carbohydrate, 3 g dietary fiber, 32 g sugar, 11 g protein.*

Mainland U.S. Favorite

Posted on: Wednesday, February 9, 2005

Crispy treat with berry medley great for Valentine's Day

I Love you Berry, Berry Much Crisp

Costco has the perfect product to use in this delicious crisp, a frozen mixture called "Nature's Three Berries." The three berries are raspberries, blueberries, and marionberries *(similar to a blackberry, but sweeter and with fewer seeds)*. It's so convenient because you can also use them in pies and smoothies. You don't have to wait to defrost the berries. Place them on the pie plate and microwave them at defrost setting *(50 percent power)* for about 6 minutes. Berries are so good for you and loaded with antioxidants.

I Love You Berry, Berry, Berry Much Crisp

Serves 6

Filling:

5 cups fresh or frozen berries *(raspberries, blueberries, boysenberries, blackberries, marion berries, or a mixture of these)*
1/8 cup Splenda®
3 tablespoons whole-wheat pastry flour

Topping:

1/2 cup whole-wheat pastry flour

Global Light Cuisine ∞ Carol Devenot

- 6 tablespoons rolled oats
- 1/2 cup Splenda® granular
- 1 teaspoon cinnamon
- 4 tablespoons Light Smart Balance™ margarine

Heat oven to 350 degrees.

Lightly coat a 9-inch pie pan with nonstick cooking spray. Spread the berries in the pie pan and mix them with Splenda® and 3 tablespoons of flour.

Mix together the flour, oats, Splenda®, and cinnamon in a medium-size mixing bowl. Cut in the margarine with a pastry blender or two knives, scissors fashion, until mixture resembles fine crumbs. Sprinkle topping over berries. Bake for 40 to 45 minutes or until the berries bubble. Serve warm with a whipped or frozen nondairy topping.

Per serving: *130 calories, 5 g fat, 22 g carbohydrates, 5 g dietary fiber, 61 mg sodium, 2 g protein.*

Desserts

Mainland U.S. Favorite

Posted on: Wednesday, June 15, 2005

Go flakier and lighter with phyllo

Crispy Apricot Turnovers

In place of puff pastry, I like to use phyllo *(or filo/fillo, pronounced FEE-low)*, a light, paper-thin pastry dough. The Athens Fillo Dough® brand produces the best quality turnover. Phyllo has virtually no fat. It contains just a little vegetable shortening to bind the dough. When you substitute phyllo for puff pastry, it produces a lighter, flakier product. You can find this dough in long, narrow boxes in the freezer section of most large grocery and health food stores.

Phyllo means leaf in Greek, indicating it's as thin and delicate as a leaf. This dough, now made by rolling machines, was once hand rolled so thin that a ball of dough the size of a fist could be made to cover a card table. It is used throughout the Mediterranean world. In eastern Europe, phyllo has been used for fruit strudels for centuries. Today it is used in fine restaurants and homes worldwide to produce a variety of appetizers, entrees, and desserts.

Crispy Apricot Turnovers
Serves 6

3/4 cup 100% real fruit apricot jam or preserves
6 (1.25-ounce) sheets whole-wheat phyllo
Butter-flavored cooking oil spray

Thaw phyllo and peel off desired number of sheets *(with perhaps one extra in case of a tear)*. Place the sheets between two damp towels to prevent drying out.

Heat oven to 400 degrees.

Lay one phyllo sheet down at a time on the work surface, with narrow ends toward you. Spray with butter-flavored cooking spray. Fold sheet in thirds lengthwise. Spray again. Spoon 2 tablespoons of real fruit jam about 1 1/2 inches from the bottom edge of the sheet. Fold the lower left-hand corner of phyllo diagonally to right side of dough, covering the filling. Continue folding in flag style until the end of the sheet. Spray both sides of the turnover and lay on baking sheet. Repeat the process with remaining phyllo sheets and real fruit jam or preserves. Bake for 15 minutes or until golden brown.

Per serving: *250 calories, 7 g fat, 0.5 g saturated fat, 0 mg cholesterol, 190 mg sodium, 45 g carbohydrates, less than 1 g dietary fiber, 42 g sugar, 3 g protein.*

Mainland U.S. Favorite

Posted on: Wednesday, December 12, 2007
Sweeten cheesecake with agave
Chocolate Swirled Cheesecake

Personal chef Alyssa Moreau and I had a great time testing the following recipe.

We made a yogurt cheese—a healthier alternative to cream cheese and easy to make by allowing the whey *(liquid)* to drain from yogurt.

We made the graham cracker crust from scratch, but you can buy the ready-made crust if you like, and you can use a higher fiber graham cereal instead to boost nutritional value. For the filling, we combined the yogurt cheese, low-fat cream cheese, a little flour for thickening and agave for sweetening.

Agave *(uh-GAH-vee)*, made from nectar contained in certain cactus leaves, has become one of my favorite sweeteners. The native inhabitants of Mexico regarded this plant as sacred. They believed that the nectar would purify their body and soul. Spaniards fermented the nectar and created a drink we now know as tequila.

Agave has a very low glycemic index level, meaning it is taken up by the body slowly. The syrup is about 90 percent fructose, and no chemicals are used in processing. Agave is sold as "syrup" or "nectar" in health food stores. Honey, brown rice syrup, and maple syrup are substitutes, though all taste a bit different.

Global Light Cuisine ∞ Carol Devenot   273

Chocolate Swirled Cheesecake
Serves 8

Crust:

2 cups graham crackers or 1 package oat bran grahams

2 tablespoons nonhydrogenated margarine *(Earth Balance®, available at health food store)* or whipped butter

3 tablespoons low-fat yogurt

1 tablespoon maple syrup

Nonstick cooking spray

Filling:

1/2 cup yogurt cheese *(1 cup' low-fat, plain yogurt with natural cultures)*

1 cup nonfat cream cheese

2 tablespoons all-purpose flour

1/3 cup agave or 1/4 cup honey

1 teaspoon vanilla

1/2 cup dark chocolate, melted in microwave

Topping:

1 ounce organically-grown frozen raspberries or strawberries

4 to 5 tablespoons agave sweetener

Pinch of sea salt

1/2 tablespoon arrowroot whisked together with 2 tablespoons water

To make yogurt cheese, place 1 cup of low-fat plain yogurt *(made with natural cultures)* in a cheesecloth-lined colander or funnel-shaped strainer or yogurt-maker basket. Allow to drain one-half hour at room temperature or cover and put in refrigerator overnight. Set aside.

Preheat oven to 350 degrees. Place crust ingredients in food processor and process until it holds together when pressed between your fingertips. Spray an 8-inch pie pan and press the processed mixture against the bottom and sides of the pie pan. Bake 15 minutes and cool.

Place the yogurt cheese, cream cheese, flour, agave, and vanilla in the food processor and process until well blended and smooth. Pour a thin layer of chocolate on the bottom of the cooled pie crust. Pour the yogurt mixture into cooled pie crust and, using a chopstick, stir carefully, swirling the chocolate up into the yogurt until it's attractive. Drizzle 1 to 2 tablespoons of chocolate on the surface of the filling and swirl again with chopstick. Place a piece of aluminum foil over the pie to prevent the crust from burning and bake at 350 degrees for 20 minutes or until firm in the center.

In a saucepan, heat together the berries, agave, salt, and arrowroot mixture. Spoon over cooled cheesecake and chill.

Per serving: *325 calories, 9 g fat, 4.5 g saturated fat, 10 mg cholesterol, 330 mg sodium, 53 g carbohydrate, 2 g dietary fiber, 40 g sugar, 90 g protein.*

Global Light Cuisine ∞ Carol Devenot

Mainland U.S. Favorite

Frozen bananas are creamy in texture. Other fruits can be frozen and puréed the same way. Experiment with mango, pineapple, and other fruits for interesting flavors and textures.

Banana Almond Cream
Serves 2

1 (6- to 7-inch) banana, frozen
1/2 to 3/4 cup almond milk
2 tablespoons grape nuts® cereal
   (wheat and barley nuggets)
2 tablespoons raisins
Mint sprigs

In a food processor, using the S blade, purée the frozen bananas. Add the almond milk as needed to soften the mixture. Purée to a "soft serve" texture. Place the banana almond cream in individual serving glasses and garnish with cereal and raisins. Top with a sprig of mint. Serve immediately.

Per serving: *150 calories, 2 g fat, 31 g carbohydrates, 2 g dietary fiber, 3 g protein.*

South Pacific/Hawaiian

A serving would be 1 to 2 *luau*-portion squares *(about 2- x 2-inch)*. I recommend using "light" coconut milk, which can be found in local markets and Chinatown, because it will reduce the number of calories and fat grams. For a gourmet touch, thaw out some frozen raspberries and heat them with pure maple syrup to taste. Drizzle it over the Haupia squares and garnish with a sprig of mint.

Jan's Haupia
(coconut pudding)
Serves 12 to 13

6 tablespoons cornstarch
3/4 cup water
1 (13.5-ounce) can light coconut milk
1/2 cup sugar

Combine the cornstarch and water. In a medium saucepan, stir together the coconut milk and sugar, and bring to a gentle boil. Add the cornstarch-water mixture and bring this to a boil, stirring constantly. Cook until thick. Pour pudding into an 8-inch square pan and chill until firm. Yields 25 squares.

Per serving (2 squares): *76 calories, 2 g fat, 16 g carbohydrates, 0 g dietary fiber, 0.4 g protein.*

Snacks and Beverages

278

Global Light Cuisine ∞ Carol Devenot

Asia/Chinese

Posted on: Wednesday, December 13, 2006

Fruit mui: Make your own for favorite holiday gifts

My Favorite Fruit Mui

The moment I tasted my friend Lavina Chow's fruit *mui*, I knew it would be a great recipe for holiday gift giving. The flavor reminded me of the days when my mom and I would go to the crack seed store to buy our favorite snacks. The rows of apothecary jars held an amazing assortment such as *li hing mui*, cherry seeds, and pickled mangoes. But I selected only my favorites, because it was expensive.

My Favorite Fruit Mui

Makes 1 gallon

2 1/2 cups dried apricots
4 1/2 cups dried cherries
4 cups dried mangoes
3 1/2 cups prunes
2 (1.25-ounce) packages seedless *li hing mui*
2 tablespoons *li hing* ginger, minced
2 cups honey
1 1/2 cups fresh lemon juice
3 tablespoons whiskey
3 tablespoons Hawaiian salt
1 tablespoon Chinese Five Spice seasoning
1 to 2 teaspoons ground cloves

Snacks and Beverages

In a large mixing bowl, mix together apricots, cherries, mangoes, and prunes. In another bowl, combine the remaining ingredients and stir thoroughly. Place both mixtures in a gallon jar and mix. Allow to season for at least two days, turning the jar occasionally. Wash smaller jars in hot, soapy water. Rinse with hot water. Transfer fruit *mui* to smaller jars.

Per serving (1 tablespoon): *35 calories, 0 g fat, 0 g saturated fat, 0 mg cholesterol, 85 mg sodium, 8 g carbohydrate, 1 g dietary fiber, 7 g sugar, 0 g protein.*

Asia/Japanese

Musubi is the local version of a Japanese snack that is an approximately 4- by 2 1/2- by 2-inch block of white rice with a slice of Spam® cooked in *soy sauce* and sugar and wrapped around the middle with a strip of *nori* seaweed to hold it all together. Spam® is high in fat and salt and not recommended. An expedient and convenient way to assemble this snack is to use a *musubi* maker *(a preformed, rectangular-shaped "rice ball" maker that is used to press the rice into a rectangular form)*.

"Make Her" Musubi
Serves 2

1 cup Hapa Rice *(page 101)*, cooked
6 *umeboshi* plums, deseeded, or pickled ginger
2 slices Japanese cucumber, sliced 1/4-inch thick
2 slices carrot, sliced 1/4-inch thick
1 sheet *nori (seaweed)*
Musubi maker

Musubi Maker

Cook rice following directions on the package and let cool. Cut the sheet of *nori* to the width of the *musubi* maker. Lay on a flat surface and place the bottom of the *musubi* maker on the sheet of nori. Place half the rice in the square of the *musubi* maker. Press the rice down with the top of the *musubi* maker. Layer *umeboshi* plums, cucumber, and carrot on the rice. Add a layer of rice to the top of the *musubi* maker and place the top of the maker on the rice and press firmly. Carefully remove the bottom of the *musubi* maker and fold the *nori* over the top to finish your *musubi*.

Per serving: *100 calories, 0.5 g fat, 21 g carbohydrates, 1 g dietary fiber, 2 g protein.*

Variations: You can substitute the *umeboshi* plums *(or pickled ginger)* with teriyaki tuna, but make sure you use water-packed tuna. Place some drained tuna in a small frying pan and add a little soy sauce and brown rice syrup to sweeten. Experiment with other fillings. Be creative when you make her *musubi*.

Hawaii Local Favorite

When you feel like you are "going bananas," why not go with the flow, and make a snack that will soothe your nerves. Try this Banana Wrap. My favorite banana is Hawai`i's own apple banana. The little bit of tartness of this fruit offsets the super sweetness of the peanut butter and honey. This wrap is also great paired with any fruit smoothie.

Banana Wrap
Serves 1

1 whole-wheat tortilla
1/2 to 1 tablespoon peanut butter
1/2 to 1 tablespoon honey
1 banana

Microwave the tortilla for 20 seconds. Spread the peanut butter over the surface of the tortilla and drizzle the peanut butter with honey. Place the banana on the tortilla and roll it up. Eat immediately, biting on each side of the roll so that the banana does not slide out.

Per serving: *360 calories, 9 g total fat, 2 g saturated fat, 0 mg cholesterol, 300 mg sodium, 73 g carbohydrate, 7 g dietary fiber, 33 g sugar, 9 g protein.*

Mainland U.S. Favorite

Posted on: Wednesday, November 23, 2005

Try brown rice syrup in `ono bars

Loco `Ono Energy Bars

In this recipe, brown rice syrup is both a sweetener and a binder. It is made by fermenting brown rice with special enzymes. These enzymes break down the starch in the rice, producing a light brown, translucent syrup that is an excellent alternative to brown or white sugar.

Conventional white and brown sugar are simple sugars—monosaccharides and disaccharides. Brown rice syrup is a complex sugar or a polysaccharide. In the body, polysaccharides are broken down more slowly than monosaccharides, avoiding rapid spikes in blood glucose. The slow absorption also uses the complex sugars for energy instead of being stored as fat for later use. The buttery flavor and delicate sweetness of brown rice syrup make it an ideal sweetener in baking and desserts.

Loco `Ono Energy Bars
Serves 24

1 1/2 cups rolled oats *(regular oatmeal)*
1 cup crispy brown rice cereal
1/4 cup sesame seeds
1/2 cup wheat germ
1 1/2 cup dried apples
1 cup raisins, or currants, or chopped dried cherries
1/2 cup nonfat protein powder

1 cup brown rice syrup
1/2 cup Splenda®
1/2 cup reduced-fat chunky peanut butter
1 1/2 teaspoon vanilla extract
1 teaspoon apple pie spice
Nonfat cooking spray

Preheat oven to 350 degrees.

Spray a 13- by 9-inch jelly roll pan with nonfat cooking spray. *(A jelly roll pan is a cookie sheet with shallow lip or edge all around it.)* Spread oats, cereal, sesame seeds, and wheat germ on the pan and toast for about 15 minutes. Turn with a spatula every 5 minutes until lightly browned.

Meanwhile, chop apples and place in a large bowl. Add raisins and protein powder and toss by hand to coat the fruit. Add the toasted oat cereal mixture to this same bowl and mix thoroughly.

Lightly spray another jelly roll pan with cooking spray.

In a large saucepan over low heat, combine rice syrup and Splenda®. When the Splenda® has dissolved, mix in peanut butter, vanilla, and apple pie spice. Add the coated fruit and oat cereal mixture to this saucepan and stir with a rubber spatula until all the dry ingredients stick together. Do not overcook.

With dampened hands and spatula, spread the warm mixture into the sprayed jelly roll pan, pressing into an even layer. Chill to desired firmness.

Cut the unbaked bars into 2- by 3-inch bars. They may be wrapped individually in plastic wrap or waxed paper. Store in an airtight container with waxed paper between layers. The bars can be refrigerated up to a month or frozen for longer storage.

Makes approximately 24 bars.

Per serving (with Splenda®): *180 calories, 4 g total fat, 1 g saturated fat, 0 mg cholesterol, 120 mg sodium, 32 g carbohydrate, 2 g dietary fiber, 17 g sugar, 4 g protein.*

Per serving (with sugar): *190 calories, 4 g total fat, 1 g saturated fat, 0 mg cholesterol, 120 mg sodium, 35 g carbohydrate, 2 g dietary fiber, 21 g sugar, 4 g protein.*

Mainland U.S. Favorites

Banana Smoothie
Serves 3

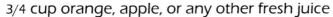

2 (large) bananas
6 to 9 ice cubes
3/4 cup orange, apple, or any other fresh juice

Break up bananas and place in blender or food processor. Add ice cubes a few at a time with the apple juice. Blend on low and graduate to high speed. Pour into three glasses. Serve immediately.

Per serving: 98 calories, 0.4 g fat, 25 g carbohydrate, 2 g dietary fiber, 0.8 g protein.

Tri-Berrie Smoothie
Serves 2

1 cup berries or choice of any three berries: raspberries, strawberries, blueberries, marionberries, etc., frozen
1 banana, frozen
1/2 cup of low-fat vanilla yogurt
1 cup of pomegranate juice or choice of apple or orange juice
1 tablespoon flax seed oil
1 to 2 tablespoons of low-fat granola *(optional)*

Place the above ingredients in a blender and blend for 30 seconds. Makes 2 cups.

Per serving (without granola): 250 calories, 8 g total fat, 1 g saturated fat, 5 mg cholesterol, 50 mg sodium, 43 g carbohydrate, 4 g dietary fiber, 32 g sugar, 4 g protein.

288 Snacks and Beverages

Glossary

Adzuki Beans: Also called adzuki, azuki or aduki beans, they are small, red Japanese beans used in dishes like *seikhan* and can easily be found canned or dried in your supermarket, perhaps in the Asian section.

`Ahi: A yellow-fin tuna commonly used for *sashimi* and *poke*.

Aburage: Deep-fried bean curd *(tofu)* slices.

Achiote Oil. Made from annatto seeds and oil that have been heated, strained, and cooled.

Almond Milk: Milk extracted from almonds. Used as a beverage, in cereals, and in smoothies.

Annato Seeds: Seeds from the lipstick tree. When soaked in oil, the oil takes on a deep reddish color and becomes *achiote* oil. Puerto Ricans use this seasoning for the flavor and the color in making *gandule* rice and *empanadillas* and *pastelles (cooked green bananas and pork)*.

Avocado: A native of Mexico, it is a fruit but tastes like a vegetable. See page 49 for more information.

Baby Bok Choy: A younger version of the Chinese vegetable bok choy, which is a mild-flavored vegetable that has dark green leaves and long, ivory white stems with tiny yellow flowers. The Chinese use it in soups and stir-fry dishes.

Bean Thread: Made of mung bean starch and similar to rice sticks only shorter. It is also known as cellophane noodles. Cooked by soaking in hot water before using and becomes translucent. See Long Rice.

Black Bean Sauce: Sauce made of fermented black beans with ginger, garlic, rice wine, and other ingredients.

Boca® Burgers: Brand name for meatless burgers made from soy protein.

Breadfruit or Ulu: One of the staples of Polynesia, it is traditionally steamed or baked in coconut milk. It can be used the same as a potato in soups and salads. *Ulu* has been made into *poi*.

289

290   Glossary

You can also find *ulu* chips locally, which are deep fried and not recommended.

Brown Rice Syrup: It's about half as sweet as ordinary table sugar. Some health food enthusiasts like it because it contains complex sugars, which are absorbed more slowly into the bloodstream. Maple syrup is a substitute: 3/4 cup plus 2 tablespoons of maple syrup for each cup of brown rice syrup.

Chapati: An East Indian unleavened flat bread that is much like flour tortillas.

Char Siu Sauce: A favorite Chinese reddish-brown sauce commercially made from sugar; water; wheat, soybeans, salt, wine, and hoisin sauce. Meat, chicken, and duck are marinated in this sauce and then baked or barbecued.

Chinese Fish Cake: Pinkish-gray fish paste that can be purchased in fish shops or local supermarkets.

Chinese Five-spice Powder: A seasoning in Chinese cuisine that incorporates the five basic flavors of Chinese cooking—sweet, sour, bitter, savory, and salty and consisting of cinnamon, powdered cassia buds, powdered star anise and anise seed, ginger root, and ground cloves. Another recipe for the powder consists of Sichuan pepper, star anise, cassia, cloves, and fennel seeds.

Chinese Parsley or Cilantro. Used as an herb and a garnish in Chinese and Spanish cooking. This herb is also known as the leaves of coriander.

Choy Sum: A bright green, leafy vegetable with short, grooved stems and yellow flowers. Used in Chinese soups and stir-fry and noodle dishes.

Chung Choy: Chinese condiment that is salted, preserved whole turnips.

Couscous: A pasta made from durum wheat. After it is milled into semolina, it is then mixed with water, and than shaped into spherical granules. Often used in place of rice, it goes well with meats, fish, and vegetables. It can also be used as a dessert.

Dasheen: See Japanese taro.

Global Light Cuisine ∞ Carol Devenot 291

Dashi Shoyu: A half-and-half mixture of *dashi (fish stock)* and soy sauce that has been heated and allowed to cool before using. It can be bought in store already prepared or made at home so when making it to taste other ingredients like *mirin* are added.

Down Dog Yoga Position: Down dog, downward facing dog, or also *mukha svanasana* can be quickly described as a dog with its front legs stretched out in front of its head at a forty-five degree angle with its rear end facing the ceiling and its hind legs stretched out in the forty-five degree angle facing the rear. The body looks like a jackknife. It is a very common position in different types of yoga.

Edamame: Soy beans.

Egg Beaters®: The commercial brand Egg Beaters® is made from the separation of egg whites from the yolks. They are fortified with vitamins and minerals. Emulsifies and thickeners such as xanthium gum and guar gum are added. The elimination of the egg yolk lowers the calories, fat and cholesterol levels.

Egg Replacer: A powder made from potato starch, tapiocas, flour, leavening *(calcium lactate calcium carbonate, citric acid)*, , sodium carcoboxymethycellulose, and methylcellulose. Calcium lactate is not dairy derived, so it does not contain lactose.

Fish Cake: Japanese deep-fried fish cake is found in refrigerated section in supermarkets. It is brown and shaped as a round ball threaded on a stick or as thick patties. The patties might come with gobo *(burdock root)*, carrots, green peas, or *char siu*. This type of fish cake is used in saimin, *musubi*, and other Japanese dishes. *See Kamaboko*, the other type of fish cake.

Fish Sauce: *See patis.*

Fructose: Sugar derived from fruit rather than sugar cane or beets. You use one-third less fructose in a recipe calling for sugar *(2/3 cup fructose equals 1 cup sugar)*. Fructose is found in local supermarkets and health food and drug stores.

Furikake: A Japanese condiment that is a mixture of *nori (seaweed bits)*, sesame seeds, salt, and sugar.

Gandul or Gandule Beans: *See* Pigeon Peas.

292 Glossary

Ginger Root: A commonly used cooking spice throughout the world, it is from a perennial plant in the family *Zingiberaceae*. The ginger plant has a long history of cultivation known to originate in China and then spread to India, Southeast Asia, West Africa, and the Caribbean

Goma: Japanese name for black or white sesame seeds. The black goma is used for poke, sushi, and other Japanese dishes.

Goya Powder: The ingredients are not listed on the package. It can be purchased at the Mexican or Spanish markets.

Hapa Rice: A rice mix that is half brown rice and half white rice.

Hawaiian Salt: White or pink course sea salt from Hawaii.

Hoisin Sauce: A Chinese sauce made from soy mash, sugar; flour; vinegar; salt, garlic chili, and spices. It is used as a flavoring in poultry and roast pork and as a side sauce for dipping or can be mixed with other Chinese sauces.

Jalapeño Pepper: A medium- to large-size chili pepper originally from Mexico which is prized for the warm, burning sensation when eaten. Ripe, the jalapeño can be 2 to 3.5 inches (5 to 9 cm) long and is commonly sold when still green.

Japanese Cucumber: This cucumber was developed in Japan, and it is longer; thinner; smoother-skinned, and crunchier than the common U.S. cucumber.

Japanese Taro or Dasheen: This Japanese taro is small and dark-brown. If not available to you, substitute other forms of taro or potato.

Jasmine Rice: An aromatic, long grain white rice from Thailand, the grains tend to cling together.

Jook: Also known as *congee, jook* is a Chinese turkey rice soup or porridge often eaten for breakfast.

Kalamata Olives: An almond-shaped, deep-purple olive imported from Greece with a rich and fruity flavor from its wine vinegar marinade.

Kamaboko: Fish cake formed in a half-tube or tube shape is packaged on blocks of wood or plastic and found in the refrigerated section of local supermarkets. It is usually sliced in half

Global Light Cuisine ∞ Carol Devenot 293

moons and served in saimin. The other definition of fish cake refers to the deep-fried version. See Fish Cake.

Ko Choo Jung Sauce: A Korean hot sauce made from chili pepper; soy bean, rice barley, water; honey, salt, and seasonings.

Kochujang or Gochujang: A savory and pungent fermented Korean hot pepper condiment in paste form. The primary ingredients are red chili powder, glutinous rice powder mixed with powdered fermented soybeans, dried barley sprout malt, and salt.

Kochu Karu: Korean hot, red pepper powder.

Konbu: Green Japanese seaweed, a kelp, comes in strips that are tied in knots about 1 inch apart then cut and put in *nishime* and other Japanese dishes.

Kosari: Korean dried fern or fernbracken.

Li Hing Mui: Dried Chinese plum coated with *li hing* powder.

Li Hing Powder: A Chinese seasoning powder made with prunes, salt, water, sugar, dextrose, preservatives, and food coloring. It is used as a sweet-sour seasoning on dried seeds, candy, fresh and dried fruit, and even in cakes. It can be found in most local stores in Hawaii.

Liquid Amino: An all-purpose seasoning made from soy protein and tastes like soy sauce. It contains 16 amino acids.

Long Rice: Bean threads or rice sticks used in Asian dishes. Cooked by soaking in hot water before using and becomes translucent.

Lychee: A small *(about 1 1/2 inches in diameter)* seasonal Chinese fruit. In most varieties the outer shell-like covering is red with little bumps. The flesh is white with a large seed in the center. It tastes a little like grapefruit and can be found fresh in season or canned in local markets.

Luau: Traditionally a Hawaiian feast and now modified into small or large family parties that celebrate a special occasion and major tourist attractions. At a *luau,* you will experience traditional *luau* food, hula dancing and music, leis, and everyone visiting and having good fun.

294 Glossary

Lu`au Leaves: Cooked taro leaves used in Hawaiian dishes such as *laulau;* chicken, pork, or *tako (octopus) luau* leaves; or Samoan *palu sami.*

Lumpia: Filipino name for small deep fried "egg rolls" or "burritos." Traditionally, meat and vegetables are wrapped in *lumpia* pastry covering called *lumpia* wraps. A dessert favorite is banana *lumpia.*

Mirin: Japanese rice wine used in cooking.

Mochi: Japanese sweet rice cake. As a New Year's Day tradition families used to pound the soaked and steamed sweet rice to make the *mochi* "dough"—a rather tricky and, potentially danger-ous process involving a huge stone mortar and wood pestle with one person pounding and the other turning the ball of *mochi* and feeling for lumps. The silky smooth dough was then filled with a paste of sweetened red adzuki beans to make *mochi* cakes.

Mochiko: Japanese sweet rice flour or glutinous rice flour.

Mui: Any preserved seed or snack that is seasoned with salt, sugar, and various Chinese spices is called *mui.* Some examples are *li hing mui, see moi,* cracked seed, and salted lemon or plum.

Musubi: Musubi is usually a rice ball. Spam® *musubi* is made with a *musubi* maker. It is approximately 4- by 21/2- by 3-inches of white rice with a slice of Spam® cooked in shoyu and sugar, and wrapped around the middle with a strip of *nori* seaweed to hold it all together. Spam® is high in fat and salt and not recom-mended.

Musubi Maker: A preformed, rectangular-shaped "rice ball" maker *(4- x 21/2- x 2-inch)* used to press the rice into a rectangular form.

Nori: A dark, almost black, dried Japanese seaweed that comes in paper-thin sheets and used to make *musubi, kakimochi,* and Japanese rice crackers.

Ogo: Hawaiian seaweed scientifically known as *Limu Manuaea. Limu* is the Hawaiian word for seaweed. *Ogo* is brownish-green in color with delicate translucent branches that have a crunchy texture. It is used as a condiment in Polynesian cooking and an ingredient in *poke,* salads or pickled.

Okinawan Sweet Potato: A small sweet potato coming to the islands from Okinawa, Japan, that has a light-beige skin and shaped like a sweet potato. When cooked the skin turns dark brown and the inside is a deep, rich purple color.

Panko Flakes: Japanese bread crumbs.

Patis or Fish Sauce: *Patis,* the Filipino name for fish sauce, is a clear brownish liquid sauce obtained from *bagoong* after it has been fermented. Brine is sometimes added to the *patis,* then aged, filtered, and bottled. *Bagoong* is the fermented sauce of small fish or shrimps. Anchovies, sardines, herring, and scad are the popular fishes used. A mixture of approximately three parts of fish or shrimp and one part of salt is fermented for four to six months to create the desired taste and pungency.

Phyllo Dough: A paper-thin dough used to make Greek dishes such as Spanakopita and Baklava. It can be found in most supermarkets and health food stores in the refrigerated food section.

Pigeon Peas or Gandul or Gandule Beans: A tropical small kidney-shaped legume used in Puerto Rican cooking; known as the *gandul* or *gandule* beans.

Poi: Steamed and mashed taro root, a staple food of the Hawaiians.

Poke: Raw fish mixed with *limu (fresh seaweed)*, green onions, Hawaiian salt, *shoyu,* and sesame oil. There are many varieties of *poki* including tofu *poki.*

Rice Paper: Round, wafer-thin sheets made from rice flour and used for Thai Summer and Spring rolls. Should be dipped in water to rehydrate before using.

Rice Sticks: Southeast Asian and East Asian countries use rice noodles. You can buy them in thin, medium, and wide noodle varieties. Thin noodles can be used in soups, salads, spring rolls, cold salads, and stir-fries. They're similar to bean threads, only they're longer and made with rice flour instead of mung bean starch. Not necessary to cook, just soak in hot water to prepare.

Saimin: A noodle soup dish developed in and unique to Hawaii. Inspired by Japanese udon, Chinese mein, and Filipino pancit, saimin was developed during Hawaii's plantation era. It is a soup dish of soft wheat egg noodles served in hot *dashi (stock from*

296   Glossary

Japanese bonito fish or shrimp). Saimin noodles tend to crinkle when cooked. It is garnished with green onions, baby bok choy or Chinese cabbage, *kamaboko (steamed fish cake)*, *Char siu (Chinese barbecue pork)*, sliced luncheon meat *(Spam® is the most popular choice)* or Portuguese sausage, and *nori*, among other additions.

Seitan: A high-protein food made from boiled or baked wheat gluten mixed with water and seasonings. It is a good meat substitute because of its chewy texture. Available at health food stores.

Shiitake Mushroom: *Shii* is Japanese for oak and *take* means mushrooms. Shiitake mushrooms have been a staple of the Asian diet for centuries. This black Japanese mushroom has a meaty texture and a pungent, woodsy flavor four times the flavor of white button mushrooms. The best shiitakes are grown on natural hardwood logs such as oak, hickory, and sweet gum. Fresh mushrooms keep in the refrigerator for two to three weeks. Most readily available are the dried shiitake mushrooms, which need to be rehydrated before using.

Shirataki Noodles: Pronounced shee-rah-TAH-kee, these noodles are very low carbohydrate, low calorie, thin, translucent, gelatinous traditional Japanese noodles made from the fiber of the roots of the Konjac plant. This plant grows in subtropical and tropical parts of eastern Asia. It is a yam-like tuber known as "Devil's Tongue." The word *shirataki* means "white waterfall," alluding to the appearance of these noodles.

Shiso Leaves: The most common species is *Perilla frutescens var. japonica* or *shiso* which is mainly grown in India and East Asia and a member of the mint family. There are both green-leafed and purple-leafed varieties which are generally recognized as separate species by botanists. The leaves resemble stinging nettle leaves, being slightly rounder in shape. In North America, it is increasingly commonly called by its Japanese name, *shiso*, in addition to being generally referred to as *perilla*. Its essential oils provide for a strong taste whose intensity might be compared to that of mint or fennel.

Sitaw: Filipino name for stir-fried long beans.

Soba (buckwheat) Noodles: Soba is the Japanese name for buckwheat noodles. The noodles are made from buckwheat

Global Light Cuisine ∞ Carol Devenot 297

flour and water and are high in iron and mineral content. They can be purchased at any local store.

Soy Nuts: Roasted soybeans that can be eaten as a snack or used as a garnish in salads and other dishes. If you can't locate them in your favorite supermarket, health food stores have them.

Soy Sauce or Shoyu: Brewed soybean sauce. *Shoyu* is the Japanese name commonly used in the islands for this sauce.

Sriracha Sauce: Thai hot chili sauce made from chili, sugar; garlic, salt, distilled vinegar; and preservatives.

Stevia: The Paraguayan herb is also known as sweet leaf. It comes to us in the health food stores as a white powder; liquid drops, or tea and is an excellent sugar substitute. It is 200 to 300 times sweeter than sugar so you only need a minute amount or it could turn bitter.

Tamari: Tamari is a soy sauce naturally brewed to be milder and less salty.

Tempura: A classic Japanese dish of deep fried battered vegetables or seafood.

Tofu: Asian product that is coagulated soybean curd. You can buy it .in soft, firm, and extra firm varieties. The amount of fat grams varies from 1.5 to 4 grams. The word tofu is derived from the Chinese word *taofu.* You mostly find it in the refrigerated section of the supermarket, but there are shelf varieties like silken tofu.

Tōgarashi, Shichimi Tōgarashi, or simply Shichimi: A seven-flavor chili pepper that is a common Japanese spice mixture. The main ingredient is coarsely ground red chili pepper, to which is typically added: mandarin orange peel, sesame seed, poppy seed, hemp seed, *nori* or *aonori,* and ground *sansho (a relative of Sichuan pepper).*

Turbinado Sugar: A type of sugar cane extract, also known as turbinated sugar, is made by steaming unrefined raw sugar. Turbinado sugar is similar in appearance to brown sugar but paler, and in general the two can be exchanged freely in recipes. A popular brand name is Sugar in the Raw.

Glossary

Tsubushi-An: Small, red Japanese azuki beans prepared with sweeteners and seasonings. You can make this at home or buy canned in Asian sections of your supermarket.

Umeboshi Plum: Japanese red, pickled plum in a jar found in Asian sections of your supermarket.

Udon: Japanese noodle that is flatter and thicker than soba *(buckwheat)* noodles and is made from white flour or whole wheat flour.

Vegetarian Stir Fry Strips: You can find White Wave® Vegetarian Stir Fry Strips in health food stores. They are made from wheat gluten called seitan. It is a low-fat, high-protein alternative to beef and poultry. Its meat-like texture and delicate flavor make it a perfect replacement for beef in your favorite recipes. Meatless strips made from wheat gluten. Another favorite product is Vitamark International's SuperSOY™ Beef Strips made from soy flour and corn. It really tastes like the original in local-style *hekka*.

Vermicelli: Can be round Italian pasta noodle smaller than spaghetti or in East Asia a thin rice noodle or rice sticks.

Wakame: A tender, leafy Japanese seaweed.

Index

Recipes by Continent / Country in Order of Appearance

Africa
Bobotie	117

Australia/New Zealand
Palagyi's Pavlova	231

Asia/Chinese
Chinese Black Mushroom and Tofu Lettuce Cups	5
Jenny's Watercress Soup	27
Mom's Comforting Jook	29
Oriental Chicken Salad	55
Kalakoa Fried Rice	85
Lynne's Quick Asian Salmon	120
Grilled Hamachi with Black Bean Sauce	122
Spicy Szechuan Eggplant	124
Broccoli Stir Fry	126
Garden Chow Mein	128
Char Siu Chicken and Char Siu Sauce	130
Garlic Asparagus and Chicken in Black Bean Sauce	132
Chinese Five Spice Chicken & Vegetables	134
Shoyu Chicken	136
Sichuan Ma Po Tofu	138
Sweet and Sour Tofu and Carol's Sweet and Sour Sauce	140
Sesame Soy Chicken and Edamame Stir Fry	142
Mango Pudding	234
Warm, Tropical Mango-Lychee Dessert	236
Almond Float	238
My Favorite Fruit Mui	279

Asia/Filipino
Lazy Lumpia and Dipping Sauce	8
Green Papaya Salad	56
Sitaw	86
Chicken Adobo	144
Veat, Not Meat Guisantes	146
New Kine Banana Lumpia	239

Asia/Indonesian
Indonesian Chicken Satay	148

Asia/Japanese
Low-carb Saimin	31
Mitsuko's Oden	33
Namasu	58
Sekihan	87
One Giant Sushi	89
Wild Salmon Shiro Misoyaki	150
Chicken Katsu	152
Simply Nishime	154
Smart Manju	241
Okinawan Sweet Potato Poi Mochi	242
Make Her Musubi	283

Asia/Korean
Korean Chicken Soup	35
Quickie Cucumber Kim Chee	59
Watercress Namul	90
Chop Chae	91
Enlightened Ja Jang Myun	156
Susan's Grilled Chicken	158

Asia/Thai
Summer Rolls with Dipping Sauce	10
Yummy Sticky Rice	93
Thai Shrimp or Tofu Curry	160
Pad Thai	162

Recipes by Continent / Country in Order of Appearance

Asia/Thai (continued)

Thai Tapioca Pudding	244
Sweet Brown Sticky Rice with Mango-Lychee	246

Caribbean/Cuban

Cuban Stuffed Zucchini	164

Caribbean/Puerto Rican

Empanadillas	12
Arroz con Gandules	166

Europe/French

Ratatouille	94
Spinach & Ricotta Crepes	168
Chocolate Mousse Pie	248

Europe/German

Sauerbraten–Crock Pot	171

Europe/Greek

Greek Couscous Salad	60
Greek Salad	62
Greek Seasoned Roasted Vegetables	96
Meatless Moussaka	173

Europe/Irish

Savvy (Savoy) Stuffed Cabbage	176

Europe/Italian

Eggplant Caponata	14
Slimmed-Down Tomato-Butternut Squash Bisque	37
Herbed White Bean Salad	64
Woodi's Caprese	65
Linguine Al Pesto Alla Moda Ligure Redo	98
Chicken Florentine a la Devenot	178
Mama Claire's Spaghetti Sauce	180
Rav-e-oli	182

Cherry Tomatoes and Penne Pasta	184
Zucchini—Swiss Chard Frittata	186
Angela's Quickie Veggie Lasagna	190

Europe/Mediterranean

Mediterranean Spinach Rice Balls	16

Europe/Portuguese

Healthy Portuguese Bean Soup	39

Hawaii Local Favorite

Dilly Dip	18
Good Kine Potato Salad	67
Tofu Mayo	69
Tofu Salad	70
Hold da Mayo Cold Slaw	71
Ceci's Tasty Sweet Potatoes	100
Hapa Rice	101
Long Rice Chicken	102
Tuna Tofu Patties	190
Lara's Mahimahi with Mango-Papaya Salsa	192
Plate Lunch Curry Stew	194
`Ono Keia Hawaiian Stew	196
What the Hekka?	198
Coffee Burger with Wasabi Mayo	201
Terry Burger with Teriyaki Sauce	205
Okinawan Sweet Potato Pie	249
Fo' Real Bread Pudding	252
Banana Wrap	285

India/Indian

Ek Handi Ka Murch Aur Masoor	205
Tandori Chicken	208

Global Light Cuisine ∞ Carol Devenot 301

Recipes by Continent / Country in Order of Appearance

Mainland U.S. Favorite

Hearty Turkey Soup	41
Light and Creamy Broccoli Soup	43
No Need Ham Split Pea Soup	45
Roasted Beet Salad with Sherry Shallot Vinaigrette and Candied Pecans	72
Microwaved Brown Brown Basmati or Long Grain Rice	104
Festive Stuffed Butternut Squash	106
Flame-broiled Fish Taco	210
Barbecue Roasted Salmon	212
Quinoa Spinach Casserole	214
Date with a Nut Bread	254
Banana Muffins for Mom	256
Yummy Rummy Oatcakes	258
Easy as 1-2-3 Pumpkin Bars	260
Raspberry and Chocolate Bars	262
Little-Bit-Butter Oatmeal Cookies	264
Soy Chocolate Fantasy	266
I Love You Berry, Berry, Berry Much Crisp	268
Crispy Apricot Turnovers	270
Chocolate Swirled Cheesecake	273
Banana Almond Cream	275
Loco `Ono Energy Bars	284
Banana Smoothie	287
Tri-Berrie Smoothie	287

Mainland U.S./American Indian

Southwestern Corn Chowder	47

Mexico

Guacamole	19
Salsa	20
Ceviche	21
Mexicano Sop A Con Rose Avos	49
Chicken Fajitas	217
Turkey Chiles Rellenos Casserole	219
Carol's Chili	222
Bostadas	225

Middle East

Harira	51
Curried Couscous Salad	75
Tzatziki	78
Flab You Less Falafel	226

Middle East/Israeli

Heal Ti Israeli Salad	80

South Pacific/Hawaiian

Lynne's Tofu Poke	23
Lomi Lomi Tomato	108
Luau Spinach	109
Baked Sweet Potato	110
Baked Taro	110
Jan's Haupia	276

South Pacific/Samoan

Lani Ulu (breadfruit)	111
Light Palu Sami	112

302   Index

Recipes Alphabetically and by Food Groupings
~ (V) indicates vegan recipe ~

Almond Float ~ 238
Angela's Quickie Veggie Lasagna ~ 190
Arroz con Gandules ~ 166

Baked Sweet Potato (V) ~ 110

Baked Sweets Recipes

Banana Muffins for Mom ~ 256
Chocolate Swirled Cheesecake ~ 273
Crispy Apricot Turnovers ~ 270
Date with a Nut Bread ~ 254
Easy as 1-2-3 Pumpkin Bars ~ 260
I Love You Berry, Berry, Berry Much Crisp (V) ~ 268
Little-Bit-Butter Oatmeal Cookies ~ 264
Loco `Ono Energy Bars (V) ~ 284
New Kine Banana Lumpia (V) ~ 239
Okinawan Sweet Potato Pie ~ 249
Okinawan Sweet Potato Poi Mochi (V) ~ 242
Palagyi's Pavlova ~ 231
Raspberry and Chocolate Bars ~ 262
Smart Manju ~ 241
Warm, Tropical Mango-Lychee Dessert ~ 236
Yummy Rummy Oatcakes ~ 258

Baked Taro (V) ~ 110
Banana Almond Cream (V) ~ 275
Banana Muffins for Mom ~ 256
Banana Smoothie (V) ~ 287
Banana Wrap (V) ~ 285
Barbecue Roasted Salmon ~ 212

Beef Recipes

Sauerbraten in a Crock Pot ~ 171

Black Bean Sauce ~ 124
Bobotie ~ 117
Bostadas ~ 225
Broccoli Stir Fry ~ 126

Buffalo Recipes

Coffee Burger with Wasabi Mayo ~ 201

Global Light Cuisine ∞ Carol Devenot   303

Candied Pecans ~ 74
Carol's Sweet and Sour Sauce (V) ~ 141
Carol's Chili (V) ~ 222
Ceci's Tasty Sweet Potatoes (V) ~ 100
Ceviche ~ 21
Char Siu Chicken and Char Siu Sauce ~ 130
Char Siu Sauce (V) ~ 131
Cherry Tomatoes and Penne Pasta ~ 184
Chicken Adobo ~ 144
Chicken Fajitas ~ 217
Chicken Florentine a la Devenot ~ 178
Chicken Katsu ~ 152

Chicken Recipes

Broccoli Stir Fry ~ 126
Char Siu Chicken and Char Siu Sauce ~ 130
Chicken Adobo ~ 144
Chicken Fajitas ~ 217
Chicken Katsu ~ 152
Chinese Five Spice Chicken and Vegetables ~ 134
Chicken Florentine a la Devenot ~ 178
Ek Handi Ka Murch Aur Masoor *(one-pot chicken, red lentils, and green beans)* ~ 205
Garden Chow Mein ~ 128
Garlic Asparagus and Chicken in Black Bean Sauce ~ 132
Harira *(Ramadan soup)* ~ 51
Indonesian Chicken Satay ~ 148
Jenny's Watercress Soup ~ 27
Korean Chicken Soup ~ 35
Long Rice Chicken ~ 102
Meatless Moussaka ~ 173
Mexicano Sop A Con Rose Avos ~ 49
Mitsuko's Oden ~ 33
Mom's Comforting Jook *(turkey rice soup)* ~ 29
Oriental Chicken Salad ~ 55
Pad Thai ~ 162
Plate Lunch Curry Stew ~ 194
Quinoa Spinach Casserole ~ 214
Ratatouille ~ 94
Shoyu Chicken ~136
Sichuan Ma Po Tofu ~ 138
Spicy Szechuan Eggplant ~ 124
Spinach and Ricotta Crepes ~ 168

304   Index

Chicken Recipes *(continued)*

 Susan's Grilled Chicken ~ 158
 Tandoori Chicken ~ 208
 Veat, Not Meat Guisantes (V) (or chicken) ~ 146

Chinese Black Mushroom and Tofu Lettuce Cups (V) ~ 5
Chinese Five Spice Chicken and Vegetables ~ 134
Chocolate Mousse Pie (V) ~ 248
Chocolate Swirled Cheesecake ~ 273
Chop Chae (V) ~ 91
Coffee Burger with Wasabi Mayo ~ 201
Crispy Apricot Turnovers ~ 270
Cuban Stuffed Zucchini ~ 164
Curried Couscous Salad ~ 75

Dairy Recipes (contain some dairy)

 Almond Float ~ 238
 Angela's Quickie Veggie Lasagna ~ 190
 Bobotie ~ 117
 Bostadas ~ 225
 Cherry Tomatoes and Penne Pasta ~ 184
 Chicken Florentine a la Devenot ~ 178
 Chocolate Swirled Cheesecake ~ 273
 Crispy Apricot Turnovers ~ 270
 Cuban Stuffed Zucchini ~ 164
 Curried Couscous Salad ~ 75
 Flame-broiled Fish Taco ~ 210
 Greek Salad ~ 62
 Harira *(Ramadan soup)* ~ 51
 Light and Creamy Broccoli Soup ~ 43
 Linguine Al Pesto Alla Moda Ligure Redo ~ 98
 Little-Bit-Butter Oatmeal Cookies ~ 264
 Mama Claire's Spaghetti Sauce ~ 180
 Mango Pudding ~ 234
 Meatless Moussaka ~ 173
 Mediterranean Spinach Rice Balls ~ 16
 Mexicano Sop A Con Rose Avos ~ 49
 Okinawan Sweet Potato Pie ~ 249
 Quinoa Spinach Casserole ~ 214
 Raspberry and Chocolate Bars ~ 262
 Ratatouille ~ 94
 Roasted Beet Salad with Sherry Shallot Vinaigrette and
  Candied Pecans ~ 72
 Slimmed-Down Tomato-Butternut Squash Bisque ~ 37

Global Light Cuisine ∞ Carol Devenot   305

Dairy Recipes *(continued)*
  Spinach and Ricotta Crepes ~ 168
  Sweet Brown Sticky Rice and Mango-Lychee ~ 246
  Tandoori Chicken ~ 208
  Tri-Berrie Smoothie ~ 287
  Turkey Chiles Rellenos Casserole ~ 219
  Tzatziki ~ 78
  Woodi's Caprese ~ 65
  Yummy Rummy Oatcakes ~ 258
  Zucchini-Swiss Chard Frittata ~ 186

Date with a Nut Bread ~ 254
Dilly Dip (V) ~ 18
Dressing for Oriental Chicken Salad (V) ~ 55

Easy as 1-2-3 Pumpkin Bars ~ 260
Eggplant Caponata (V) ~ 14
Ek Handi Ka Murch Aur Masoor *(one-pot chicken, red lentils,*
  and green beans) ~ 205
Empanadillas ~ 12
Enlightened Ja Jang Myun ~ 156

Festive Stuffed Butternut Squash (V) ~ 106
Flab You Less Falafel (V) ~ 226
Flame-broiled Fish Taco ~ 210
Fo' Real Bread Pudding (V) ~ 252

Fruit Recipes (contain some fruit)
  Almond Float ~ 238
  Banana Almond Cream (V) ~ 275
  Banana Muffins for Mom ~ 256
  Banana Smoothie (V) ~ 287
  Banana Wrap (V) ~ 285
  Barbecue Roasted Salmon ~ 212
  Bobotie ~ 117
  Ceviche ~ 21
  Chicken Fajitas ~ 217
  Chocolate Mousse Pie (V) ~ 248
  Chocolate Swirled Cheesecake ~ 273
  Crispy Apricot Turnovers ~ 270
  Cuban Stuffed Zucchini ~ 164
  Date with a Nut Bread ~ 254
  Dilly Dip (V) ~ 18
  Easy as 1-2-3 Pumpkin Bars ~ 260

306   Index

Fruit Recipes *(continued)*

Ek Handi Ka Murch Aur Masoor *(one-pot chicken, red lentils, and green beans)* ~ 205

Festive Stuffed Butternut Squash (V) ~ 106

Flab You Less Falafel (V) ~ 228

Flame-broiled Fish Taco ~ 210

Fo' Real Bread Pudding (V) ~ 252

Greek Salad ~ 62

Green Papaya Salad ~ 56

Guacamole (V) ~ 19

Harira *(Ramadan soup)* ~ 51

I Love You Berry, Berry, Berry Much Crisp (V) ~ 268

Lara's Mahimahi with Mango-Papaya Salsa ~ 192

Little-Bit-Butter Oatmeal Cookies ~ 264

Loco `Ono Energy Bars (V) ~ 284

"Make Her" Musubi (V) ~ 281

Mango Pudding ~ 234

Mexicano Sop A Con Rose Avos ~ 49

My Favorite Fruit Mui ~ 279

New Kine Banana Lumpia (V) ~ 239

Pad Thai ~ 162

Palagyi's Pavlova ~ 231

Raspberry and Chocolate Bars ~ 262

Sauerbraten in a Crock Pot ~ 171

Southwestern Corn Chowder (V) ~ 47

Soy Chocolate Fantasy ~ 266

Sweet Brown Sticky Rice and Mango-Lychee ~ 246

Tandoori Chicken ~ 208

Tofu Mayo ~ 69

Tri-Berrie Smoothie ~ 287

Tzatziki ~ 78

Warm, Tropical Mango-Lychee Dessert ~ 236

Yummy Rummy Oatcakes ~ 258

Garden Chow Mein ~ 128

Garlic Asparagus and Chicken in Black Bean Sauce ~ 132

Good Kine Potato Salad ~ 67

Grain and Grain Product Recipes

Angela's Quickie Veggie Lasagna ~ 190

Arroz con Gandules ~ 166

Banana Almond Cream (V) ~ 275

Banana Muffins for Mom ~ 256

Banana Wrap (V) ~ 285

Grain and Grain Product Recipes *(continued)*

Bobotie ~ 117
Bostadas ~ 225
Cherry Tomatoes and Penne Pasta ~ 184
Chicken Fajitas ~ 217
Chicken Florentine a la Devenot ~ 178
Chicken Katsu ~ 152
Chocolate Swirled Cheesecake ~ 273
Coffee Burger with Wasabi Mayo ~ 201
Crispy Apricot Turnovers ~ 270
Cuban Stuffed Zucchini ~ 164
Curried Couscous Salad ~ 75
Date with a Nut Bread ~ 254
Easy as 1-2-3 Pumpkin Bars ~ 260
Enlightened Ja Jang Myun ~ 156
Empanadillas ~ 12
Festive Stuffed Butternut Squash (V) ~ 106
Flab You Less Falafel (V) ~ 226
Flame-broiled Fish Taco ~ 210
Garden Chow Mein ~ 128
Greek Couscous Salad (V) ~ 60
Grilled Hamachi with Black Bean Sauce ~ 122
Hapa Rice (V) ~ 101
Harira *(Ramadan soup)* ~ 51
Hearty Turkey Soup ~ 41
I Love You Berry, Berry, Berry Much Crisp (V) ~ 268
Kalakoa Fried Rice (V) ~ 85
Lazy Lumpia and Dipping Sauce ~ 8
Linguine Al Pesto Alla Moda Ligure Redo ~ 98
Little-Bit-Butter Oatmeal Cookies ~ 264
Loco `Ono Energy Bars (V) ~ 284
"Make Her" Musubi (V) ~ 281
Mama Claire's Spaghetti Sauce ~ 180
Meatless Moussaka ~ 173
Mediterranean Spinach Rice Balls ~ 16
Mexicano Sop A Con Rose Avos ~ 49
Microwaved Brown Basmati or Long Grain Brown Rice (V) ~ 104
Mom's Comforting Jook *(turkey rice soup)* ~ 29
New Kine Banana Lumpia (V) ~ 239
Okinawan Sweet Potato Pie ~ 249
Okinawan Sweet Potato Poi Mochi (V) ~ 242
`Ono Keia Hawaiian Stew (V) ~ 196
Pad Thai ~ 162

308   Index

Grain and Grain Product Recipes *(continued)*

    Plate Lunch Curry Stew ~ 194
    Quinoa Spinach Casserole ~ 214
    Raspberry and Chocolate Bars ~ 262
    Savvy (Savoy) Stuffed Cabbage (V) ~ 176
    Sekihan (V) ~ 87
    Sesame Soy Chicken and Edamame Stir Fry ~ 142
    Shoyu Chicken ~ 136
    Sichuan Ma Po Tofu ~ 138
    Smart Manju ~ 241
    Spinach and Ricotta Crepes ~ 168
    Summer Rolls with Dipping Sauce ~ 10
    Sweet and Sour Tofu and Carol's Sweet and Sour Sauce (V) ~ 140
    Sweet Brown Sticky Rice and Mango-Lychee ~ 246
    Terry Burger and Teriyaki Sauce ~ 203
    Tri-Berrie Smoothie ~ 287
    Turkey Chiles Rellenos Casserole ~ 219
    One Giant Sushi ~ 89
    Warm, Tropical Mango-Lychee Dessert ~ 236
    What the Hekka? (V) ~ 198
    Woo's Southwest Orzo (V) ~ 223
    Yummy Rummy Oatcakes ~ 258
    Yummy Sticky Rice (V) ~ 93

Green Papaya Salad ~ 56
Green Papaya Salad Vinaigrette Dressing ~ 56
Greek Couscous Salad (V) ~ 60
Greek Couscous Salad Dressing (V) ~ 61
Greek Salad ~ 62
Greek Salad Lemon Dressing (V) ~ 63
Greek Seasoned Roasted Vegetables (V) ~ 96
Grilled Hamachi with Black Bean Sauce ~ 122
Guacamole (V) ~ 19

Hapa Rice (V) ~ 101
Harira *(Ramadan soup)* ~ 51
Healthy Portuguese Bean Soup (V) ~ 39
Heal Ti Israeli Salad ~ 80
Hearty Turkey Soup ~ 41
Herbed White Bean Salad ~ 64
Hold da Mayo Cold Slaw (V) ~ 71
Hold da Mayo Cold Slaw Vinaigrette Dressing (V) ~ 71

I Love You Berry, Berry, Berry Much Crisp (V) ~ 268

Global Light Cuisine ∞ Carol Devenot   309

Indonesian Chicken Satay ~ 148
Indonesian Satay Dipping Sauce (V) ~ 148

Jan's Haupia ~ 276
Jenny's Watercress Soup ~ 27

Kalakoa Fried Rice (V) ~ 85
Korean Chicken Soup ~ 35

Lani Ulu (V) ~ 111
Lara's Mahimahi with Mango-Papaya Salsa ~ 192
Lazy Lumpia and Dipping Sauce ~ 8

Legume Recipes (contain beans or peanuts)
Arroz con Gandules ~ 166
Banana Wrap (V) ~ 285
Carol's Chili (V) ~ 222
Chop Chae (V) ~ 91
Ek Handi Ka Murch Aur Masoor *(one-pot chicken, red lentils, and green beans)* ~ 205
Flab You Less Falafel (V) ~ 226
Garlic Asparagus and Chicken in Black Bean Sauce ~ 132
Greek Couscous Salad (V) ~ 60
Grilled Hamachi with Black Bean Sauce ~ 122
Harira *(Ramadan soup)* ~ 51
Healthy Portuguese Bean Soup (V) ~ 39
Hearty Turkey Soup ~ 41
Herbed White Bean Salad ~ 64
Indonesian Chicken Satay ~ 148
Loco `Ono Energy Bars (V) ~ 284
Long Rice Chicken ~ 102
No Need Ham Split Pea Soup (V) ~ 45
Pad Thai ~ 162
Sekihan (V) ~ 87
Sichuan Ma Po Tofu ~ 138
Smart Manju ~ 241
Soy Chocolate Fantasy ~ 266
Summer Rolls with Dipping Sauce ~ 10
Turkey Chiles Rellenos Casserole ~ 219
What the Hekka? (V) ~ 198
Woo's Southwest Orzo (V) ~ 223

Light and Creamy Broccoli Soup ~ 43
Light Palu Sami ~ 112
Linguine Al Pesto Alla Moda Ligure Redo ~ 98

310   Index

Little-Bit-Butter Oatmeal Cookies ~ 264
Loco `Ono Energy Bars (V) ~ 284
Lomi Lomi Tomato ~ 108
Long Rice Chicken ~ 102
Low-carb Saimin ~ 31
Luau Spinach (V) ~ 110
Lynne's Quick Asian Salmon ~ 120
Lynne's Tofu Poke (V) ~ 23

"Make Her" Musubi (V) ~ 281
Mama Claire's Spaghetti Sauce ~ 180
Mango-Papaya Salsa (V) ~ 193
Mango Pudding ~ 234
Meatless Moussaka ~ 173
Mediterranean Spinach Rice Balls ~ 16
Mexicano Sop A Con Rose Avos ~ 49
Microwaved Brown Basmati or Long Grain Brown Rice (V) ~ 104
Mitsuko's Oden ~ 33
Mom's Comforting Jook *(turkey rice soup)* ~ 29

Mushroom (fungus) Recipes (contain mushrooms)
Angela's Quickie Veggie Lasagna ~ 190
Broccoli Stir Fry ~ 126
Chinese Black Mushroom and Tofu Lettuce Cups (V) ~ 5
Curried Couscous Salad ~ 75
Light Palu Sami ~ 112
Mama Claire's Spaghetti Sauce ~ 180
`Ono Keia Hawaiian Stew (V) ~ 196
Quinoa Spinach Casserole ~ 214
Rav-e-oli (V) ~ 182
Shoyu Chicken ~136
Simply Nishime (V) ~ 154
Spicy Szechuan Eggplant ~ 124
What the Hekka? (V) ~ 198

My Favorite Fruit Mui ~ 279

Namasu (V) ~ 58
Namasu Dressing (V) ~ 58
New Kine Banana Lumpia (V) ~ 239
No Need Ham Split Pea Soup (V) ~ 45

Noodle Recipes
Angela's Quickie Veggie Lasagna ~ 190
Cherry Tomatoes and Penne Pasta ~ 184

Global Light Cuisine ∞ Carol Devenot   311

Noodle Recipes *(continued)*
Curried Couscous Salad ~ 75
Enlightened Ja Jang Myun ~ 156
Greek Couscous Salad (V) ~ 60
Linguine Al Pesto Alla Moda Ligure Redo ~ 98
Low-carb Saimin ~ 31
Mama Claire's Spaghetti Sauce ~ 180
Pad Thai ~ 162
Rav-e-oli (V) ~ 182
Sesame Soy Chicken and Edamame Stir Fry ~ 142
Woo's Southwest Orzo (V) ~ 223

Nuts and Seeds Recipes (contain some nuts or seeds)
Banana Almond Cream (V) ~ 275
Banana Muffins for Mom ~ 256
Bobotie ~ 117
Candied Pecans ~ 74
Chinese Black Mushroom and Tofu Lettuce Cups (V) ~ 5
Curried Couscous Salad ~ 75
Date with a Nut Bread ~ 254
Easy as 1-2-3 Pumpkin Bars ~ 260
Fo' Real Bread Pudding (V) ~ 252
Hold da Mayo Cold Slaw (V) ~ 71
Linguine Al Pesto Alla Moda Ligure Redo ~ 98
Little-Bit-Butter Oatmeal Cookies ~ 264
Loco `Ono Energy Bars (V) ~ 284
Lynne's Tofu Poke (V) ~ 23
Oriental Chicken Salad ~ 55
Quinoa Spinach Casserole ~ 214
Sekihan (V) ~ 87
Sesame Soy Chicken and Edamame Stir Fry ~ 142
Soy Chocolate Fantasy ~ 266
Susan's Grilled Chicken ~ 158
Sweet Brown Sticky Rice and Mango-Lychee ~ 246
Tofu Salad ~ 70
Watercress Namul (V) ~ 90
Wild Salmon Shiro Misoyaki ~ 150
Yummy Rummy Oatcakes ~ 258

Okinawan Sweet Potato Pie ~ 249
Okinawan Sweet Potato Poi Mochi (V) ~ 242
One Giant Sushi ~ 89

312   Index

`Ono Keia Hawaiian Stew (V) ~ 196
Oriental Chicken Salad ~ 55

Pad Thai ~ 162
Palagyi's Pavlova ~ 231

Pies
Chocolate Mousse Pie (V) ~ 248
Okinawan Sweet Potato Pie ~ 249

Plate Lunch Curry Stew ~ 194

Pork Recipes
Empanadillas ~ 12
Enlightened Ja Jang Myun ~ 156

Pudding Recipes
Almond Float ~ 238
Jan's Haupia ~ 276
Mango Pudding ~ 234
Soy Chocolate Fantasy ~ 266
Thai Tapioca Pudding (V) ~ 244

Quickie Cucumber Kim Chee (V) ~ 59
Quinoa Spinach Casserole ~ 214

Raspberry and Chocolate Bars ~ 262
Ratatouille ~ 94
Rav-e-oli (V) ~ 182
Roasted Beet Salad with Sherry Shallot Vinaigrette and
Candied Pecans ~ 72

Salsa (V) ~ 20

Salad Dressings
Dressing for Oriental Chicken Salad (V) ~ 55
Greek Couscous Salad Dressing (V) ~ 61
Green Papaya Salad Vinaigrette Dressing ~ 56
Greek Salad Lemon Dressing (V) ~ 63
Hold da Mayo Cold Slaw Vinaigrette Dressing (V) ~ 71
Namasu Dressing (V) ~ 58
Sherry Shallot Vinaigrette Dressing (V) ~ 73
Tofu Salad Dressing (V) ~ 70

Sauce for Spicy Szechuan Eggplant (V) ~ 125

Global Light Cuisine ∞ Carol Devenot   313

Sauces

Black Bean Sauce ~ 124
Carol's Sweet and Sour Sauce (V) ~ 141
Char Siu Sauce (V) ~ 131
Indonesian Satay Dipping Sauce (V) ~ 148
Mango-Papaya Salsa (V) ~ 193
Salsa (V) ~ 20
Sauce for Spicy Szechuan Eggplant (V) ~ 125
Summer Rolls Dipping Sauce (V) ~ 11
Teriyaki Sauce (V) ~ 203

Sauerbraten in a Crock Pot ~ 171
Savvy (Savoy) Stuffed Cabbage (V) ~ 176

Seafood Recipes (contain some seafood)

Barbecue Roasted Salmon ~ 212
Ceviche ~ 21
Flame-broiled Fish Taco ~ 210
Good Kine Potato Salad ~ 67
Green Papaya Salad ~ 56
Grilled Hamachi with Black Bean Sauce ~ 122
Heal Ti Israeli Salad ~ 80
Jenny's Watercress Soup ~ 27
Lara's Mahimahi with Mango-Papaya Salsa ~ 192
Lomi Lomi Tomato ~ 108
Low-carb Saimin ~ 31
Lynne's Quick Asian Salmon ~ 120
Lynne's Tofu or `Ahi Poke ~ 23
Mitsuko's Oden ~ 33
One Giant Sushi ~ 89
Sitaw ~ 86
Thai Shrimp or Tofu Curry ~ 160
Tofu Salad ~ 70
Tuna Tofu Patties ~ 190
Wild Salmon Shiro Misoyaki ~ 150

Sekihan (V) ~ 87
Sesame Soy Chicken and Edamame Stir Fry ~ 142
Sherry Shallot Vinaigrette Dressing (V) ~ 73
Shoyu Chicken ~136
Sichuan Ma Po Tofu ~ 138
Simply Nishime (V) ~ 154
Sitaw ~ 86
Slimmed-Down Tomato-Butternut Squash Bisque ~ 37

314   Index

Southwestern Corn Chowder (V) ~ 47
Soy Chocolate Fantasy ~ 266

Soy Product Recipes (contain some soy)

Angela's Quickie Veggie Lasagna ~ 190
Banana Muffins for Mom ~ 256
Bostadas ~ 225
Carol's Chili (V) ~ 222
Cuban Stuffed Zucchini ~ 164
Enlightened Ja Jang Myun ~ 156
Healthy Portuguese Bean Soup (V) ~ 39
Lazy Lumpia and Dipping Sauce ~ 8
Meatless Moussaka ~ 173
Oriental Chicken Salad ~ 55
Savvy (Savoy) Stuffed Cabbage (V) ~ 176
Sesame Soy Chicken and Edamame Stir Fry ~ 142
Terry Burger and Teriyaki Sauce ~ 203
Thai Tapioca Pudding (V) ~ 244
Tofu *(see Tofu recipes)*
Veat, Not Meat Guisantes (V) *(or chicken)* ~ 146
Warm, Tropical Mango-Lychee Dessert ~ 236
Woo's Southwest Orzo (V) ~ 223
Yummy Rummy Oatcakes ~ 258

Spicy Szechuan Eggplant ~ 124
Spinach and Ricotta Crepes ~ 168
Summer Rolls Dipping Sauce (V) ~ 11
Summer Rolls with Dipping Sauce (V) ~ 10
Susan's Grilled Chicken ~ 158
Sweet and Sour Tofu and Carol's Sweet and Sour Sauce (V) ~ 140
Sweet Brown Sticky Rice and Mango-Lychee ~ 246

Tandoori Chicken ~ 208
Teriyaki Sauce (V) ~ 203
Terry Burger and Teriyaki Sauce ~ 203
Thai Shrimp or Tofu Curry ~ 160
Thai Tapioca Pudding (V) ~ 244

Tofu Recipes

Angela's Quickie Veggie Lasagna ~ 190
Chinese Black Mushroom and Tofu Lettuce Cups (V) ~ 5
Chocolate Mousse Pie (V) ~ 248
Dilly Dip (V) ~ 18
Korean Chicken Soup ~ 35

Global Light Cuisine ∞ Carol Devenot   315

Tofu Recipes *(continued)*
Low-carb Saimin ~ 31
Lynne's Tofu Poke (V) ~ 23
Rav-e-oli (V) ~ 182
Sichuan Ma Po Tofu ~ 138
Simply Nishime (V) ~ 154
Soy Chocolate Fantasy ~ 266
Spinach and Ricotta Crepes ~ 168
Summer Rolls with Dipping Sauce ~ 10
Sweet and Sour Tofu and Carol's Sweet and Sour Sauce (V) ~ 140
Thai Shrimp or Tofu Curry ~ 160
Tofu Mayo ~ 69
Tofu Salad ~ 70
Tuna Tofu Patties ~ 190
What the Hekka? (V) ~ 198

Tofu Mayo (V) ~ 69
Tofu Salad ~ 70
Tofu Salad Dressing (V) ~ 70
Tri-Berrie Smoothie ~ 287
Tuna Tofu Patties ~ 190
Turkey Chiles Rellenos Casserole ~ 219

Turkey Recipes
Arroz con Gandules ~ 166
Bobotie ~ 117
Hearty Turkey Soup ~ 41
Herbed White Bean Salad ~ 64
Mom's Comforting Jook *(turkey rice soup)* ~ 29
Sichuan Ma Po Tofu ~ 138
Turkey Chiles Rellenos Casserole ~ 219

Tzatziki ~ 78

Veat, Not Meat Guisantes (V) *(or chicken)* ~ 146

Vegan Recipes
Baked Sweet Potato (V) ~ 110
Baked Taro (V) ~ 110
Banana Almond Cream (V) ~ 275
Banana Smoothie (V) ~ 287
Banana Wrap (V) ~ 285
Carol's Chili (V) ~ 222
Carol's Sweet and Sour Sauce (V) ~ 141
Ceci's Tasty Sweet Potatoes (V) ~ 100

316   Index

Vegan Recipes *(continued)*

Char Siu Sauce (V) ~ 131
Chinese Black Mushroom and Tofu Lettuce Cups (V) ~ 5
Chocolate Mousse Pie (V) ~ 248
Chop Chae (V) ~ 91
Dilly Dip (V) ~ 18
Dressing for Oriental Chicken Salad (V) ~ 55
Eggplant Caponata (V) ~ 14
Festive Stuffed Butternut Squash (V) ~ 106
Flab You Less Falafel (V) ~ 226
Fo' Real Bread Pudding (V) ~ 252
Greek Couscous Salad (V) ~ 60
Greek Couscous Salad Dressing (V) ~ 61
Greek Salad Lemon Dressing (V) ~ 63
Greek Seasoned Roasted Vegetables (V) ~ 96
Guacamole (V) ~ 19
Hapa Rice (V) ~ 101
Healthy Portuguese Bean Soup (V) ~ 39
Hold da Mayo Cold Slaw (V) ~ 71
Hold da Mayo Cold Slaw Vinaigrette Dressing (V) ~ 71
I Love You Berry, Berry, Berry Much Crisp (V) ~ 268
Indonesian Satay Dipping Sauce (V) ~ 148
Jan's Haupia ~ 276
Kalakoa Fried Rice (V) ~ 85
Lani Ulu (V) ~ 111
Loco `Ono Energy Bars (V) ~ 284
Luau Spinach (V) ~ 110
Lynne's Tofu Poke (V) ~ 23
"Make Her" Musubi (V) ~ 281
Mango-Papaya Salsa (V) ~ 193
Microwaved Brown Basmati or Long Grain Brown Rice (V) ~ 104
My Favorite Fruit Mui ~ 279
Namasu (V) ~ 58
Namasu Dressing (V) ~ 58
New Kine Banana Lumpia (V) ~ 239
No Need Ham Split Pea Soup (V) ~ 45
Okinawan Sweet Potato Poi Mochi (V) ~ 242
`Ono Keia Hawaiian Stew (V) ~ 196
Rav-e-oli (V) ~ 182
Salsa (V) ~ 20
Sauce for Spicy Szechuan Eggplant (V) ~ 125
Savvy (Savoy) Stuffed Cabbage (V) ~ 176
Sekihan (V) ~ 87

Global Light Cuisine ∞ Carol Devenot   317

Vegan Recipes *(continued)*

Sherry Shallot Vinaigrette Dressing (V) ~ 73
Simply Nishime (V) ~ 154
Southwestern Corn Chowder (V) ~ 47
Summer Rolls Dipping Sauce (V) ~ 11
Summer Rolls with Dipping Sauce (V) ~ 10
Sweet and Sour Tofu and Carol's Sweet and Sour Sauce (V) ~ 140
Teriyaki Sauce (V) ~ 203
Thai Tapioca Pudding (V) ~ 244
Tofu Salad Dressing (V) ~ 70
Tofu Mayo (lemon juice) (V) ~ 69
Veat, Not Meat Guisantes (V) ~ 146
Watercress Namul (V) ~ 90
What the Hekka? (V) ~ 198
Wild Salmon Shiro Misoyaki ~ 150
Woodi's Caprese ~ 65
Woo's Southwest Orzo (V) ~ 223
Yummy Sticky Rice (V) ~ 93

Vegetable Recipes

Baked Sweet Potato (V) ~ 110
Baked Taro (V) ~ 110
Ceci's Tasty Sweet Potatoes (V) ~ 100
Chop Chae (V) ~ 91
Easy as 1-2-3 Pumpkin Bars ~ 260
Eggplant Caponata (V) ~ 14
Greek Salad ~ 62
Greek Seasoned Roasted Vegetables (V) ~ 96
Heal Ti Israeli Salad ~ 80
Hold da Mayo Cold Slaw (V) ~ 71
Lani Ulu (V) ~ 111
Light and Creamy Broccoli Soup ~ 43
Light Palu Sami ~ 112
Luau Spinach (V) ~ 110
Namasu (V) ~ 58
No Need Ham Split Pea Soup (V) ~ 45
Okinawan Sweet Potato Pie ~ 249
Okinawan Sweet Potato Poi Mochi (V) ~ 242
`Ono Keia Hawaiian Stew (V) ~ 196
Quickie Cucumber Kim Chee (V) ~ 59
Ratatouille ~ 94
Roasted Beet Salad with Sherry Shallot Vinaigrette and
    Candied Pecans ~ 72

Vegetable Recipes *(continued)*
Salsa (V) ~ 20
Simply Nishime (V) ~ 154
Slimmed-Down Tomato-Butternut Squash Bisque ~ 37
Southwestern Corn Chowder (V) ~ 47
Tzatziki ~ 78
Watercress Namul (V) ~ 90
What the Hekka? (V) ~ 198
Woodi's Caprese ~ 65
Zucchini-Swiss Chard Frittata ~ 186

Warm, Tropical Mango-Lychee Dessert ~ 236
Watercress Namul (V) ~ 90

Wheat Gluten Products Recipes
`Ono Keia Hawaiian Stew (V) ~ 196
What the Hekka? (V) ~ 198

What the Hekka? (V) ~ 198
Wild Salmon Shiro Misoyaki ~ 150
Woodi's Caprese ~ 65
Woo's Southwest Orzo (V) ~ 223

Yummy Rummy Oatcakes ~ 258
Yummy Sticky Rice (V) ~ 93

Zucchini-Swiss Chard Frittata ~ 186